Authority and the
Mountaineer in
Cormac McCarthy's
Appalachia

Authority and the Mountaineer in Cormac McCarthy's Appalachia

GABE RIKARD

McFarland & Company, Inc., Publishers
Jefferson, North Carolina, and London

LIBRARY OF CONGRESS CATALOGUING-IN-PUBLICATION DATA

Rikard, Gabe.
    Authority and the mountaineer in Cormac McCarthy's Appalachia / Gabe Rikard.
      p.   cm.
    Includes bibliographical references and index.

    ISBN 978-0-7864-7459-2
    softcover : acid free paper ∞

    1. McCarthy, Cormac, 1933– —Criticism and interpretation. 2. Appalachian Region—In literature. I. Title.
PS3563.C337Z85 2013
813'.54—dc23   2013025864

BRITISH LIBRARY CATALOGUING DATA ARE AVAILABLE

© 2013 Gabe Rikard. All rights reserved

No part of this book may be reproduced or transmitted in any form or by any means, electronic or mechanical, including photocopying or recording, or by any information storage and retrieval system, without permission in writing from the publisher.

Front cover: pants (Brand X pictures/Thinkstock); boots (iStockphoto/Thinkstock); background (Stockbyte/Thinkstock)

Manufactured in the United States of America

McFarland & Company, Inc., Publishers
  Box 611, Jefferson, North Carolina 28640
    www.mcfarlandpub.com

Table of Contents

Abbreviations vi
Preface 1
An Historical Prelude: The Whiskey Rebellion 7
Introduction: An Archeology of Authority and Appalachia 21

One. Spatializing Conduits: The Roads of Appalachia 41
Two. Modernizing Discipline: Mill Villages,
    Metropolises and Mountaineers 86
Three. A Case of the Superlative: Lester Ballard,
    Mountaineers, Children of God and Men 131
Four. The Construction and Maintenance of an
    Icon, or Fantasizing the Mountaineer 167

Coda: Atavising the Mountaineer: The Road 207
Notes 227
References 229
Index 237

Abbreviations

***BOC**—Birth of the Clinic*
***COG**—Child of God*
***DP**—Discipline and Punish*
***GS**—The Gardener's Son*
***HS**—The History of Sexuality*
***MAC**—Madness and Civilization*
***OD**—Outer Dark*
***OK**—The Orchard Keeper*
***TR**—The Road*

Preface

Like many scholars attempting to discover the reasons they have written a certain text, I find that my connections to my current academic project began long before I read the first page of Cormac McCarthy or studied the first theory of Michel Foucault or latched onto the first recounting of Appalachian cultural history. My connections begin with topography.

The Shoals, Alabama, gets its name from a nearby section of the Tennessee River that, until the building of Wilson Dam in 1933, dropped over one hundred feet in fourteen miles along a rapids that made navigation impossible; now, nearly one hundred feet deep in places, Wilson Lake provides the Shoals with "recreation possibilities"—fishing, boating, sailing, golfing—where the now-dammed Tennessee once ran quick and clear. Bordering the river, farmland still stretches out, as it always has, both north to the Tennessee state line and south to the small foothills which rise one hundred feet above the surrounding land. Those "mountains" are the northern tip of the southwestern terminus of the Appalachians; I grew up on one of those mountains—Wheeler Mountain, to be exact. The Appalachians stretch from Maine in the north to Georgia in the south, and while Alabama is rarely included as part of that range, the hills surrounding Birmingham, Huntsville, and, yes, the Shoals, are connected topography.

Growing up in the western corner of North Alabama, I spent my summers traipsing through woods of oak and hickory and maple and ash, navigating patches of blackberry briars and honeysuckle vines, and climbing over barbed-wire fences and limestone bluffs all over Wheeler Mountain, much like John Wesley Rattner and Warn Pullam of McCarthy's *The Orchard Keeper* on Red Mountain. My summers mirrored theirs, and probably McCarthy's childhood summers on Brown's Mountain as well. The Shoals area, known as the Quad Cities among the locals, consists of four small towns—Florence, Sheffield, Tuscumbia, and Muscle Shoals. The Tennessee River, that same river Cornelius Suttree fishes between alcoholic binges in *Suttree,* flows between these cities. I crossed that river via O'Neal Bridge or Wilson Dam almost every day. So, well before I encountered McCarthy's work, I knew the mountains and the river about which he writes.

Topography might be my first connection to this project, but it is not the only one. Another major connection takes the form of one of the Shoals' major exports — music. After all, Muscle Shoals, according to the tourism brochures, is the "hit recording capital of the world." Percy Sledge ("When a Man Loves a Woman"), Aretha Franklin, Paul Simon, Absylom Rising, and the Muscle Shoals Rhythm Section (known forever as "The Swampers") have recorded in Muscle Shoals, and both *Muscle Shoals Sound* and *Fame* recording studios were instrumental in the creation of that great American musical collaboration, rock 'n' roll. Like the region of its birth, the "Muscle Shoals sound" is an amalgamation of regional influence: in it one hears the up-tempo electrified blues of the Mississippi hill country to the west and the plaintive acoustic guitar–driven Delta blues even further to the south and west; the throaty, gutsy praise and lamentation of the South's gospel traditions mark the vocal tracts of "Muscle Shoals soul"; steel guitars from Nashville's country scene thread through many musical numbers; and banjos, fiddles, and mandolins from bluegrass, or "hillbilly" music — popular in the mountains to the east — buckdance through Muscle Shoals' cadences. All of these varieties make up my personal musical heritage, but the last of these styles figured heavily into my childhood and probably oriented me toward the Appalachians during my formative years.

A story: my sisters and I spent many a Saturday night at my paternal grandparents' house in states of consternation. The predicament we faced on those nights was what to watch on TV. Because our house was set back in the woods, we had terrible TV reception from our "rabbit ear" antennae. My grandparents' reception was appreciably better — they got four channels to our two. So, around six o'clock, my mother would drive us around the corner, slow down as she rounded my grandparents' circular drive, and sling us out of the open door and into my grandparents' yard, glad to be rid of us for a couple hours, no doubt. OK, perhaps I exaggerate; but thus began many a great Saturday night debate — and my education in hillbillydom.

My grandfather, Papaw as we called him in the Southern fashion, loved "hillbilly" music: enter the great commercialized, commodified presentation of all things hillbilly — *Hee Haw,* hosted by country and bluegrass greats Buck Owens and Roy Clark. We kids, on the other hand, preferred the fast-paced flash-and-glamour of *Solid Gold,* Dionne Warwick and/or Marilyn McCoo's expose of pop and R&B talent. The major problem for my grandparents, at least as they presented it, was one of exposure, literally. They claimed *Solid Gold* had entirely too many scantily clad women making entirely too many suggestive gyrations for their stolid, conservative tastes. In retrospect, I realize that it was more about the music and dancing than the outfits because *Hee Haw* had its share of Daisy Dukes-wearing temptresses. So, as my grandfather relaxed and often dozed off in his La-Z-Boy recliner, we surreptitiously changed the channel to CBS (*Solid Gold*) and then back to NBC (*Hee Haw*) when he chastised us in his waking moments. I hated *Hee Haw* back then. Now, however, I realize that the music it promoted runs in my blood; for me it serves as the first conscious connection to the Appalachian literature of this current project. The irony is certainly not lost on me.

I could conclude that the influence from my mother's side of the family had something to do with my tastes in music, and eventually literature, as well. My Papa D — mother's father — played fiddle and mandolin, and both of my mom's brothers were multi-instrumentalists, mainly guitar and banjo. Even though we visited them less often than my father's parents (mom's family lived ninety miles to the east in Huntsville), when we all got together for holidays, especially Thanksgiving, out came the instruments, and the playing of bluegrass, folk, and blues commenced. I always remained in awe of my uncles' instrumental talents (and I still do), and I vowed to "play guitar like them" one day. As the years passed, I became more and more involved in these musical sessions, though admittedly I was more interested in heavy metal than bluegrass: that is, until I purchased my first Martin guitar (just like my uncle Ken's) when I headed off to college as an undergraduate. By then, I understood the influence bluegrass, blues, country, and folk had on my musical musings and tastes. However, it took me several years to understand how that influence played into my choice of dissertation topics.

My first real foray into Appalachian *literature* came at the University of Mississippi. Having finished my master's in Shakespeare at Florida State, I went to Oxford with the intentions of studying her native son, William Faulkner. I had always planned to study Shakespeare and Renaissance literature for my master's and Southern literature, especially Faulkner, for my doctorate, reasoning that it might make me a more marketable job candidate. However, once I sunk my teeth into Faulkner studies, I realized that the breadth of the writing about Faulkner's body of work would make it extremely difficult to carve out a niche for myself in Faulkner studies. I began to focus elsewhere.

Donald Kartiganer introduced me to Cormac McCarthy's work in an American novels class at the University of Mississippi. We read *Child of God* and I was enamored with how McCarthy created sympathy for the sociopathic necrophile Lester Ballard by making it obvious that *even he* was a product of his socialization. Then I truly began to focus on Appalachia and her people when I studied the marginalization of American poor whites in a class we students called the "white trash" class. Jay Watson led us through the various manifestations of the poor white figure in American culture and literature and I began to hear echoes of my own past. Even though I personally could not identify myself or my immediate family with this class distinction — we were solidly middle class thanks to my parents' hard work — I knew many "poor whites" growing up; furthermore, the attitudes — social, political, and economical — evident in literature about and by poor whites surrounded me growing up in my North Alabama enclave. Certainly, the class discovered, poor whites were not isolated in the Appalachian Mountains or in the red clay hills of Georgia or in the plateau of Alabama's Sand Mountain or in the hill country of North Mississippi or even in the American South as a region; according to the literature we read, they lived next door or down the road in any rural area, any town, or any city anywhere in the United States. While "poor white trash" had become a rhetorical identity not geographically isolated, reading *Child of God* and later *Outer Dark* nonetheless made me believe that there was something exceptional about the southern Appalachian mountains and the mountaineers who live(d) there. Perhaps the mountains and the river affected me more deeply than I consciously understood; perhaps listening to and playing hillbilly music conditioned my literary proclivities more than I knew.

Reading more McCarthy, I began to notice the recurring relationships between figures in positions of authority and the characters over whom they exert their power. McCarthy's Appalachian novels evidence this tendency most prevalently. Whether it be Marion Sylder punching Jefferson Gifford in the face as he sleeps, or Arthur Ownby shooting an X in the government tank, or Culla Holme stealing the squire's boots, or Lester Ballard attempting to break up the county's auction of his land, the relationships between these mountaineer characters and the authorities who would discipline them remain the most intriguing aspects of these novels to me. Perhaps my own socialized propensity for questioning the veracity of authority made me sensitive to this interpretation, or perhaps using Michel Foucault to interpret Shakespeare while working on my master's thesis heightened my consciousness of these interactions; regardless, I noticed a pattern which mirrors sentiments expressed in a John Cougar song: when authorities and the mountaineer clash, no matter the context, the mountaineer usually loses. So I set out to excavate how and why the mountaineer, or the "hillbilly" — a cultural "loser" from antiquity until the present — serves as a disciplinary tool for authority both historically and in McCarthy's work.

Essentially, that inquiry led me to this project, which I consider to be, in Foucault's terms, an archeology of the [Appalachian] present. Many scholarly publications highlight the philosophical or spiritual underpinnings of McCarthy's world: Vereen Bell's *The Achievement of Cormac McCarthy* sets the standard for such readings, and Diane Luce's recent work *Reading the World: Cormac McCarthy's Tennessee Period* follows in that vein; others — specifically David Holloway's *The Late Modernism of Cormac McCarthy* and John Cant's *Cormac McCarthy and the Myth of American Exceptionalism* — unpack the postmodern sensibilities of his texts. These works, along with several of the essay collections compiled by James D. Lilley, Rick Wallach and Wade Hall, and Sabine Anders, reveal interesting insights into McCarthy's work, and certainly all of them influence this current study, even if only tangentially. None of these approaches is, however, the focus of this project. I am more intrigued by social surfaces. I am more interested in the pistons of culture that make up the social machine, the resources that fuel it, the libations that lubricate it, and the by-products of its combustive interactions.

This is a text which interrogates historical, cultural, and social contexts — McCarthy's, his characters,' the Appalachian region's, the mountaineers' — and deconstructs the mechanizations of power and resistance that stem from centuries of manipulation and reaction, determinism and subversion, movement and stasis. This project focuses on representations of culture and society rather than linguistics or philosophy or spirituality; it delves into how geographical and topographical spaces, limited physical and social mobilities, occupational and political choices (or the lack thereof), and cultural and commercial iconographies shape, pinion, and cultivate the very real lives of Appalachian mountain people. Through these avenues I seek to understand how, in Anthony Harkins's terms, the mountaineer can serve "the dual and seemingly contradictory purposes of allowing a 'mainstream,' or generally nonrural, middleclass white, American audience to imagine a romanticized past, while simultaneously enabling that same audience to recommit itself to modernity by caricaturing the negative aspects of premodern, uncivilized society" (Harkins 7).

No novel, no screenplay, no art at all, in fact, is constructed in a vacuum; so it is also with an academic treatise. In addition to the subconscious contributions of my childhood to this book, I have a list of people to thank for their very conscious influence and assistance on this project, many of whom have no idea that they inspired or helped me along at some point down the line. Michael Leslie, Jennifer Brady and the late Cynthia Marshall shepherded me through the gestational phases of my academic career; Laura Rosenthal, James O'Rourke, and Bruce Boehrer helped me construct a theoretical foundation that has ultimately produced this project. Donald Kartiganer, David

Galef, and Tristan Denley asked all the right questions; Jay Watson helped me answer them. Heath Mahan, Jonathan Williams, Deric Murphy, and Warren Waldrip slept through many turned pages, many loudly-made pots of coffee, and many early mornings filled with cursing and book throwing, while lodging few complaints, as I researched this project from the bunk of a tour bus. Thanks to Mich Abraham for his sage legal advice. My colleagues at SUNY Sullivan — Cindy Linden, Lynne Crockett, Lisa Linquist, Lisa Collero, Tim Russell, Tom Martin, Amy Colon, and Anne Ruskawitz — continually model what it means be *great* teachers. Paul, Tara, and Noah Reifenheiser treat me like part of the family — albeit like *that* crazy redneck uncle — and that kindness should never be underestimated. I could not ask for better mentors, friends, and extended family.

Then there is my biological family. My paternal grandparents — Mamaw and Papaw, neither of whom finished high school themselves — showed me what hard work and diligence mean in concrete terms; Papa D, my maternal grandfather, and my mother's brothers Jim and Ken Dowdy inspired me musically and provided what I now know is my first connection to Appalachia. Gran Gran, my mother's mother, just plain inspired me — and continues to inspire me — with her indefatigable spirit. Shylock, the sixteen-pound orange ball of feline terror who has accompanied me through all the years of this project, enduring innumerable moves and dodging a variety of angrily tossed projectiles, has always reminded me — whether it be with a clawed swipe or a purred note of satisfaction — not to take myself too seriously, since that food bowl or that catnip-infused toy is really the most important article in the universe.

Finally, my immediate family — Glenn, Dorlea, and Kiley Rikard, Meagan and Jason Haney: all of my verbosity could not sum up the debt I owe to you. You never once doubted my abilities and never once failed to strengthen my resolve. This *first* one is for you.

An Historical Prelude
The Whiskey Rebellion

The Declaration of Independence states that "all men are created equal, that they are endowed by their Creator with certain unalienable rights, that among these are life, liberty and the pursuit of happiness." Yet the Constitution of the United States of America, a document written nearly a decade after the American Revolution, makes no mention of this equality (795). Why? Furthermore, why did many of the patriots who fought to free the colonies not support the ratification of the Constitution? The Declaration of Independence separated the colonies from Great Britain and had nothing to do with the establishment of laws or government. In the twelve-year interim between the Declaration and the writing of the Constitution, the writers of said documents found themselves in substantially different roles. In 1776 they were rebels who sought to throw off King George III's tyranny, but in 1788 they found themselves in positions of authority. Many therefore became voices for a strong central government. The Articles of Confederation gave most powers to the individual states, making it difficult for the country as a whole to form a formidable international presence, and exposing the country to potential threats from both foreign powers and domestic rebels. Men like George Washington, Alexander Hamilton, John Adams, and even Thomas Jefferson now had vested interests in maintaining their hold on power; gone were the proclamations of universal equality. They were replaced with a desire for order — an order these men dominated as landholders and men of material wealth. Perhaps they saw the Constitution and the strong federal government it established as the reinstitution of a power structure much like the one against which they had fought a bloody war. An experiment in democracy, in the United States the enforcement of laws and social mores could not be carried out in traditional ways: there was no monarchy wherein "crime attacks the sovereign: it attacks him personally, since the law represents the will of the sovereign" (*DP* 47). In such a democracy, new forms of social manipulation and law enforcement, a new "political economy," developed to ensure the peace and prosperity of a fledgling nation. Michel Foucault analyzes the genesis of such new forms of power when he states:

> The "invention" of this new political anatomy must not be seen as a sudden discovery. It is rather a multiplicity of often minor processes, of different origin and scattered location, which overlap, repeat, or imitate one another, support one another, distinguish themselves from one another according to their domain of application, converge and gradually produce the blueprint of a general method [*DP* 138].

The Constitution was one part of this new political anatomy that gave the federal government the power to enact other "minor processes." Many of the United States' western inhabitants saw the Constitution as an attempted power grab by the eastern elite that already owned vast quantities of the western lands *in absentia*; perhaps those western settlers understood that under this new Constitution, "no longer would westerners be free to treat taxes and collectors as they wished. No longer could they expect to deny rents to landlords without legal consequences. No longer could they exist outside the pale of eastern laws and eastern law enforcers, as had been their practice for decades prior to ratification of the Constitution" (Slaughter, *Whiskey Rebellion* 74).

Acceptance and ratification of the Constitution was not a monolithic event. In fact, Patrick Henry, made famous by the quote "give me liberty or give me death," stuck to his independent guns after the Revolution. He did not support the strong centralized government established by the Constitution. Like Henry, many patriots had their doubts about the wisdom of a strong central government. Other "Friends of Liberty" like Albert Gallatin, William Findley, and George Logan joined Henry in opposition to the strong Federal government as embodied by the Constitution. In fact, many felt the states should "adopt a bill of rights for the Constitution, reject indirect taxes levied by remote central governments, maintain strong local militias to protect against the encroachment of mercenary armies, and the nation and liberty might again be safe" (131). Most of these men, though they were themselves extensive speculators in the western lands, represented the quarters of the populace less dominated by the Eastern elite — rural areas west of the mountains where the economy and individual existence were less stable than along the Eastern coast and in the larger metropolises like Philadelphia, Boston, and New York. Their frontier constituencies would be the ones adversely affected when Alexander Hamilton, using the newly minted power of the federal government, enacted an excise on domestically distilled liquor. The Treasury secretary did act, and a conflict of interests brewed. This conflict eventuated in the Whiskey Rebellion, the "first large-scale resistance to a law of the United States under the Constitution"; subsequently, "the federal government's response represented the first exercise of the internal police power of a president under the Constitution" (Slaughter, "Friends of Liberty" 10).

A deconstruction of the Whiskey Rebellion uncovers subtle, gestate Foucauldian disciplinary techniques and demonstrates how and where they began to be birthed in the United States' sociopolitical arena. As George Washington's Treasury Secretary, Hamilton's decision to place an excise tax on whiskey — a product universally identified as important to the economy of the frontier of the western mountains — set a precedent for disciplinary relationships between authorities and the people of the then "western" mountains who eventually became identified as "mountaineers." The whiskey excise became a way to delineate between law-abiders and lawbreakers, and the inhabitants of the frontier "saw the excise as a conspiracy of men in the more settled, urban, mercantile, cosmopolitan East against the economic interest of the Country — the rural, agricultural, especially the western hinterlands" (*Whiskey Rebellion* 131). This episode in American history also served as the genesis for the federal attitude toward untaxed liquor and its makers from 1791 until the present day. Hamilton's law initiated this facet of government taxation. For the people of the eighteenth-century American frontier, turning corn into whiskey was the most desirable, cost-efficient way to transport and sell their grain crops; they saw its manufacture both as a birthright and as a staple of their barter-based economy: "commercial sale of the beverage was only a secondary function of distillation. To tax whiskey at the point of production was, therefore, an untoward burden in the West because much liquor was never sold, and the quantities that reached the local markets seldom brought much cash" (*Whiskey Rebellion* 73). Thereafter the taxation of liquor became an increasingly important aspect of federal revenue collection. According to Wilbur Miller, by Reconstruction, "the whiskey tax had become the leading source of internal revenue, rising from 30 percent of the collections in 1868 to 63 percent in 1884. The whiskey tax seemed to be a permanent contributor to an expanded government's daily functioning" (148).

But Hamilton wanted more than just taxes out of the whiskey excise; he wanted to strengthen the federal government politically. He understood that the enforcement of a whiskey excise would require the saturation of the frontier by agents of the federal government and recommended that "it is desirable to have an office accessible (within the distance of ten miles) to every owner of a still, in order that the entry contemplated by the law may be made by each" (Hamilton, *Papers, Vol. 8* 368). The frontiersmen needed to be utilized in the eastern economy of the "Founding Fathers" if the nation was to survive and flourish. Hamilton's whiskey excise itself, and *how* its enforcement engaged the government with the citizens of the frontier, initiated the disciplining of both the frontier and the general population by forcing the frontier population, whose opposition to the law remained outspoken and sometimes violent, into positions of alterity in relation to the law-abiding population.

The furor surrounding the whiskey excise also marks a political beginning to the creation of *Appalachia* as an "othered" region that continues to serve as a discursive oppositional to national social norms. When Thomas Slaughter contemplates the reasons for tensions between the eastern elite and the frontiersmen, he echoes the sentiments of Appalachian scholars who discuss the absentee land ownership of Appalachia; he notes: "Most of the great landowners who profited from the consolidation of wealth in the western countries were outsiders. Few of the great residential landholders of the 1780s were able to hold their ground against eastern speculators" (Slaughter, *Whiskey Rebellion* 65). Those "eastern speculators" included the men who wrote the Constitution. Hamilton's excise was intended to make certain that the men of the frontier not only contributed to the coffers of the federal government, but that they remained connected to the East economically and politically via a web of excise offices, taxmen, and other representatives of federal authority.

After the Revolutionary War, the grievances of the frontier inhabitants were longstanding and not without merit. These men had spearheaded westward expansion, fought the natives at great personal expense and danger, and served in the Continental Army; their "activism had shifted westward after the war—[to] mountainous regions [which had] remained in depression during the postwar recovery of the east" (Hogeland 52). In many cases they received land grants as payment for their services, but they felt that the Congress had abandoned them at the least and had targeted them at the worst when it approved the whiskey excise. The men of the frontier had grievances with a government that could not protect them from Indians, that could not open the Spanish-controlled Mississippi River so that they could more easily get their products to market, and that, in some instances, could not even pay them for their service in the Revolution. These trailblazers wished to retain their independence from the Easterners' intrusions, and besides, taxing the *production* of their whiskey, and not its sale, seemed unfair to them. The westerners saw themselves "as the most beleaguered of citizens and worthy of an exemption from additional burdens" (93).

To policy makers and other Easterners, on the other hand, the western settlers began to be identified with the wildness of the mountainous lands they occupied. Katherine Ledford claims that she sees "evidence of a deepening association of Appalachian frontiersmen and residents with the mountainous landscape that they inhabited, an equation that says more about the explorers and travelers and their cultures than it does about either the geographic reality of the Appalachian Mountains or the people who inhabited them" (Ledford 48). The explorers and surveyors, often employed by Eastern speculators or colonial governments, maintained the objectives and prejudices of those employers. Ledford writes that between 1669 and 1670, "John Lederer was one of the first colonists to explore the Appalachian Mountains, and his description of the landscape emphasizes danger and uncertain natural order" (52). Lederer, commissioned by Virginia governor William Berkley, allowed the social and political environment of his day to color his characterization of the mountains: "In a colony troubled by the agitation of frontiersmen in the Piedmont and the hostility of Indians beyond them, Lederer finds a difficult landscape that he characterizes as dangerous and uninviting, a serious physical barrier that the colonial government would have to contend with" (53). Sixty years later,

> as exploitation of the region's natural resources became less of a passing remark and more of a reason for serious pause, positive descriptions of the Appalachian Mountains became a necessity. Social and economic anxiety did not disappear, just a negative geographical terrain for mapping anxiety as that land became more desirable. Another site had to take its place. This time, Appalachian settlers became the physical entity for transference of social and economic unease [55].

The Appalachian Mountains *began* to become a site of *social geography* and not merely a physical impediment for the growing nation to overcome. This change in outlook toward the western lands on the part of the Easterners begins fifty years *before* the Revolutionary War because people like "William Byrd II proved adept at making this cultural switch." He and others helped change the attitude of the colonialists towards the physical mountains, making the inhabitants the major impediments to speculation rather than the geography: "As Byrd discovers the value of the mountain land, his descriptions of the settlers who were beginning to inhabit the land [in the 1720s and 1730s] become increasingly negative" (55). Men like Byrd lay the ideological and iconographical groundwork for post–Revolutionary War attitudes toward western settlers who otherwise resemble "normal" colonists.

Perhaps not surprisingly, some historians contend that Hamilton and other members of the governing elite *did* have ulterior motives. Hogeland lays much of the blame for the Whiskey Rebellion, a direct result of the whiskey excise, at Hamilton's feet. He sees Hamilton in league with Philadelphia financier and Constitution signer Robert Morris. Having noted how state legislatures' wills crumbled at the first sign of popular resistance to tax enforcement, especially when it concerned tax collection from the poorer quarters of the population, Hamilton and Morris sought to strengthen the *financial* role of the federal government by having it take on the debts of all the states. They held the purse strings of the federal government and could ensure that all of the national debts would be repaid. They resisted the "people's movement" in American politics, one which wanted to write laws "to dictate fair and equal distribution of wealth and credit ... to limit the profits that a few money men could reap" (Hogeland 34). Ideologically, Hamilton, Morris, John Adams and other Federalists saw the strengthening of the federal government as essential to the survival of the United States. Financial stability was a large part of their survival strategy. Accordingly, they sought to solidify the power of the eastern moneyed men who had floated the finances of the Revolution, and part of that process meant destabilizing the power of the inhabitants of the frontier. Hamilton's philosophy for many of his political moves stemmed from his knowledge of David Hume's economic philosophies; Hume "argued that the key to a nation's prosperity is concentrating wealth in the hands of the few people who can use it to finance ambitious projects" (33). Hamilton identified Hume's ideal in Robert Morris, who had overseen much of the business of the Continental Congress and the financial dealings inherent in the execution of the Revolution. Hamilton's loyalty to the financiers remained unequivocal: "Creditors came first: Morris officially suspended army pay, already shaky enough, and he prohibited legislatures from paying their own soldiers, insisting states send all money to Congress, to be distributed as he saw fit" (33). Hamilton's use of the whiskey excise, therefore, "meant to give the debtor class no further chance for resistance" to paying their creditors regardless of their ability to pay (Hogeland 52).

The West was essential to the United States. Washington himself "perceived that the fate of his personal finances, the nation, and indeed the world were inextricably bound to the frontier; and he interpreted threats to the West as menaces to them all" (*Whiskey Rebellion* 78). The men in charge of the federal government had personal business stakes in the development of the lands west of the mountains. Slaughter notes, "Washington would own over 63,000 acres of trans–Appalachia, becoming one of the largest absentee landlords the western country knew during his day" (82). Robert Morris, the very man who helped guide Hamilton's hand in government monetary policy, "engaged in the practice of dodging, by which the speculator sold lands in Europe before acreage or warrants were actually purchased on Appalachian frontiers" (Dunaway, "Speculators and Settler Capitalists" 57). So, with Hamilton installed as the Federalists' first Secretary of the Treasury, who had the ear of a rather receptive President Washington, the Eastern financiers' success was all but assured. It is arguably naive to suggest that the Founding Fathers had no motives in suppressing the Whiskey Rebellion besides the defense of the new nation.

At the same time Hamilton introduced his tariff on domestically produced spirits, the Washington administration, at the behest of Secretary Hamilton, set about establishing a banking system that would centralize economic and financial power in the eastern metropolises. A national bank would solidify the essential status of the federal government in lending and debt situations and set up a financial system where the men of the west were financially beholden to those of the east.[1] Hamilton wrote to President Washington: "It is manifest that a *large commercial City* with a great deal of *capital* and *business* must be the fittest seat of the Bank. It is morally certain that for twenty years to come Philadelphia will continue to have as good pretensions as any of the principal trading Cities now established" (*Papers, vol. 8* 221). Issuing currency and controlling the financial markets would saturate the new country with the influence of the federal government. Likewise, Hamilton claimed his central banking institution "will interweave itself into the monied interest of every State, which will by its notes insinuate itself into every branch of industry and will affect the interests of all the classes of the community; ought to produce strong prepossessions in its favor in all who consider the firm establishment of the National Government as necessary to the safety and happiness of the Country" (*Papers, vol. 8* 223). Such a monetary system, bolstered by enforceable taxes, would tighten the connective tissues between the federal government and the frontier while simultaneously weakening the relative position of the men who lived on the frontier, men who, in the words of Judge Alexander Addison, "talked wildly. These, without property to secure their attachment to the government or the country, unaccustomed to a regular industry, and trained to a rambling life, had the arms in their hands" (qtd. in Kohn 55). In the eyes of the easterners, the frontiersmen were dangerous vagrants and squatters of ill repute. They owned nothing and had little stake in the economy's success. They could not be trusted to properly develop the land of the West, so they needed to be disciplined.

Wilma Dunaway's analysis of "pre-capitalist" America, *The First American Frontier*, helps to lay bare the motivations of the Founding Fathers, thereby complicating their reasons for solidifying power in the federal government. The acquisition of land was the key element for these men, and Dunaway demonstrates why:

> [F]our major alterations occur to effect the capture of territory through the commodification of land. First, indigenous people are displaced so that property rights can be redefined to permit the sale and transfer of ownership in the marketplace. Second, public commons are eliminated through various forms of pri-

vate enclosure, thereby increasing landlessness among a sizable segment of the population. Third, land tenure arrangements are modified to encourage the agglomeration of large landholdings. Finally, as a result of the commodification of land, the environment of the frontier is also articulated with the world economy. Natural resources and land are exploited to generate exports for global markets, thereby shifting previous ecological balances and relationships [19].

This process, of course, did not occur at the exact moment the colonists cast off the yoke of King George III; it took years of reinforcing, decades of manipulation, and centuries of growth. After the ratification of the Constitution, parallel political and economic developments — the implementation of the whisky excise and the creation of a national bank — worked to disenfranchise the frontiersmen while simultaneously bringing them into closer contact with the controls of the eastern elite.

Hamilton "became intent on imposing on *all* the people, throughout the states, direct federal taxes, payable by the people to Congress — in coin. These taxes would be collected not by weak state governments but *by a powerful cadre of federal officers*" (Hogeland 33, emphasis added). The excise tax on domestic distillation served three purposes: (1) It gave the federal government much-needed revenue; (2) It increased the presence of the federal government in the western lands in the persons of excise collectors; (3) It placed economic, social, and political pressures on farmers and frontiersmen in and west of the Alleghenies.[2] These economic competitors held, if only by their physical presence, lands coveted by the Easterners. Those Easterners with newly ratified *political* power sought to enhance their *economic* power and vice versa.

While Hamilton's central banking institution infiltrated the economic markets, the federal government sent men to the frontier to find distillers and collect the excise. Hamilton wrote that the "following plan, afterwards successively put in execution, was about this time digested for carrying if possible the laws into effect, without the necessity of recurring to force":

> 1.) to prosecute delinquents in the cases in which it could be clearly done for non compliances with the laws 2.) to intercept the markets for the surplus produce of the distilleries of the non complying counties, by seizing the spirits in their way to those markets, in places where it could be effected without opposition 3.) by purchases through agents for the government for the use of the army (instead of deriving the supply through contractors as formerly) confining them to spirits in respect to which there had been a compliance with the laws [qtd. in Boyd 39].

This outlines a policy for law enforcement's handling of liquor sales from 1792 until post–Prohibition: arrest those who refuse to pay the tax, seize their products, and ensure that those who abide by the law have a stable market in which to conduct their sales. Farmers turned grain into alcohol all over the western frontier, but selective enforcement created an opposition between the government and the distillers who paid the excise (mostly the larger operations who saw the tax as a limit on competition) and the distillers who refused to pay (whose distillation of smaller quantities of whiskey made them simultaneously competitors with the larger distillers and unable to pay the excise). Men considered patriots years earlier when they fought Great Britain over taxes and representation, men who now resisted the whiskey excise as undue taxation, became sociopolitical "delinquents" when they opposed the will of the United States government — the newly ratified representative of the people.

The government's policies and national events leading up to the Whiskey Rebellion present a concerted effort by those who set policy for the new nation to weave a web of unequal national interdependence. Frontiersmen became identified with their specific region, a land on the outskirts of "civilization" though still somewhat close to it, and as rebels themselves who ignored the laws of the land. Juxtaposed by the agents of governmental authority to the law-abiding majority of the nation, the illegal distillers of this certain region and population left (in the words of Hamilton, posing as "Tully" in letters he published in the *American Daily Advertiser* in August 1794) "the government of the Union in the prostrate condition of seeing the laws trampled under foot by an unprincipled combination of a small portion of the community, *habitually disobedient* to laws, and itself destitute of the necessary aid for vindicating their authority" because they refused to pay taxes on one of their only barterable products (*Papers, vol. 17* 135, emphasis added). So, in the first six years of the American democracy, the wealthy and those in positions of authority — especially those within the government — colluded to disenfranchise poorer citizens, especially those on the frontiers, by writing and enforcing laws that cast the frontiersmen into roles of alterity and delinquency.

This seems eerily Foucauldian. The authorities infiltrated the frontier lands with representatives who observed the populace and collected what the federal government claimed the frontier distillers owed it; otherwise stated, "by means of such surveillance, disciplinary power became an 'integrated' system, linked from the inside to the economy and to the aims of the mechanism in which it was practiced" (*DP* 176). The Eastern elites controlled both the banking system and the government, and the excise presents an intimate connection between them all. This supposition is not a conjecture and it is not a theory of conspiracy; an archeology of the historical interactions between the people of the Appalachian Mountains and persons in positions of authority bears out this relationship. The Whiskey Rebellion marks the point where the authority of the federal government can be specifically and intimately connected to disciplinary technique.

This moment in the history of the United States marks the birth of the mountains as a site of *white* transgression. Since the first settler entered the mountains, the region had served as an essential part of the new United States, one that buffered the eastern "civilized" regions from the Indians and from the Spanish, English, and French. In the process of quelling the Whiskey Rebellion, the mountains west of "civilization" became more than a space controlled by the "noble savages"; it became identified as a place full of *American* rebels — white western inhabitants who disrespected the laws ratified by the rest of the country. Hamilton wrote Washington, "I hope there will be found characters fit for examples and who can be made so" (*Papers, vol. 17* 366). Despite the waning of the rebels' resolve after burning General John Neville's house and gathering militiamen in Braddock's field, General Richard Henry "Lighthorse" Lee (ironically a signer of the Declaration of Independence), and Hamilton himself led 15,000 troops to the Three Forks (Pittsburgh) area, where they made arrests and interrogations and generally terrorized the western Pennsylvania population with the power of the federal government. In the frontier regions of Virginia, North Carolina, and Georgia, as in western Pennsylvania, the excise tax was largely ignored. Hamilton chose western Pennsylvania as the site of enforcement because of its proximity to the seat of the central government, Philadelphia, and perhaps because of Washington's substantial personal holdings in the area. After quelling the "insurrection," Lee and Hamilton marched a score of "rebels" back to Philadelphia, making them public examples of frontier delinquency and of federal punishment. When the rebellion officially ended, "only twelve cases went to trial, and ... only two rebels were convicted" (Hogeland 238).

George Washington magnanimously pardoned these two because actual punishment for individual crimes was not important. An example had to be made out of an entire region's delinquency, proving the superior power of the federal government: "Holding large numbers of lesser-known people in Philadelphia for long periods of confusion and fear, and then sending them home, extended the policy" whereby frontiersmen were subjected to the federal government's power. "The idea was to destroy the will of an enemy that, though stubborn, had in the end been no match for the energy and scope of the national government" (238). The "leaders" of the Whiskey Rebellion were never brought to justice because it was more important that the followers realize that *they too* were subject to the arm of the law. With agents of federal enforcement prowling the western country, any citizen could be potentially under surveillance and subject to prosecution at any time; the power of and obedience to the federal government needed to be instilled in the consciousness of the people, and such selective prosecution made that possible.

Richard Kohn argues that the Whiskey rebellion was "'a clear-cut case of the failure of law and the necessity for coercion.' The question facing the government was not whether to suppress the rebellion, but how" (qtd. in Slaughter, "Friends of Liberty" 21). The application of fifteen thousand troops to put down an insurgency of fewer than one thousand western citizens certainly represents a display of power antithetical to Foucauldian disciplinary techniques. The oppression of the frontiersmen in the Three Forks area of Pennsylvania, however, was beside the point: it was a by-product of the desire to instill willful obedience in the population. Everyone in the new country became distinctly aware of the government's power in his or her daily life. When little-known men, and not just the leaders of the rebellion, could be taken into custody to answer for the crime of sedition, any and all citizens could and would be subject to the law. The display itself reveals that the disciplinary techniques employed by Hamilton and his peers had a gradual effect. The excise pushed the frontiersmen to open rebellion, which in turn forced the federal government to mobilize, which ultimately reinforced the federal government's position in relation to the states and the citizens.

The federalization of state militias, including those of Virginia, North Carolina, and Pennsylvania, further helped to solidify the federal government's powers by circumscribing the powers of state governments. This could never have happened under the Articles of Confederation. Hamilton and Washington utilized the powers given to the federal government by the newly ratified Constitution through (a) the whiskey excise itself— federal government's ability to tax individuals within separate states without their direct approval (under the federal government's right to regulate interstate commerce — Article I, Section 8 of the Constitution); and (b) the federalization of militias (the president could call on the states to provide men and arms for the protection of the republic — Article II, Section 2 of the Constitution). Just as importantly, though, both of these measures initiated a type of micro-politics wherein the law-abiding citizen was conditioned into identification with and internalization of the authority of the government. As it concerns the micro-politics of the militias, Foucault would say that "they carve[d] out individual segments and establish[ed] operational links; they mark[ed] places and indicate[d] values" (*DP* 148). Each militia member had his specific place and his specific responsibility in the service of his government. The *federalization* of the state militias conditioned the members of those militias to willingly do the bidding of the *federal* government despite the fact that the people they marched to suppress had so recently been their brothers-in-arms.

Moreover, the advent of an insurgency against taxation by the federal government made the mountains on the western outskirts of civilization a realm of resistance. This resistance made it easy to label the region as "backward" and as opposed to "progress." It helped those in power hone the descriptions of mountain inhabitants William Byrd II had initiated. The whiskey excise stigmatized noncompliant distillers as "delinquents" (in both Hamilton's and Foucault's terms) and pitted them against the federal government. More importantly it compartmentalized citizens who rebelled against the newly formed republic: they became rebels against the common good, while the authoritative position of the federal government became further solidified. The mountain region became an example for the rest of the nation, categorized and compartmentalized and enclosed *beyond the pale*. In this context and thereafter, overtly challenging the authority of the federal government with a display of force was futile.

At a cursory glance, Hamilton's implementation of the whiskey excise appears largely ineffective. Resistance cropped up all over the frontier where geography made enforcement largely impossible, and eventually the excise was repealed when Thomas Jefferson assumed the presidency. However, Hamilton's use of the excise tax, his knowledge that it would disproportionately affect the settlers west of the mountains, and his eventual decision to execute the tax in a well-defined and enclosed region, set up a model for disciplining the American population, a model that has been used, consciously or unconsciously, to discipline the mountaineer since. The federal government could have never enforced the whiskey excise throughout the entire frontier. However, by enclosing the Whiskey Rebellion both *geographically* and *ideologically*, by making its perpetrators outlaws and delinquents, and by subjecting only *some* of the whiskey rebels to the talons of the law, Hamilton and his fellow Federalists began to train the American population to identify with the law and order represented by the federal authorities. The frontier represented a lawless place and the potential anarchy posed by the Whiskey Rebels helped the government alienate those who would stand against the republic. The entire episode created a dichotomy between the law-abiding people of the surrounding regions and the lawlessness of both the geographical mountains and the frontier people who inhabited them. People who, like the Founding Fathers, sought to profit financially from such a rendering of the soon-to-be-labeled-*Appalachian* region and its people would quickly exploit its reported lawlessness.

And thus begins the archeology of *Appalachia* and the Appalachian region. The relationships between the mountain inhabitants and the various authorities who have sought to take advantage of the geographical, natural, and human resources of the region have ever been contentious and remain so to this day. Corporations, utilities, the government, and individuals all vie for the same land, so conflict is inevitable. Power and resistance circle and spar. Back and forth they dart and feint. Organizations plan for the future. Typically, those with the least power find themselves most disfranchised as a matter of course. Mike Clark and Jim Branscombe maintain that in Appalachian history,

> you couldn't call it a conspiracy, but when the planners finally get around to doing something, it meshes perfectly with the wishes of the corporations. You don't need to prove a conspiracy to see the effect. You don't need to prove that the governor of a state sat down with his planners and said, 'Okay, we're gonna get these bastards out of the hills and hollows.' The conspiracy doesn't have to happen, because the result is automatic. Ultimately, the interests of the planners and the politicians and the corporations merge, and the people are the victims [qtd. in Egerton 239].

The Whiskey Rebellion was not a conspiracy either, but it established the foundations for interactions between those in positions of power and those in the mountains who resist that power. Any scholar, critic, or writer who delves into the realm of the Appalachian region or *Appalachia*, wades through these histories of power and resistance. Cormac McCarthy, a writer of some uncommon skill, excavates the relationships between authority and the mountaineer in his Appalachian works—*The Orchard Keeper, Outer Dark, Child of God, Suttree, The Road* and *The Gardener's Son*—providing the critic with one site of *Appalachian* archeology.

Introduction
AN ARCHEOLOGY OF
AUTHORITY AND APPALACHIA

When Alexander Hamilton sent federal regulators into the mountains to make mountain whiskey distillers pay taxes, those mountain people resisted the intrusion. Later in the history of federal alcohol regulation, the enforcers of Prohibition became known as "revenuers"; their presence in rural America, especially in Appalachia, and their opposition to mountaineer "bootleggers" stems from the implementation of laws similar to those that spurred the Whiskey Rebellion. The unwanted presence of such government officials has induced in the mountaineer the idea that he has been constantly watched by "outsiders" and by the government and its agents; Jack Weller claims that the mountaineer historically "finds it difficult to understand the bureaucracies of business and government. He has a certain fear of them, as if those who run them were out to get him or were interested only in doing things to their own advantage and at his expense" (56). In one specific relationship between the mountaineer and authority, the attempted regulation of "un-bonded" Appalachian liquor, produced a resentment in the mountaineer toward authority, a desire to avoid encounters with revenuers, and an urge to subvert legal mandates. The Whiskey Rebellion and the conflict it initiated was merely the beginning of a tumultuous relationship between Appalachian mountain people and figures of authority who have sought to define, confine, educate, discipline, and otherwise use the mountaineer. For the industries who wanted to extract timber and coal and other natural resources from Appalachia, for the proponents of social uplift who saw the mountaineer as a potential convert outside their back door, for the government who recognized the utilitarian value of the region, and for the academic who makes the study of such relationships his work, the mountaineer inhabitants of Appalachia present(ed) a paradoxical predicament: white, Anglo-Saxon, Christian Americans who barely engaged in the historical sweep of modernizing American capitalism and who remained isolated, undisciplined "primitives" within a few hundred miles of modernizing American metropolises. A peasant exception to American exceptionalism. Who these authorities are, what constitutes their ulterior motives, and how the indigenous mountaineer has responded to them is one focus of this study.

Cormac McCarthy's "Appalachian" works—*The Orchard Keeper, Outer Dark, Child of God, Suttree, The Gardener's Son,* and to some extent his most recent novel, *The Road*—all reflect the process of modernization as it occurred in the Appalachian mountains in the mid-twentieth century, an era when both scholars and politicians became preoccupied with the saga of the region. Like much Appalachian scholarship, McCarthy's novels reflect the conflicts between the modernizing agents of authority and the mountaineer. David Paul Ragan concludes: "McCarthy depicts a world in which traditional embodiments of value—religion, community, relationships, agrarian connections with the earth—have deteriorated as a result of the increasing pressure of urban culture, commercial interests and governmental intrusions upon the lives of the novel's essentially rural characters" (17); further, "the intrusion of the new, alien authority jeopardizes" the traditional existence of many of McCarthy's characters just as the implementation of the whiskey excise challenged the economic viability of the early mountain frontiersmen and as the later intrusion of extractive industries displaced them (23). McCarthy's work seems especially sensitive to the role that "discipline" plays in the modernization of the Appalachian region because, as Christopher Walsh notes, "McCarthy situates much of his narrative action in the conflict that ensues when archaic ways of mountain life come up against the agencies of modernization, which include the emergence of a robust finance capitalism, industrialization (and the ecological disasters that follow), and large-scale intervention from state and federal government agencies" (*In the Wake of the Sun* 13). Not surprisingly, the interactions between mountain characters and authority in McCarthy mirrors authority's dealings with mountaineers historically, as this study will show.

The rise of the capitalistic democracy of the United States accelerated in the late eighteenth century, continued unabated through the nineteenth, and steamed into the twentieth; power throughout the social strata shifted from old-world, traditional royalty to a new group of landowners and financial barons who controlled both the means and processes of production, and the labor force. They pressed for a modernization that held efficiency as central to economic growth and profit. A political system that touted the freedom of the individual was established at the expense of the "divine right" of monarchies, and the economic system shifted to an "open market" and the unmitigated movement of goods and services. Traditional American history posits that economic outcasts, religious émigrés, and some borderlanders — persons who lived in areas between the jurisdictions of governments — all limited by their social standings in Europe, along with their descendants, rose to become the eastern American elites via their own hard work and savvy. Landowners and financiers ascended to power in a New World system free of Old World social moorings. In the New World, allegiances were not to kings but to self-determination and the accumulation of personal material wealth. Old regimes of power predicated on economic, political, and social oppression began losing their efficacy. The solitary laborer gained new prominence in the machine of progress on whose back the barons of industry established their economic, political and social dominance. But this laborer still needed guidance. The new elite in America could not depend on the old forms of domination over the masses.

The disciplinary techniques Michel Foucault names and the advent of both American self-governance and American capitalism go hand in hand. When Foucault speaks of capitalism in general, he maintains that "the growth of a capitalist economy gave rise to the specific modality of disciplinary power, whose general formulas, techniques of submitting forces and bodies, in short, 'political anatomy,' could be operated in the most diverse political regimes, apparatuses or institutions" (*DP* 221). The American republic was one of those diverse political regimes. American political ideology has maintained a theoretical egalitarianism, but capitalism ensures economic and social stratification. American political constructions of personal liberty and autonomy made wholesale oppression and suppression of the poorer, often transient classes by the wealthier, landed ones nearly impossible; the American experiment demanded more subtle forms of coercion. Allen Batteau claims that "at the internal periphery of a mature capitalist economy, power is exercised less by force or cooptation, and more by manipulation of regressive and self-defeating impulses within the dependent class" ("Rituals of Dependence" 144). As the nineteenth and twentieth centuries progressed, America became a mature capitalist economy and the Appalachian region sat squarely on its "internal periphery." Batteau discusses Appalachia's economic relationship to the rest of America, stating:

> The larger structure in question is the set of relationships of objective dependency between the regional economies of Appalachia and lowland metropoles. These relationships establish a subservient position for the region in financial, commercial, and regulatory transactions. Whether this is a matter of "dependent development," the creation of "internal periphery," or "internal colonialism" is of

less interest to us than its aggregate result: It has precluded industrial diversification and regional autonomy in Appalachia, because all capital formation has flowed into channels of greatest profit to lowland commercial and financial centers ["Rituals of Dependence" 142–143].

This trend started with Alexander Hamilton's manipulation of the banking system and the whiskey excise.

Therefore, Foucault's ideas about discipline can shed light on social and economic relationships within nineteenth- and twentieth-century America, especially the relationships between persons in positions of authority and how they have dealt with inhabitants of geographical Appalachia — persons often called "hillbillies" and other derisive names. These persons are known in academic circles as mountaineers, and as Walsh reminds us, "It is precisely these marginal cultures and characters overlooked ... and ridiculed by the culture outside of the South that McCarthy brings to center stage" (*In the Wake of the Sun* 8).

The eastern mountains, one hundred and fifty to two hundred miles inland from the Atlantic coast of the North American continent, now known as the Appalachians, have existed for millennia; not so *Appalachia*. While *Appalachia* falls roughly within the geographical boundaries and immediately surrounding areas of the mountains that bear the name, and despite having been so long a part of the American consciousness and vernacular, *Appalachia* "is not simply something that is immediately 'out-there' in the southern mountains. Rather, much of what we take to be 'Appalachia' is a complex, multi-layered, and intertextual reality. In other words, it is a social construction produced and reproduced — often without much interference or assistance by locals — in an ongoing set of discourses about the actual place and its peoples, i.e., a body of interpretation and discussion" (Blee and Billings 119).

Appalachia is not a specific region of the continent, but a spatial metaphor and a domain of discourse. Likewise, the mountaineer as we know him, this wayward scion of the American Adam, is a fiction, a device, and a tool: "Every society has a battery of social types that its members use to classify one another, but what we might call the economy of social types has been profoundly affected by mass literature and the mass media of communication," and the mountaineer remains the perfect example of just such a social type whose status has been "enhanced" by literature and mass media (Reed 8). Loosely grounded in the mountain reality, he is an icon used in the disciplining of the Appalachian mountain region, its people, and rest of American culture. Deconstructing the discursive ontology of *Appalachia* and its mountaineer inhabitants allows a critic "to capture the process by which knowledge functions as a form of power and disseminates the effects of power," as Foucault would say; the act of trying "to decipher discourse through the use of spatial, strategic metaphors enables one to grasp precisely the points at which discourses are transformed in, through and on the basis of relations of power" (*P/K* 69–70).

Appalachia as an image was created and has been subsequently employed to disfranchise the mountaineer, causing the rest of society to view him as an "other." The problem of mountaineers is the position of social ambivalence they occupy: they do not hold power positions, but they enable positions of power to exist through their alterity. While being used as a rhetorical oppositional to the dominant culture, however, mountaineers can also seize their rhetorical identity and wield it as a weapon against their own reification and against the hegemonic culture that keeps them in a station of economic, political, and social obscurity. Simultaneously, though, this seizure of identity and of name can be manipulated by the hegemonic culture to confirm the preconceived notions and stereotypes of the mountaineer as Other. The relationship between the mountaineer and the authorities that have historically dealt with him presents a classic example of Foucauldian resistance and power, one that is reflected and deconstructed in McCarthy's Appalachian novels, in which McCarthy engages in a "discourse which implores us to reconsider the [Appalachian] region's relationship to America as a whole, especially those narratives about the disempowered and marginalized" (Walsh, *In the Wake of the Sun* 21).

Foucauldian Power Relations

Power in a Foucauldian analysis is not an insidious, prohibitive, restrictive force that acts on individuals. To the contrary, power is an ambivalent element in dialogic relationship. In *The History of Sexuality*, Foucault defines power and power relations as the

> [m]ultiplicity of force relations immanent in the sphere in which they operate and which constitute their own organization; as the process which, through ceaseless struggles and confrontations, transforms, strengthens, or reverses them; as the support which these force relations find in one another, thus forming a chain or a system, or on the contrary, the disjunctions and contradictions which isolate them from one another; and lastly as the strategies in which they take effect, whose general design or institutional crystallization is embodied in the state apparatus, in the formation of the law, in the various hegemonies [92].

Power relations are a web; they are not an isolated entity. They course through the social strata playing off one another, connecting every individual. Custom molds behavior; law strengthens custom; extra-legal social stigmatization and punishment reinforce "proper" actions and eliminate "improper" ones, and so on. All of these elements sculpt the behavior patterns of individuals within society. Discipline is not the piston in the cylinder or even the gasoline in the combustion chamber; rather, it is the oil that lubricates the entire engine mechanism.

Further, disciplinary power functions not from the top down as an oppressive control over individuals; it functions discreetly through them, utilizing each individual as a source, a point and an object of surveillance. Foucault makes this explicit:

> [D]isciplinary power became an "integrated" system, linked from the inside to the economy and to the aims of the mechanism in which it was practiced. It was also organized as a multiple, automatic and anonymous power; for although surveillance rests on individuals, its functioning is that of a network of relations from top to bottom, but also to a certain extent from bottom to top and laterally; this network "holds" the whole together and traverses it in its entirety with effects of power that derive from one another: supervisors, perpetually supervised.... [T]his enables the disciplinary power to be both absolutely indiscreet, since it is everywhere and always alert, since by its very principle it leaves no zone of shade and constantly supervises the very individuals who are entrusted with the task of supervising; and absolutely "discreet," for it functions permanently and largely in silence. Discipline makes possible the operation of a relational power that sustains itself by its own mechanism and which, for the spectacle of public events, substitutes the uninterrupted play of calculated gazes [*DP* 176–177].

In disciplinary power relations, the "norm" sets a standard for homogenization and makes possible the definition of variations from that norm: "It individualizes by making it possible to measure the gaps, to determine levels, to fix specialties and to render the differences useful by fitting them one to another"; it makes possible "all the shading of individual differences" (184). "Calculated gazes," reproduced in individuals throughout the social strata, create a power relationship wherein they establish "over individuals a visibility through which one differentiates them and judges them" (184). Such visibility enables differentiation.

Discipline in the Foucauldian sense certainly curbs social misbehavior; additionally, though, it creates order and stability within the social and economic system. If each individual has his own space, then each has a specific purpose within a specified economy — he can be supervised individually, as can his associates, who also have their specified space within the specified economy. In this way, disciplines ensure efficiency. They "carve out individual segments and establish operational links.... [T]hey guarantee the obedience of individuals, but also a better economy of time and gesture"; they organize both obedience and economies: "The first of the great operations of discipline is, therefore, the constitution of '*tableaux vivants*,' which transform the confused, useless, or dangerous multitudes into ordered multiplicities" (148). By dividing, compartmentalizing, and hierarchizing, discipline isolates individuals and then connects them together so that they can be used with systematic efficiency.

The disciplines employ a variety of techniques — enclosure, examination, training, panopticism; they create delinquents and use illegalities to distinguish and compartmentalize citizens. Discipline "sometimes requires *enclosure*, the specification of a place heterogeneous to all others and closed in upon itself. It is the protected place of disciplinary monotony" (141). Individuals are compartmentalized and disciplinary situations create juxtapositions that illuminate difference; discipline "'trains' the moving, confused, useless multitudes of bodies and forces into a multiplicity of individual elements.... [T]he success of disciplinary power derives no doubt from the use of simple instruments; hierarchal observation, normalizing judgment and their combination in a procedure that is specific to it, the examination" (170). Discipline employs the *gaze*. Illustrating the ideal of this idea, Foucault cites Jeremy Benthum's architectural mechanism "the Panopticon" to explain how this gaze works in a society:

> The panoptic mechanism arranges spatial unities that make it possible to see constantly and to recognize immediately.... [The individual] is seen, but he does not see; he is the object of information, never a subject in communication.... [H]ence the major effect of the Panopticon: to induce in the inmate a state of consciousness and permanent visibility that assures the automatic functioning of power.... [T]he inmates should be caught up in a power situation of which they are themselves the bearers [200–201].

He is quick to add, however, that panopticism is not limited to an architecture, but that it pervades the social strata and the consciousness of each individual (205). Panopticism works because the individual interiorizes the idea that he or she might be watched at any given moment and acts accordingly.

Disciplinary measures show themselves in places where efficiency remains a major goal. However, the disciplines are not oppressive in any traditional sense; they increase the efficiency of functions: they "increase the possible utility of individuals ... [they] increase aptitudes, speeds, output and therefore profits" (210). The cotton mill town disciplines the existence of its laborers. Each industry worker's material existence is virtually identical, as is his or her relationship to the owners of the town. Addressing coal mining specifically, Appalachian advocate Harry Caudill laments that

> the miner was only a licensee of the company in the occupancy of his camp house. He had always spent at least three quarters of his pay in the company

stores. He and his family found recreation in the company-owned movie theaters and when he managed to finance a secondhand automobile he bought tires and gasoline for it at the company-owned service station. His children were delivered by company doctors and if the birth occurred in a hospital, the hospital was company owned [Caudill 174–175].

Like the coal towns of which Caudill speaks, "in the mill towns the mountaineers could find community and its institutions, including schools, churches, recreation facilities, and sanitary conditions" (Shapiro, *Appalachia on Our Mind* 170). These institutions, controlled by the mill owners, regimented the millhand's life outside the mill, while the regimentation of the mills themselves categorized the mountaineer-turned-millhand's vocational existence. Mirroring historic reality, in McCarthy's *The Gardener's Son*, the mill bell tolls out the workers' shifts and only mill laborers could live in the Greggs' mill houses (33, 32). A factory time clock regiments the minutes of a laborer's day; a school bell separates those who efficiently use their time between classes and those who do not; collective exercise, marching drills, and stringent dress code requirements make the military what it is — regimented. These institutions enclose and train individuals to the point that discipline becomes second nature. Each institution runs most smoothly when this internalization occurs and the individuals enforce the discipline all by themselves. This internalization extends a web of disciplined relations to modern society

> [n]ot because the disciplinary modality of power has replaced all others; but because it has infiltrated the others, sometimes undermining them, but serving as an intermediary between them, linking them together, extending them and above all making it possible to bring the effects of power to the most minute and distant elements.... [I]t is not that the beautiful totality of the individual is amputated, repressed, altered by our social order, it is rather that the individual is carefully fabricated in it.... [Society's members are] in the panoptic machine, invested by the effects of power, which we bring to ourselves since we are part of its mechanism [216–217].

Like the inmates of the Panopticon, citizens of a community both comprise and exist in the disciplinary machine. Drawn out of the isolation of his backwoods existence by economic factors beyond his control, the mountaineer came to civilization and entered into this disciplinary situation, whether in a mill town or a mining camp.

In the nineteenth century, Appalachia served as a delinquent Other against which American culture was defined. Though the rationale was economic, the introduction of modern roads, railways, and industrial processes brought to the Appalachian region the disciplinary training Foucault sees fitting so perfectly with capitalism. They brought the mountaineer into closer contact with modernizing America. Eller reminds us that "the arrival of the railroads after 1880 stimulated a variety of nonagricultural developments — including furniture, textile, tourism, oil, chemical, and mineral-related industries — which combined to pull large numbers of mountaineers into the new industrial system" (*Miners* 121). Old economic habits like bartering were replaced by a wage- and coin-dictated economy, an economy in which the mountaineer was disadvantaged. As the extractive industries conducted their ecologically unfriendly business, the value of the already meager farmland depreciated and the mountaineer could not maintain his agrarian/sylvan lifestyle; he was forced to enter the modern economy, to take jobs in timber mills, coal camps, and cotton mills, where he felt the full brunt of modernity. The McEvoys in *The Gardener's Son* are the perfect examples of this phenomenon; Chris Walsh states, "The McEvoys are inexorably caught up in the enforced pattern of migration from mountain farms to industrial milltowns that characterized this period in Appalachian history" (*In the Wake of the Sun* 334). Because things became so bad in the Appalachian mountains, whole families would journey to the mill towns or coal camps, only to discover that there was no work for them. While the McEvoy family luckily finds work, James Gregg turns another such family away (21–24).

In addition to spatializing populations, categorizing deviance, and compartmentalizing individuals, discipline creates *delinquents* whose entire lives become the focus and locus of observations that "condemn them to recidivism" (*DP* 267). Delinquency and regulated illegalities are disciplinary functions that help sustain domination because those who control and manipulate politics and economics proscribe the ways delinquents and illegalities are both characterized and punished. This works in three ways: (a) delinquents come primarily from the lower classes, against whom the weight of law is often thrown; (b) delinquents themselves require supervision; and (c) delinquents' disbursal throughout society necessitates and legitimates the infiltration of society by the observing agents of the hegemony: the police. Certainly these characterizations of delinquents in society present themselves in an Appalachian mountain context and in literature about the Appalachian region. The image of the region as "backward," and its citizens as prime examples of sloth and degeneracy, comes in handy to a society that wishes to promote the capitalist values of hard work, thrift, and efficiency.

A system of discipline cannot be implemented overnight, of course: "It is rather a multiplicity of often minor processes, of different origin and scattered location, which overlap, repeat, or imitate one another, support one another, distinguish themselves from one another according to their domain of application, converge and gradually produce the blueprint of a general method" (138). The genius of discipline, of course, is that it is not heavily oppressive or overtly coercive. It is not draped over the society from an authoritarian objectivity; rather, "it is the specific technique of a power that regards individuals both as objects and as instruments of its exercise" (170). All of these disciplinary techniques can be observed in McCarthy's work with respect to the mountaineer.

Disciplining the Mountaineer

In his "Afterword" to Foucault's *Power/Knowledge*, Colin Gordon states, "'Madness' does not signify a real historical-anthropological entity at all but is rather the name for a fiction or a historical construct: the problem which it addresses is hence that of the series of conceptual and practical operations through which madness, as mental illness, has been constituted in our societies and an object of certain forms of knowledge and a target of certain institutional practices" (235). Were one to replace "madness" with "hillbilly," or "the mountaineer," Gordon's quote could be read in the same way. The image of the mountaineer, replete with the political, economic, and social imperatives of those who have helped create and sustain this image, has become synonymous with reality: "The southern mountains have been missionarized, researched, studied, surveyed, romanticized, dramatized, hillbillyized, Dog-patched, and povertyized" throughout American history (West 12). Though not merely passive objects in the westward expansion of the United States, mountaineers have encountered disenfranchisement, displacement, and discrimination in their economic, social, cultural, and political interactions with the American culture at large. The mountaineer presents society with a paradox and has ever done so: how can a people so similar and simultaneously dissimilar to the rest of the nation—"contemporary ancestors" both strange and peculiar—exist on the periphery of modern society economically, socially, culturally, and politically? The answer is that they cannot and they do not. The truly paradoxical answer rests in the convolution of the "real" mountaineer and the "iconic" mountaineer.

The Appalachian region does have real social and economic difficulties, and several different explanations for Appalachian challenges have been put forth in both academic and policy conversations: (a) genes vs. environment; (b) a subculture of poverty; (c) regional development (or a lack thereof); and (d) internal colonialism (Walls and Billings 42–43). Ironically, though, the real problem stems from the fact that academia, benevolent organizations, writers (even sympathetic ones), industries, and the government have continually confused the mountaineer of literature and myth with the people of the Appalachian mountains, and they are *not* one and the same. Ronald Eller claims that

> [t]he great mass of existing historical literature has simply failed to provide an authentic record of the mountain experience or of mountaineers' perceptions of that experience. Neglected by professional historians, Appalachian history has been reduced to popular legends and myths perpetuated in romantic novels, missionary tracts, and social surveys. Central to this reality is the fact that much of the traditional literature on mountain life has been written from the perspective of outsiders — people whose cultural views were more in line with the outer, mass society than with the culture of the mountain people themselves ["Appalachian Oral History" 2].

The mountaineer, subsequently, has been disciplined by a fiction. Authority and its agents have used the image of the mountaineer to justify the exploitation, displacement, study, disciplining, and depopulation of an entire population of Americans. And this image has allowed the mountaineer to shoulder the blame, because as Eller notes, "Our efforts to explain and deal with the social problems of the region have focused not on economic and political realities in the area as they have evolved over time, but on the supposed inadequacies of a pathological culture that is seen to have equipped mountain people poorly for life in the modern industrial world" (*Miners* xviii). Thus, the mountaineer has *become* a deviant in relation to normative American society; he has *become* enclosed in a stereotype as a delinquent who must be observed and policed. John Shelton Reed says that "the mass media," who have been instrumental in facilitating the internalization of the mountaineer iconography, "have proven to be voracious consumers of social types, picking them up, legitimating them, amplifying them, and feeding them back to the audience as categories for thought" (9). For over two hundred years, the audience has ingested particular ideas about mountaineers, and only recently has anyone challenged those ideas. Echoing John Cant's claim in his *Cormac McCarthy and the Myth of American Exceptionalism*, I will argue that McCarthy is one author who starts with "the mountain people of isolated Appalachian Tennessee, and writes them into the discourse of America in a way which no-one [has] previously attempted" (Cant 71). Both Cant and Chris Walsh note that McCarthy challenges Appalachian mythologies by giving "a voice to those excluded from official historical records" grounding his work in an interpretation of the historical record that reflects his own personal experiences with the culture of East Tennessee (Walsh, *In the Wake of the Sun* 56). That is why "an understanding of the social, historical, cultural, and environmental issues evoked by the subtly presented nuances of time and place" in McCarthy's

Appalachian works is so vitally essential to any understanding of them (Luce, *Reading the World* vii).

In the mid-nineteenth century, "the progress of civilization in America, and Americans' self-consciousness of their progress, was such that the apparent persistence of pioneer conditions among the mountain people made Appalachia seem a strange land inhabited by peculiar people" (Shapiro, *Appalachia on Our Mind* xiii). In this era of discipline, deviance from a norm became an increasingly potent concept; there was no color difference and little class difference between mountaineers and other American whites, so

> [c]onventional modes of resolving the dilemma posed by the perception of "deviance" from the American norm by a region or a people — ascription of geographic, chronological, or ethnic distance which made such "deviance" seem natural and normal — could not be utilized to explain the "deviance" of white, Anglo-Saxon, Protestant, native-born Americans [x].

In order to distinguish them, to compartmentalize them and to discipline them, their difference and deviance had to be invented. Appalachia *became* a place of difference. In the case of the local colorists — writers who used Appalachian oddity for their own financial gain — Appalachia provided fodder for creativity; in the case of those involved with denominational benevolence — "home" missionaries of Christian denominations — Appalachia provided the impetus for financial contributions. For the mountaineer to be fully enclosed and properly distributed, he had to be rhetorically objectified. In the preface of *Appalachia on Our Mind*, Shapiro discusses early conceptions of the Appalachian region. He maintains that the designation of Appalachian mountain difference arose in the 1870s. The first chapter of Shapiro's text looks at how the culturally accepted regional stereotypes were actually constructed by these "local color" writers who were more concerned with making money than telling the truth about mountain existence. He cites Will Wallace Harney's 1873 article for *Lippencott's Magazine*, "A Strange Land and Peculiar People" (a phrase since overused to describe the inhabitants and land of Appalachia), as one of the instigators of this phenomenon. Perhaps it is no coincidence that Harney's "peculiar people" resemble George Washington Harris's Sut Lovingood, the "Nat'ral Born Durn'd Fool" Harris last published stories about in 1869, the year of his death. Harney's "research" also took place in 1869. Perhaps this is an early incident of "reality" mirroring fiction.

Further development of the mountaineer image came from the writings of "local colorists" and from the needs of "home missionaries." Shapiro says of local-colorist Mary Noailles Murfree, "the popularity of Murfree's sketches did not depend on the validity of her private experience so much as the ability to establish the otherness of Appalachia as a matter of fact rather than of mere unfamiliarity" (*Appalachia on Our Mind* 20). Harris, Murfree, Harney, James Lane Allen, John Fox Jr., and other "local color" writers exploited the perceived differences between the Appalachian region and the rest of America, and in so doing proliferated the mythic status of Appalachian alterity, framing the mountains and their people in an iconographic, rhetorical enclosure. Some of the first instances of feuds, of conflicts between revenuers and moonshiners, and of the general depravity of the mountain people occur not within the realm of reality, but within the context of fiction. When they were reported in the historical record, they often became colored with the attitudes and preconceptions of people who came to the mountains looking to verify the ideas about hillbillies they gleaned from fiction.

When Natalie Grant says of Cormac McCarthy's characters, "They are alienated, often by choice, from their culture and their individual communities, and isolated by geography in remote rural areas," she could be talking about the iconography of the historical mountaineer as well as his representation in McCarthy (75). My convolution here of the literal and literary mountaineer reproduces the historical confusion of reality and myth. Power resides in this confusion: "Although myths are the product of human thought and labor, their identification with venerable tradition makes them appear to be products of 'nature' rather than history — expressions of a transhistorical consciousness or some form of 'natural law'" (Slotkin 6). If Appalachian degeneracy and squalor are "natural" occurrences rather than results of economic deprivations or rhetorical creations, then the "fault" for them can be placed on Appalachian inhabitants themselves. The inhabitants themselves become the focus of change rather than their economic realities or their iconographic images as constructed in the social psychology of a society at large.

Shapiro speaks of "cognitive dissonance" wherein the "conception of reality and reality as perceived [as it concerns Appalachia] do not seem to agree" (*Appalachia on Our Mind* xvi). The geographical Appalachian enclosure and the "cognitive dissonance" demonstrated in the prolific writing about Appalachian peculiarity compartmentalize the hill people, allow them to be defined in relation to the norm and vice versa. Whether or not the material reality of existence — and make no mistake, the Appalachian mountaineer has been physically isolated — coincides with the rhetorical reality created in fiction and denominational benevolence, the mountaineer has become enclosed by such attitudes; such compartmentalization advances both his own discipline and his usefulness in the disciplining of the rest of American society.

Enabling Access and Assigning Space

Vereen Bell suggests, "The phrase 'beyond the pale' is one [McCarthy] uses; and it is worth pausing over, for the idea inherent in it is metaphorically central to everything McCarthy has written. In fifteenth-century Ireland beyond the pale meant outside the jurisdiction of the English monarch — hence, to the English and in fact, unadministered and uncivilized" (11). From a disciplinary standpoint, much the same could be said about the entirety of the Appalachian mountains prior to the coming of the roads, timber companies, railroads, mill towns, and coal camps. As Bell mentions, the spaces "beyond the pale" are "unadministered" and are, therefore, uncontrolled and undisciplined. Herein lies one of the difficulties of the Appalachian enclosure: the mountaineer, inside his demarcated homespace of the mountains, enjoyed relative freedom from discipline and from contact with a capitalistic culture. The geographical isolation kept mountaineers from "coagulating" with other populations from impoverished areas of the United States: poor blacks and rednecks of the deep South, southern and eastern European immigrant minorities in the Northeast and Midwest, Native American communities in the plains states and on various reservations throughout the country, Chicano immigrants in the southwest, and Asian immigrants in the Pacific west. Though the mountaineer had contact with these groups, especially via the coal mining industry at various points in history, he remained separated from them both geographically and ideologically. Nevertheless, the mountaineer's isolation was not enough to ensure his discipline. As Foucault concludes, even within enclosure, the individual must be further compartmentalized for discipline to be most effective. In the Appalachians, further physical compartmentalization of individuals was at first impossible. The territory was too vast and too geographically varied. At the founding of the United States, these mountains were much like the rest of the territory of the continent: unknown, unexplored, unmapped.

Ronald Eller notes, "During the twentieth century, 'hillbilly culture' would become the standard means of rationalizing the poverty of an exploited region. In the late nineteenth century, it became a major justification for the swift acquisition of mountain land and resources by outsiders" (*Miners* 43). Mountaineers became the new Indians. The construction of railroads and roads enabled this acquisition of land. The rhetorical image created by local color writers and denominational philanthropists — that of educational depravity, cultural backwardness, fiscal poverty, mental and physical squalor — encouraged the exploitation of the mountain region and its resources. The building of roads facilitated this exploitation. Ambivalent and inorganic constructions, roads provided industry with easy access to the natural resources of the Appalachians. However, they also gave the mountaineer mobility and the ability to resist the manipulations of authority. While roads demarcate and compartmentalize spaces, they can be used to subvert authority, as the mountaineer tradition of bootlegging demonstrates. Ultimately, though, roads bring mountaineer and authority into contact with one another, and in that space many of the conflicts between the two parties play out.

McCarthy's work centers on the space of the road. The Green Fly Inn, a roadhouse in *The Orchard Keeper,* attracts mountaineers and bootleggers and delinquents and constables. Like this saloon, both standing on the side of the road and perching over the mountain hollow behind it, "the citizens of Red Branch cling to a precarious place in American life" (Cant 65). Many of McCarthy's characters — Arthur Ownby, Marion Sylder, Kenneth Rattner, Culla and Rinthy Holme, Lester Ballard, Bobby McEvoy, and Cornelius Suttree — all utilize roads just as the historical mountaineer has, in spite of his marginal sociocultural status. Chapter One of this study examines the roads of the Appalachian region and how they have helped facilitate the modernization of the Appalachian Mountains and the disciplining of the mountaineer.

Fleeing to Modernization and Discipline

When extractive industries displaced the mountaineer, he took the roads of Appalachia to cotton mill villages and regional cities looking for work. Both village and city life were more regimented and disciplined than the farm and forest. Separated and compartmentalized from his fellow employees, the individual mountaineer's actions, attitudes, and way of life became readily discernable from the actions, attitudes, and ways of life of those other individuals around him. Though still isolated from the rest of American society, coal camps and cotton mill villages placed the mountaineer in a living and working situation that, in the words of John Gaventa, allowed "the development of a system of controls" over the mountaineer (86). Gaventa remarks that the isolation from the rest of America did not singularly ensure the functioning of these controls. However, these controls were

> found in the nexus between the job and the community. A worker in the coal camp was reminded of that nexus every two weeks when he received his pay slip, for from his wages were docked rent, services, goods purchased at the store, medical bills, even funeral expenses — all by the same employer. The slip symbolically fused the miner's dependence as worker, tenant, consumer, and citizen. This unitary structure meant that power exercised in one part of the system could evoke a response in another: misbehaviour in the job could cause the loss of a home; failure to shop at the company store (where prices were often higher)

could mean the loss of work; disobedience of a single rule could mean eviction from the game altogether [89].

This pervasive web of relations created in the coal camp community by the operators certainly represents a form of Foucauldian disciplinary control. As in other instances, this institution of discipline "secreted a machinery of control that functioned like a microscope of conduct; the fine, analytical divisions that they created formed around men an apparatus of observation, recording and training" (*DP* 173). Standards were established and quiescence was ensured because when the mountaineer-turned-miner internalized this power relationship, as he invariably did, he came to depend on the coal company and to defer to its wishes in the political and economic realms of life. For the coal companies and the mountaineers they employed, "the establishment of power meant more: it meant the instillation of an ideology that would more permanently serve to shroud the inequalities and help to ensure non-challenging participation by the non-elite in the new order" (Gaventa 81).

Cotton mill villages operated in much the same way.

Chapter Two considers how the mountaineer becomes disciplined once he leaves the mountain enclaves for cotton mill towns and regional cities. Like so many historical mountaineers who were displaced or could not otherwise remain on their homesteads, the McEvoys of McCarthy's screenplay *The Gardener's Son* take positions in the regimented cotton mill industry, where they discover the difficulties of acclimating to modernization. Like the coal camp, the cotton mill village served as a laboratory for the implementation of disciplinary power; the mountaineer and his fictional counterparts in McCarthy find themselves subject to the time clock, to the spatial compartmentalization of the housing, and to the gazes of their fellow workers in such a village. In *Suttree*, the Appalachian regional city of Knoxville, Tennessee, serves as a repository for mountain folk as it did historically. Slums like McAnally Flats sprang up around the textile and ore mills that skirted the edges of Knoxville's downtown. The people who sought employment and escape from agricultural failure in such spaces found themselves often relegated to those areas of town where they could be more easily subjected to the prying eyes of the authorities and their fellow citizens. Chapter Two looks at how the Greggs' cotton mill town in *The Gardener's Son* and Knoxville in *Suttree* model Foucault's panoptic schema and how they also reflect an historical reality.

The Superlative Delinquent

Discipline can transform the convict into a delinquent via documentation of his entire existence: the convicted criminal becomes "the delinquent whose slow formation is shown in a biographical investigation"; this biography "establishes the 'criminal' as existing before the crime and even outside it," as he is "linked to his offense by a whole bundle of complex threads (instincts, drives, tendencies, character)" (*DP* 252–253). He is no longer merely an individual who commits illegal acts, but a delinquent *type* who is predisposed to illegal activity. If the objective of the modern penal system is rehabilitation, the modern penitentiary has failed miserably. Foucault comes to the conclusion that the penitentiary's failure advantages society more than its success might; in classic disciplinary form, the prison "is not intended to eliminate offenses, but rather to distinguish them, to distribute them, to use them"; "it is not so much that they render docile those who are liable to transgress the law, but that they tend to assimilate the transgression of the laws in a general tactics of subjugation" (272). At the basest levels, the "failure" of the penal system serves the interests of the controlling social hegemony — in the case of an industrialized society like that of the United States — merchant capitalists and the bourgeoisie and those who aspire to such status. Otherwise stated, the "prisons manufactured delinquents, but delinquents turned out to be useful, in the economic domain as much as the political. Criminals come in handy" (*P/K* 40). As Foucault refuses to limit his discussion to the prison itself, so I contend that discipline and delinquency cannot be exclusive to penal architecture; rather, discipline and delinquency pervade society, and in this discussion, the society of Appalachia. Lester Ballard of *Child of God* is the poster child of the delinquent Appalachian type. Chapter Three examines Lester's fabrication in, of, and by his society, despite how his "judgmental community consistently tries to explain Lester's acts in such a way as to prove his constitutional difference from them" (Luce, *Reading the World* 168).

Cormac McCarthy demonstrates and dramatizes this phenomenon when he has his characters objectify and compartmentalize Lester Ballard as they tell stories about him around the courthouse steps. Like the social category of the "hillbilly" in relation to the rest of American society, Ballard becomes enclosed in a position of alterity in relation to the economically, politically, and socially secure mainstream of his society. Both the mythology of Lester's indiscipline and his superlative delinquency help discipline other members of the population. Such characterization defines Lester's relationship to his society and the mountaineer's relationship to American society as a whole. It rhetorically encloses each in a way that geography cannot: it conscripts the construction of perceptions that in turn color the view that society adopts toward these subjects. Such representations of frontier mountain people were already encapsulating real people as early as the last decade of the eighteenth century, when Alexander Hamilton penned his "Tully" letters in defense of the federal government's position on the whiskey excise, and they became more entrenched as the decades progressed. Because Lester Ballard is the quintessential mountaineer delinquent, his case study in *Child of God* deserves special attention in Chapter Three.

Iconography, or the Genesis of All Things Hillbilly

Chapter Four looks at the creation of Appalachian iconography. In *Gunfighter Nation: The Myth of the Frontier in Twentieth-Century America*, Richard Slotkin says, "Myths are stories drawn from a society's history that have acquired through persistent usage the power of symbolizing that society's ideology and of dramatizing its moral consciousness" (5). Slotkin details how the myth of the American frontier has helped to shape the history and politics of twentieth-century America. Appalachia has an intimate role in that myth, of course; it was, after all, the original American frontier. Like the image of the frontier in Slotkin's work, Appalachia has become in many respects a myth and a metaphor. Like the myth of the frontier, the iconography of Appalachia has helped construct the material reality of the region; it has shaped public policy toward the region as well. The construction of *Appalachia* and Appalachian iconography is no accident because "the actual work of making and transmitting myths is done by particular classes of people; myth-making processes are therefore responsive to the politics of class difference" (8). Certain segments of the American population have been instrumental in the creation of *Appalachia*—in most instances, outsiders and others who have some vested interest and ulterior motives for approaching the Appalachian region from a particular theoretical perspective. The inherent problem, of course, with myth-making of this nature, is that it can have palpably negative effects on real people. McCarthy foregrounds this tendency when he "deliberately sets out to give his texts mythic form" and writes characters "in such a way as to point out the destructive consequences of structuring the consciousness of the individuals by means of powerful mythologies which they are not in a position to live out" (Cant 9). Image and reality duel in his work.

Nevertheless, until recently, *Appalachia* and the mountaineer icon have been accepted as truths of Appalachia. Ronald Lewis maintains, "Appalachia is a region without a formal history" (21). Therefore, *Appalachia* could be "invented in the caricatures and atmospheric landscapes of the escapist fiction [local colorists] penned to entertain the emergent urban middle class. The accuracy of these stories and travelogues—the dominant idioms of this genre—generated little or no critical evaluation of their characterizations of either mountain people or the landscape itself" (21). Chapter Four attempts to deconstruct the iconography of *Appalachia*. It examines how the myth has been historically constructed, exposes McCarthy's complicity in and mythoclastic use of this construction, and then demonstrates *Outer Dark*'s manipulation of the myth by revealing how the landscape and action of the novel are projections of character psychology just as the invention of *Appalachia* and mountaineer iconography remain projections of the collective American psychology.

Within the last thirty years, scholars have begun to dig out an archeology of the mountaineer construct. As Billings notes, "Appalachia even before the modern era of coal mining and industrialization was not more economically isolated, nor was its population more homogenous than the populations of other rural sections of the United States" ("Introduction" 12). He and other scholars and writers reveal how "the persistent belief in Appalachian distinctiveness thus results from a persistent way of writing about the mountain region rather than from the region's actual past.... [T]he discourse on Appalachia creates the very reality it purports to describe" (12). McCarthy, of course, is a part of this process of construction, but not one who can be so easily pigeonholed. Like some of the chroniclers of *Appalachia*, McCarthy documents a literary and historical domain while subverting its traditional construction. The poor, degenerate mountaineer was created from a fiction and for a purpose, and the convolution of myth and reality reveals as much about those who have propagated the mountaineer iconography as it does about the mountaineer subjects themselves. The people and entities that have continued to propagate the iconography of Appalachian otherness assist in the disciplining of Appalachia and America. They serve the interests of authority whether they mean to or not.

(Re)Envisioning Appalachia (?)

As a coda to this project, I look at McCarthy's latest work, *The Road*, a return to the geographical region and mythical *Appalachia* of his earlier works. This post-apocalyptic reimagining of Appalachia strips away many of the cultural constructions that have posited the Appalachian mountains as a land that time forgot and the people there as so "strange and peculiar." In it, evidence of the ultimate failure of modernity and of the discipline that made modernization more efficient reveal that all of humanity possesses characteristics so often attributed to the mountaineer. In the novel, the end results of unmitigated industrialization have turned the entire landscape into a wasteland remarkably similar to images associated with areas of Appalachia where mineral extraction and other modernizing influences have destroyed the natural environment. The coda examines whether or not Foucauldian disciplinary measures can survive the destruction of society in McCarthy, and wrestles with how *The Road* manifests a re-visioning of both McCarthy's version of *Appalachia*, of his previous Appalachian writing, and of his version of Appalachian culture, generally. It asks the same question Chris Walsh posits: "Who is prepared to adhere to, or who can possibly enforce, these foundations of a cultural order in a world so brutally cultureless?" (*In the Wake of the Sun* 285).

Appalachia and the mountaineer as rhetorical constructs reveal telling things about the historical interactions of power and resistance within a modernized (or modernizing) society. They also demonstrate the often precarious relationships between history and fiction and myth and other cultural artifacts. Foucault has excavated power relationships in archeologies of prisons, mental health conceptualizations, medical histories, and other institutions whose very existences seem as originary within our society as the cold metal dome in Arthur Ownby's back yard. His critiques reveal as much about modern society as they do about their specified topics. McCarthy's Appalachian works function in many of the same ways. As cultural artifacts themselves, his fictions expose the scaffolding of the modernization of the mountains and their inhabitants; they bring the disciplining of the mountaineer to the surface and into the bright light of direct scrutiny.

One
Spatializing Conduits
The Roads of Appalachia

The Green Fly Inn, resting "on a scaffolding of poles over a sheer drop, the front door giving directly onto the road" (*OK* 12), highlights a roadside "space of lingering impacts and unseen forces" (Stewart 32). Incidents happen in this space straddling two worlds: the prodigal son, out-migrant Marion Sylder, nouveau-riche, reappears to buy his old acquaintances drinks (*OK* 14); Ef Hobie returns after a year and a half in the state penitentiary for possessing bootlegged booze, only to lose his pants (and his money — to Kenneth Rattner) when the entire back porch falls into the holler (23–26). People drink and carouse in the old place that remains "animate as any old ship to her crew and it bred an atmosphere such as few could boast, a solidarity due largely to its very precariousness" (13). After the porch caves in, the back door of the establishment opens to the drop behind it, and "at night the proprietor opened the back door and swept all litter out into the yawning gulf.... [T]he refuse collected there cascaded down the mountain to a depth undetermined, creeping, growing, of indescribable variety and richness" (13). Both the inn and the yawning holler behind it store the detritus of the mountains; they are places "where the effects of capitalism and modernization pile up on the landscape" (Stewart 4). The inn, perched precariously on both the edge of the ancient holler and the modern road, is an Appalachian space through and through. Built as a roadhouse — a literal and linguistic paradox, a house where no one lives — it collects the Ef Hobies, the Marion Sylders, and the Kenneth Rattners, delinquents all, of the mountaineer world. Even the name suggests the cast-off and the scatological: green flies lay their eggs in waste. Refuse above, refuse below. Cultural anthropologist Kathleen Stewart would call it "a space on the side of the road." Bootlegger Marion Sylder drives up to it and so does Deputy Jefferson Gifford. This roadside space, like others in

McCarthy's work, becomes the liminal area of conflict; it "stands as a graphic model to think with. It narrativizes social and moral orders and makes a text not just an object of knowledge, but the very place where the social code is continually dissolved and reconstructed" (Stewart 38).

The Orchard Keeper takes place in a time of great change in the Appalachian Mountains. At the end of Prohibition, straddling the Great Depression, and sandwiched between the two World Wars, in the era of *The Orchard Keeper*, the Appalachian region watched as its inhabitants left for industrial jobs in the northern cities during the nineteen-thirties, abandoning the farms that had been their livelihoods. K. Wesley Berry notes, "True to historical conditions, *The Orchard Keeper* reveals this agricultural decline through such details as the wrecked orchard and farms of Red Branch.... [T]he fictional abandoned farms evoke the historic mass migrations of the yeomanry into towns to claim factory jobs" (51). Roads took those migrants out of the hills; they brought development into the mountains; simultaneously, they created a space on the *edge of the pale* where characters like Marion Sylder, Arthur Ownby, Jefferson Gifford, and Kenneth Rattner could exist.

The main action of *The Orchard Keeper* opens in such a space. Kenneth Rattner, vagrant, highwayman extraordinaire, walks down a roadway near Atlanta and watches as the form of "a pickup truck, whipped past and receded into the same liquid shape by which it came" (*OK* 8). Rattner thrives in this roadside space and he tells those he meets story after story, or from another viewpoint, lie after lie about his plight: "Had he been asked his name he might have given any but Kenneth Rattner, which was his name" (10). He makes the ambivalent space on the side of the road his own and takes advantage of those who come into his realm, beating them and stealing their money. As the reader finds out later in the novel, Rattner is "wanted in three states" (235), but on the roadside he recreates his story to Marion Sylder: "My mother been real bad sick too, she ... doctor's bills is higher'n ... so I sure do appreciate [the ride]" (34–35). Certainly Sylder does not believe him, but Rattner's manipulation of his circumstances via his storytelling — his interpretation of events — demonstrates how such narrative meanderings "catch up cultural conventions, relations of authority, and fundamental spatio-temporal orientations in the dense sociality of words and images in use and produce a constant mediation of the 'real'" (Stewart 29–30). The social construct *Appalachia* itself sits squarely in just such a mediation. Further, all four of McCarthy's Appalachian novels stream from places like Stewart's "space on the side of the road," with characters making sorties both into society and into the areas beyond "proper" society, on and because of the roads of the Appalachian Mountains.

Roads: Dirt. Gravel. Macadam. Concrete. Pavement. Metaphor. Byways of travel. Grids of demarcation. John Alexander Williams notes, "History, the French poet Hilaire Belloc once wrote, belongs to those who control the roads. The road 'controls the developments of strategies and fixes the site of battles.' And shapes the strategy of development, it might be added, for roads have usually proved as important economically as militarily" (143). The ancient Romans knew this and American policy makers of the twentieth century learned from them. When the Romans wanted to hasten both the deployment and retraction of their power throughout the empire, they built great thoroughfares. The roads on which Roman troops moved stood as constant reminders to would-be insurgents that the Empire's response to subversion could and would be swift and staggering; surely the psychological shadows those thoroughfares cast quelled many rebellions before they started.

Well into the twentieth century, poor roads and huge inaccessible tracts of the American continent made the movement of personnel and supplies difficult, especially in the Appalachian mountain region. Jack Weller notes, "Turnpikes, then great railroads spanned and crisscrossed the continent, moving goods, people, and ideas from place to place—except in the mountains. Commerce, industry, education, and culture increased in the nation—but not in the mountains" (13). After the great military mobilization of World War II, American authorities realized that the vast and often inaccessible countryside of the United States impeded the nation's defense. The Eisenhower administration began remedying this American insufficiency: "The interstate system, as it is now called, is 40,000 miles of limited access highways that were built on the premise of being faster and safer routes for transit than the existing roadways" (McKenna and Anderson 274). During the time frame addressed in most of McCarthy's Appalachian novels, however, road construction throughout the Appalachian region remained woefully underdeveloped.

Theoretically, roads advantage everyone. All citizens have access to roads and the mobility that they afford; accordingly, anyone unhappy with his or her lot in life can hit the road in search of betterment. But reality is much more complex. A mountaineer, with no money to purchase seed for his crops, would have a hard time acquiring an adequate mode of transportation: he would have to trade a lot of ginseng for a car, or even a mule, and one can only walk so far or fast and carry only so much. Roads, like so many other facets of Appalachian "uplift," help those able to help themselves. As with other infrastructural projects, "public investment [in Appalachian roads] has generally increased the ability of corporations and government to exploit Appalachia's natural resources rather than improve the social welfare of its people" (Fowler 94). Germane to this study, Interstate 75/40, running from the southwest to the northeast through Knoxville, quickens the pace of transportation and the distribution of consumer products through the region, but in its building, many poor mountain people found themselves displaced. Constructed in the 1950s and depicted in *Suttree*, I-75/40 still cuts directly through McAnally Flats, where "pale concrete piers veered off, naked columns of some fourth order capped with a red steel frieze. New roads being laid over McAnally, over the ruins" (463). The poor of the neighborhood—black and white—remain the dispossessed "sad chattel." The dwellers of McAnally Flats had no resources to get out of the way of progress, much less to take advantage of it. Suttree finds "people out of doors that would as soon stayed in" as the supports for the Interstate rise above the slums (416). Suttree, unlike many of the poorest of Knoxville's residents, takes advantage of this new road, moving elsewhere to other opportunity, while "behind him the city lay smoking, the sad purlieus of the dead immured with the bones of friends and forebears" (471). But Suttree is not truly a mountaineer; he has resources: an upper-middle-class background, an education, knowledge of the world outside of McAnally and Knoxville. The huntsman's hounds sniff his footprints, not his boots.

Roadspace: Official and Unofficial

In the modern United States, road construction is both a capital-intensive and a labor-intensive endeavor, so those who control capital make roads happen: thus, governments—federal, state, or municipal—oversee road construction. Government codes regulate the positioning, construction, and use of roads; government entities can declare eminent domain and seize the property of private citizens if it is deemed that a potential thoroughfare requires that parcel of private land. Governments, of course, are also responsible for making the society and economy stable, so they listen closely to the admonitions and desires of private industry. Thus, "in the United States, transportation systems have traditionally been developed at the behest of the private sector. The transportation system development has necessarily been tied closely to commerce" (McKenna and Anderson 270). It would certainly be a stretch to say that those who control capital—those in positions of authority in American culture—control roads. However, well-constructed roads do facilitate commerce; the movement of goods and services enhances the economy, which pads the pockets of those who control capital. Furthermore, as they do with commerce, roads make *policing* the populace far easier; they make the far-reaching extension of authority more efficient. When roads cut into a particular geography, they provide access both into and out of that place; representatives of authority can thereby infiltrate that territory. At the very least, they help organize "an analytical space" (*DP* 143). In an essay titled "Questions of Geography" collected in *Power/Knowledge: Selected Interviews and Other Writings 1972–1977*, Foucault discusses the notion of how many of the spatial metaphors he employs — territory, field, domain, soil, region, etc. — correspond with terms used in relation to geography. In that essay, he suggests, "If one or two of these 'gadgets' of approach or method that I've tried to employ with psychiatry, the penal system or natural history can be of service to you, then I shall be delighted" (*P/K* 65). Foucault's interviewer in this essay then notes, "If there are such [genealogical] points of collision, tensions and lines of force in geography, these remain on a subterranean level because of the very absence of a polemic in geography," and I am not so bold as to suggest a universal polemic (64). However, for Americans, "a race of road builders," *roads* are a disciplinary technique *par excellence* (Rovetch and Gaskie 3). These thoroughfares that superimpose a knowable grid on geography allow authorities to map spaces; well-defined, well-kept byways allow speedier transit; authorities can identify illegalities more easily and can subsequently pursue them more quickly and more efficiently, while lawbreakers can continue to attempt to evade the law's long arms. The identification grids that roads create enable authority to situate, individuate, and locate people. Roads are political connectors in the web of human power relations, superimposed on physical geography by and for authority. They allow the mapping of the circulation of power, and they can be manipulated like so many other conduits of power — prone nearly as equally to resistance as to domination.

Roads are human stamps on geography, always already political in nature and ideology. On every official document citizens and noncitizens fill out in the course of their lives, two questions mark the top of the form: What is your name? What is your street address? This development in social services illustrates an interesting facet of the ideological ramifications of something as seemingly mundane as a road. Having a specified address and being connected to the thoroughfare grid in such a way benefits an individual: it increases one's security and it brings the individual into the fold of domestic social relationships. It allows the authorities to better protect citizens from undesirable events and persons, while simultaneously allowing the authorities — in this case both government and consumer representatives (as the number of sale catalogs on my coffee table proves) — to know where individuals spend the majority of their time. The late-twentieth-century advent of the 911 emergency response systems has focused this knowledge even further.

Roads form an intersection between capitalism and discipline; they rationalize and organize geographical spaces and movements in much the same way the placement of weaving-room machinery and mill villages organized the body movements and living spaces of cotton-mill workers. Capitalism has always needed efficiency; it "would not have been possible without the controlled insertion of bodies into the machinery of production and the adjustment of the phenomena of population to economic processes," and discipline provides that type of manipulation (*HS* 141). As Foucault further states:

> If the development of the great instruments of the state, as *institutions* of power, ensured the maintenance of production relations, the rudiments of anatomo- and bio-politics, created in the eighteenth century as *techniques* of power present at every level of the social body and utilized by very diverse institutions (the family and the army, schools and the police, individual medicine and the administration of collective bodies), operated in the sphere of economic processes, their development, and the forces working to sustain them. They also acted as factors of segregation and social hierarchization, exerting their influence on the respective forces of both these movements, guaranteeing relations of domination and effects of hegemony [141].

Roads are one of these "techniques" of power: they help manage populations, their distributions, their availability, and their docility. Historical Appalachia shows how this works. Appalachia has provided a laboratory for venture capitalism and population discipline in the eighteenth, nineteenth, and twentieth centuries, and the selective placement of roads has functioned within that laboratory.

Conversely, however, individualized transit also enables the subversion of authority and resistance to its power. Roads "carry huge symbolic and mythical import in American culture, associated with the dream of the open road and the promise of mobility and prosperity" (Walsh, *In the Wake of the Sun* 261). Like authority, individuals can use roads for their own ends. Roads are inanimate, they are ambivalent; they allow resistances to authority's rule(s) to become as widespread and as effective as the actions of the agents of authority themselves. According to Foucault, "Power comes from below; that is, there is no binary and all-encompassing opposition between rulers and ruled at the root of power relations.... [O]ne must suppose rather that the manifold relationships of force that take shape and come into play in the machinery of production, in families, limited groups, and institutions, are the basis for wide-ranging effects of cleavage that run through the social body" (*HS* 94). Power depends on the interplay of authorities and resistances; each legitimates the other and they not only co-exist, but *must* co-exist for power relations to exist at all. It should come as no surprise that the discipline manifested by roads reveals the manipulations of authority and the subversions of that authority. Resistances to authority can evade capture and prosecution by having better knowledge of the roads and moving more quickly on them. Further, as is the case with legal and licensed commerce, byways facilitate more efficient illegal and unlicensed exchanges.

Bootlegging provides one excellent exposition of the relationship between authority, resistance, and discipline in American history. In frontier America, and especially in the geographical territory named Appalachia, mountaineers have perceived the distilling of unlicensed booze as a birthright, and they have continued to make liquor subversively despite federal, state, and local laws against that activity. For years this illegality remained a cottage (or holler) industry, but that changed with the coming of roads to the region. Just like legal commerce, bootlegging became more profitable as transportation of the product became easier because "a dependable and well-managed transportation system was required to get the whiskey out of the narrow valleys of the highlands and into the big city markets" (Caudill 153). A bootlegger with a fast car and familiarity with local routes could outrun or outfox many a lawman. Marion Sylder's whiskey running in *The Orchard Keeper* exemplifies the story of the historical blockade-runner. Watery gas causes his downfall, not the long arm of the law. Always adaptive, the mountain folk like Sylder figured out how to take advantage of opportunity when it presented itself. Running moonshine in souped-up cars supplemented many a mountaineer's income, but roads provided points of contact between such deviance and those who wished to police it. Roads remain the fields on which power plays. McCarthy's novels demonstrate these power relationships.

In-Roads/Out-Roads

Roads accelerated the implementation of a modern economy in Appalachia when extractive industries took advantage of the fact that in Appalachia levels of "economic production and consumption, which by traditional standards was appropriate, represented 'poverty' by market standards" (Precourt 99). For years absentee landowners patiently waited for the technology to catch up to their land speculations in Appalachia; they first found that technology in the railroad, which was "foremost among the elements that transformed Appalachian life" (J. Williams 229). The mountaineers themselves, who still relied heavily on inefficient agriculture for their existence, became an issue that the absentee landowners and industrial barons — the authorities in this case — had to address. Despite major absentee land ownership in the Appalachian Mountains, sometimes where "valuable raw materials were waiting to be exploited ... local Appalachians owned the land containing the valuable resources; thus, the local people represented an obstacle to exploiting the resources — they were 'in the way'" (Precourt 101). These authorities had more profitable uses for the Appalachian land, and the people who occupied those lands became impediments to progress. Walter Precourt says it best:

> The problem boils down to this: Something must be done with the people in order to get the resources. One solution to this problem in some cases has been actual genocide. More often, however, indigenous people are "corralled" into reservations or otherwise forced off their land. Such exploitation never occurs without a rationale. Most often, the rationale is that, because the exploited peoples are culturally or biologically inferior, they must be "saved" or "modernized" [101].

Forced removal might have occurred sporadically in the Appalachian Mountains, but overall, such oppressive methods would have met with a vehement public outcry. White Anglo-Saxon Protestants could not be marched to the Ohio River or sent to reservations in Oklahoma. The authorities could have used the railroads to disperse the population, but it would have required draconian methods: forcing the people onto boxcars and shipping them elsewhere — maybe into work camps where they could concentrate on more efficient methods of agricultural and industrial production. And that would have never worked for "our contemporary ancestors."

The mountaineer needed to be modernized, though, so over time, a methodology developed to discipline this populace in ways that reinforced the seemingly natural progression of economic events. The changing economy of the Appalachian region set in motion a plethora of events that, in retrospect, can be analyzed as disciplinary measures. Roads became the key disciplinary tool in this endeavor. Road building was never an exclusively altruistic effort to uplift the region and bring it into the twentieth century. Roads mean money and they always have: "From the beginning [of the United States] a federal role in the expansion of economic activity was accepted.... [H]ence, the continuous series of acts to 'open up the West' to *trade and commerce*" (*Appalachian Experiment* 17, emphasis added). I am not suggesting that this was a concerted effort by the agents of authority to depopulate the mountains so that they could rape and pillage the land; however, as David Holloway notes, the tacit involvement of the government in the modernization of Appalachia and of the South as a whole is undeniable. It started when the first railroad sped up the extraction of timber and coal and made the extractive industries in Appalachia profitable on a large scale. Subsequently, road construction, which advanced greatly during the 1930s, only spurred the interests of these industries. Holloway indicates:

> Since the crisis of the 1930s the "modernizing" impacts of the state's underwrit-

ing of capital in regional economies of the United States has been even more pronounced in the south. Under the New Deal, distribution of Agricultural Adjustment Administration money and the redistribution of farm credit strengthened the assets of large landowners and the position of banks and insurance companies (Daniel 400–403), prompting the final breakdown of plantation agricultural and the penetration of southern production by "modern" capitalist class relations. As land became concentrated in fewer hands and production was mechanized, the planters who dominated much of the flatland and hill south converted their plantations into capitalist "neoplantations" (Kirby 51–79), breaking apart the old networks of dependency relations, converting paternal forms of labor control into commodity labor (133–53), and shifting the economy of the south from a labor intensive to a capital intensive mode of production [Holloway 68].

Yet the sweep of events seems to have colluded with industrialists making more money, and the end result has been the disciplining of the mountaineer.

The relative isolation of mountaineers kept them outside the purview of discipline in many of the same ways they remained outside the purview of the capitalist economy; they needed to be plugged into both. Discipline "makes any apparatus of power more intense: it assures its economy (in material, in personnel, in time); it assures its efficiency" (*DP* 206). Roads are the disciplinary function within a function that facilitates this event. They allow the entrance of the capitalist economy and its modernization; the mobility they encourage creates preferable spatial arrangements; their material existence helps to define the categorization and compartmentalization of the individual. The farmers of the Appalachian Mountains herded their livestock to market like the drovers of *Outer Dark* (*OD* 213–218), and like Arthur Ownby, mountaineers used roads for commerce even if they used them for few other things — Ownby's long traverse to the "Harrykin" (*OK* 188–195) and his general wanderings in the woods show how he can keep off the roads if he must, but in order to *trade* the ginseng for what few supplies he does need, he takes to the road. In the Appalachian region, this disciplinary mechanism functions in three ways: (1) Appalachian inhabitants recognize the economic opportunities in coal and timber camps, mill towns, and industrial (regional or Midwestern) cities and they use roads to move there, forsaking their inefficient agriculture for an existence more ensconced in the capitalist economy; (2) mountaineers use roads to resist discipline in the mountains or in the cities, and the stronger side of the power binary — authority — manipulates this resistance to legitimate itself via policing and incarceration or institutionalization; and (3) mountaineers refuse to join the tide of the modern economy and they move deeper into the hills and hollows where they are disciplined by the classic image of the mountaineer, as I will show in a later chapter.

They head off-road and off the grid. It should come as no surprise, therefore, that the authors of *The Appalachian Experiment: 1965–1970* maintain, "A final standard for comparing [Appalachian Regional] Commission projects against the expectations for them is not mentioned explicitly in the Act but rather is found in the underlying assumption that the highway system should serve as a framework for future Appalachian development" (77). The grid frames, bisects, and organizes the mountain space.

The Founding Fathers of the United States made this assumption, as did both the fathers of the steel and coal industries and the policy makers of the twentieth century. Commerce leads the reasons George Washington thought the solution to the absence of markets and the general backwardness of the western country "was clearly to establish better routes of communication and trade with the West" (Slaughter, *Whiskey Rebellion* 86). Washington did not live long enough to see the "internal improvements" that opened the Appalachians to industry, but he helped establish a policy of governmental involvement in road building that advanced the objectives of private industry. Washington, Jefferson, and other early American leaders encouraged this relationship, and like-minded entrepreneurs certainly took advantage of these opportunities. Later, in the second half of the nineteenth century, "the timber barons helped to create the free market for land and natural resources, and the federal government financed the railroads that opened the region to subsequent mineral extraction and manufacturing" (Malizia 193).

In the late twentieth century, the pattern remained. The Appalachian Land Ownership Study estimates "the federal government is the single largest owner in Appalachia, holding over 2 million acres.... [C]orporate ownership is the greatest in the counties with the greatest coal reserves; government ownership is associated with tourism and recreation counties" (177–178). The government and corporations are the entities of authority in Appalachia that benefit from the discipline of the populace and from the commerce stimulated by a pervasive grid of roads. They are the "colonizers" so many critics, Helen Lewis for instance, talk about when they discuss Appalachia; as Lewis claims, "Although many writers on Appalachia speak of the outside control of wealth, the degree and extent to which this is true has been only slightly and sporadically documented. There are no systematic, thorough studies of the land and mineral ownership for the region. This 'oversight' itself might be considered 'evidence' of the protection provided colonizers" (184). In many instances, these entities of authority have taken advantage of the Appalachian situation with the aid and blessing of the American public, not because the public wanted to further disadvantage the mountaineer, but ostensibly because it wanted to help the mountaineer. Here is one possible scenario: the public wants to help Appalachia, the government that allocates the public's funds determines that road-building will best aid the region, and the public goes along with the plan. McKenna and Anderson note, "The political system of the United States is designed in such a way that transportation policy has been effectively a form of 'indirect subsidy.' The system of contracts, land acquisition, and regulation, purported to provide benefits for all citizens, actually assists in maintaining a high degree of entrepreneurialism which primarily benefits smaller segments of society." In other words, while the population as a whole helps finance and build roads via taxes, etc., and while they certainly do benefit from that construction, some — read corporate America — benefit *more* from such infrastructure. Appalachian regional highway development and the roads built under such development serve as a framework for disciplining the Appalachian mountain population. A Foucauldian reading of Appalachian discipline allows for this. Authority can take advantage of the power of roads as a disciplinary tool; however, that does not presuppose that in doing so they entirely repress or suppress resistance. Examples of these phenomena are present in the history of the Appalachian Mountains and in the work of McCarthy, and they will shed light on why road building has been an oft-preferred way of dealing with the problems of the Appalachian region.

Conduits of Power, or the Solution to the Problem

The Appalachian region, of course, has always had a problem with roads — mountains: "East of Knoxville, Tennessee, the mountains start, small ridges and spines of the folded Appalachians that contort the outgoing roads to their liking," and those mountains grow taller and thicker farther to the east and north (*OK* 10). Crossing the mountains has always been difficult, but the promise of land and wealth on the western side kept the stream of settlers moving from east to west: "Appalachia was the first 'West' that national policy tried to 'open.' That early attempt placed central emphasis on the opening of highway access" (Newman 19). Newman further states, "Albert Gallatin, Jefferson's Secretary of the Treasury, proposed a series of highways and canals to open the mountainous heartland of Appalachia to development" (19). Like Washington and others, both Gallatin and Jefferson understood the importance of access to and through the mountains and to the hinterlands of America. Rovetch and Gaskie conclude that Gallatin "delivered a report to the Congress dealing with the need for a system of transportation improvements to penetrate the Appalachians and to connect the Atlantic Seaboard to the continental interior" (Rovetch and Gaskie 3). While the first Appalachian roads provided a way in and out of Appalachia, the system of roads was hardly pervasive. Most of the roads in the eighteenth and nineteenth centuries went directly *through* the mountains. Little infrastructural development came to the interior of the Appalachians at that time, but Gallatin's proposal proves transportation through Appalachia has been on the minds of the authorities at least since the founding of the United States.

Brown and Hillary venture an interpretation: "The Region's topography has played two chief roles in migration patterns: it has acted as a barrier on the one hand and an isolator on the other" (70). The mountain region did not develop industrially as quickly as the rest of the nation, so people outside of Appalachia came to see the Appalachian inhabitants as uncultured and "backward." According to Wilma Dykeman, "One explanation of this 'backwardness' was isolation. Used without qualification, the term robbed Appalachian people of any choice or free will; they became solely victims of geography" ("Appalachia in Context" 37). They lacked the arteries of commerce and communication available to other regions of the country that had fewer topographical challenges. Appalachian scholar and apologist Jack Weller, in his book *Yesterday's People: Life in Contemporary Appalachia*, maintains that Appalachian settlers came to the mountains with certain preconceived notions of independence and culture. Weller states

> Those who came to the tight valleys were generally not the ones interested in settling down to a stable way of life and accumulating wealth and comfort and the benefits of a regulated society.... [T]he mountain settlers were more the perennial frontiersmen, interested in freedom from the restraints of law, order, and a differing culture. These were often the people who had been embittered by civilized life in England and Scotland and had come to these shores in rebellion against the very kind of society which they found already entrenched on the eastern shore" [10].

But there are problems with Weller's interpretations, as Allen Batteau suggests: "*Yesterday's People* was widely accepted, not because it accurately portrayed Appalachia but because it portrayed Appalachia in a way that middle-class readers wanted Appalachia portrayed. Hence, as myth, *Yesterday's People* offers a better guide to the preconceptions of the American middle class than to the social life of the Appalachian people" (Batteau, "Concept" 110). Nevertheless, it seems that the images of the Appalachian mountaineer have been exacerbated by his isolation.

The lack of roads through Appalachia has been one cause of this isolation because the difficulty of transportation throughout the Appalachian region has limited interaction between mountaineers and people outside the mountains and it also insulated the mountain people from the pressures of America's burgeoning capitalist economy, an economy that helped shape the personality of the growing United States and its citizens. Limited connections to an increasingly mechanized and commercialized modern culture allowed the mountaineer to continue at an economic level only marginally beyond subsistence. If, as Foucault suggests, "the individual, with his identity and characteristics, is the product of a relation of power exercised over bodies, multiplicities, movements, desires, forces," then "there is much that could be said as well on the problems of regional identity and its conflicts with national identity" (*P/K* 74). To "regionalize" is to discipline. Insulation and isolation further shaped how the rest of America perceived the personality of the mountaineer; these two factors have allowed the exploitation of the perceived differences between the mountaineer and other Americans, which in turn have enhanced the exploitation of the Appalachian region and her people.

For most of the nineteenth century, the people in the hills and hollers of Appalachia farmed. They were self-sufficient farmers, not subsistence farmers. Mountaineer agriculturalists kept limited numbers of livestock and often engaged in commercial market culture, using existing roads to drive their livestock to market. Pigs "dominated livestock holdings in the Carolina mountains" because "whereas a single cow required fully fifteen acres of pine forest to survive during the winter months, a hog could survive on much less pine forest" (Salstrom 7). The abundance of hogs in Appalachia surely gives rise to the legend of the "mulefoot" hog the drover speaks of in *Outer Dark*, the "mountain hog from north of here," as well as various less savory Appalachian stereotypes (*OD* 214). Critics have tried to place *Outer Dark* geographically and there are certainly historical connections; Ronald Eller maintains, "Each year, drivers herded thousands of head of cattle, sheep, hogs, chickens, and turkeys over these main stock roads, destined for sale on the great tobacco and cotton plantations of the South" (*Miners* 14). So perhaps "the howling polychrome tide of hogs that glutted the valley from wall to wall" and eventually go over the bluff into the [French Broad?] river helps localize the novel's events in the southern Appalachian mountains (*OD* 214, 217). Salstrom claims, "The year 1827 marked a breakthrough in the commercial life of western North Carolina. In that year the Buncombe Turnpike, largely following the French Broad River, reached completion from Greeneville, Tennessee, through to Greenville, South Carolina. This new turnpike greatly facilitated livestock drives out of the mountains toward the coastal plain of South Carolina" (Salstrom 8). This development continued well into the nineteenth century so that "in 1849 alone some 124,000 hogs passed through Cumberland Gap and Asheville, North Carolina, on their way to market" (McWhiney 53). That the drovers took this route is entirely plausible.

In the latter half of the nineteenth century, mountaineers' continued insistence on agriculture kept the mountaineer on the periphery of the capitalist system and to some extent outside of the discipline of modern American society. Walter Precourt theorizes that the differences between the mountaineers and the society around them results from this difference in economic ideology and practice:

> Self-sufficient farming is virtually the *antithesis* of a market-based productive system; it is not based on wage labor and cannot possibly provide the monetary means to acquire what the market defines as necessity. In fact, the subsistence economy is integrated according to an entirely different set of principles. Motivation to work is rooted in institutions other than the market, i.e., the family and community-based networks of mutual aid. Thus, prestige is not based on acquiring market goods and services; appropriate productive behavior is defined in terms of an adequate contribution to family and community [99].

Roads like the Buncombe Turnpike connected them to the larger culture, but even when the mountaineers came into contact with the monetary economy, it was often to trade rather than buy or sell. Eller notes: "During the late summer, before the crops were harvested, families spent much of their 'lay-by' time collecting ginseng, yellow-root, witch hazel, sassafras, galax, goldenseal, and bloodroot. Most local merchants were willing to accept these plant products in exchange for store commodities" (*Miners* 21–22). Arthur Ownby of *The Orchard Keeper* is the perfect example of a mountaineer who does not engage the monetary system. He trades. Nevertheless, at least theoretically, more roads through the Appalachian wilderness bring mountaineers into contact with modernizing culture and its system of monetary exchange and would advance their assimilation into that system, and Ownby is no exception to this.

McCarthy's Appalachian novels demonstrate how isolated mountaineer characters can be socially and economically problematic. Poor, isolated, and insulated — so much so that they violate the taboo of incest — Culla and Rinthy Holme live far off the beaten path where "there had been no one to the cabin for some three months.... [Culla] himself slogging through the new spring mud four miles to the store and back once a week for such few things as they needed" (*OD* 6). Though greatly exaggerated, the "incest tendency" of the hillbilly did exist, as Harry Cauldill summarizes: "The mountaineer had little contact with life far from his front door; he rarely sought a woman from another county or district. The animosities of the feuds shut a prospective bridegroom off from adversary clans, so that he tended to turn to the womenfolk of his own blood-line or of others friendly to the faction to which he gave his allegiance" (84–85). Limited thoroughfares, limited choices, limited gene pools. Even the tinker — himself a social pariah who lives a solitary life of virtual exile but remains on the roads (*OD* 192–193) — cannot fathom the magnitude of Culla and Rinthy's deviance and abjection (193–194). Their sin against the mores of society evidences their isolation.

No doubt the storeowner keeps a ledger for Culla as Mr. Fox does for Lester Ballard in *Child of God* (*COG* 124–126). Culla pays him via trade since he "ain't got no money," as he tells the tinker (*OD* 7). When Culla abandons Rinthy, he sells his father's old shotgun to Buddy Sizemore, according to the store clerk (56); perhaps he knows that his ramblings amongst society will require monetary exchange. The gun is the only commodity he possesses. Culla and Rinthy Holme, Lester Ballard, Arthur Ownby, and Marion Sylder all demonstrate the mountaineers' need for discipline; roads help the agents of authority administer such discipline.

In McCarthy, these characters epitomize the people "farthest up the hollows, where the creek bed may often serve as the road.... [I]t is these families — isolated by distance, by lack of roads, and by choice — that most clearly display the characteristics of the folk culture" (Weller 88). The roads themselves provide one of the few connections these people have to American cultural norms. McCarthy describes the habitations of such people as "jerrybuilt shacks strewn about the valley in unlikely places, squatting over their gullied purlieus like great brooding animals rigid with constipation, yet endowed with an air transient and happenstantial as if set there by the recession of floodwaters" (*OK* 11). He labels the people themselves as "families of gaunt hollow-eyed and darkskinned people, not Mellungeons and not exactly anything else, who reproduced with such frightening prolificness that their entire lives appeared devoted to the production of the ragged line of scions which shoeless and tattered sat for hours at a time on the porch edges, themselves not unlike the victims of some terrible disaster" (12). The people who inhabit McCarthy's books are hillbillies who resist authority when they come in contact with it. George Guillemin concludes, "Although his shotgun assault on the storage tank may represent a traditional reaction against outside intrusion," Ownby's "apparent defiance seems to be motivated not so much by impotent rage against, or misanthropic grief over, the human destruction of pastoral space, as by a mystical primitivism whose agenda includes defiance and escapism" (*Vision* 31). One might think Guillemin's "mystical primitivism" is actually a product of the "folk culture" Weller recognizes, that it is something inherent in the mountaineer psyche. Regardless of what motivates such resistances, they stand as reminders of why such Appalachian inhabitants need discipline.

If discipline is a function of the interaction between members of a society and authority within that society, if commerce enhances that function, and if roads perform a vital function within that function, then Appalachia has been *underdisciplined*. However, where roads do run in McCarthy, they are the physical spaces where characters like Ownby, Kenneth Rattner, Lester Ballard, Culla Holme, and Marion Sylder most frequently come into contact with authority. They are zones of conflict and spaces of encounter where "in the schizophrenic space of desire of the bourgeois imaginary, the 'Other' literally embodies both authenticity and a degraded state of nature" (Stewart 119). When McCarthy's characters try to escape society's ire or try to avoid contact with the authorities, they leave the roads. In those unmapped, undisciplined places authority has a hard time following. Eventually, though, the mountaineers return to the roads where discipline takes effect.

The Modern Solution

Appalachian regional discipline goes hand-in-hand with Appalachian regional "improvement." The twentieth-century approach to Appalachian improvement differs little from the eighteenth- and nineteenth-century approach for which road building served as the centerpiece. In some ways, these developments gave rise to the cultural situations chronicled in *The Orchard Keeper*. John F. Kennedy established the President's Appalachian Regional Commission (PARC) to study the problems of twentieth-century Appalachia and to recommend ways to rectify Appalachia's poverty. This commission concluded that the same problems that cursed Appalachia throughout its history still cursed it in the twentieth century. According to Monroe Newman, "The President's Appalachian Regional Commission highlighted six major problems of the Region ... Low Income ... High Unemployment ... Lack of Urbanization ... Deficits in Education ... Deficits in Standards of Living ... Changing Population" (29–30). The access in and out of the region provided by roads was seen as a legitimate solution to the region's problems, so the commission came up with some of the same recommendations for correcting the difficulties. The new roads built in the 1950s had not been enough. The Appalachian region needed more of them. A deconstruction of the PARC's recommendations (recommendations later followed by the Appalachian Regional Commission in 1965), however, shows how business and industry, rather than the mountaineers themselves, benefited most from the undertakings of Appalachian uplift. According to the *PARC* recommendations,

> [f]our priority goals requiring significant investments were recognized. These were: (1) the provision of access both to and within the Region; (2) the utilization of the Region's natural resources of coal, timber, and tillable land; (3) the

utilization of the Region's rainfall and water resources; and (4) the improvement of the education and health of the people. In line with these priorities, the *PARC* report recommended a $1.2 billion highway program to link Appalachia with the major metropolitan markets lying just outside the Region [*Appalachian Experiment* 10].

Roads facilitate these goals. These goals may not be ranked in order of importance, but it remains telling that the first three recommendations only tangentially help the people of Appalachia while they prioritize investments that immediately benefit industry. As a solution to Appalachia's problems, economic and otherwise, and "in response to these conditions, Congress authorized construction of an Appalachian Development Highway system, designed to connect major federal highways and to open up areas of significant rural population ignored by the Interstate routes" (Appalachian Regional Commission 15). Again, however, only those with the means to take advantage of transportation and industrial opportunities could do so.

New roads make it easier to transport resources out of the mountains and tourists into recreation areas. Newer, bigger, wider roads connecting to major metropolitan areas just outside Appalachia also make out-migration a more attractive option for mountaineers who can no longer live off the land. The Appalachian Regional Commission's claim that "in recommending the construction of such a [highway] system, PARC clearly ruled out the option of simply allowing existing migration trends to depopulate the most depressed sections of the Region.... [W]hile migration from the most isolated areas was expected to continue, it was hoped that this flow would be redirected to 'growth areas'" seems disingenuous (*Appalachian Experiment* 67). Between 1940 and 1970, "the net loss through migration from the Southern Appalachians was more than three million persons," so how the ARC could convince themselves that more, higher quality roads could possibly truncate this trend is baffling (McCoy and Brown 35). Truthfully, that claim was lip service, even for the commission itself. As Rovetch and Gaskie have noted, the Appalachian Regional Commission "faced up to the realities of out-migration ... the primary emphasis of the program budget ... was two-fold: to make people more capable of high quality work at home, and thereby help to attract jobs to the home area; or, failing to attract enough jobs, to make the people capable of landing a job in some other area to which they might migrate" (Rovetch and Gaskie 49). Therefore, "government policy focused not upon rural reform but upon building highways to connect rural regions with urban centers and on establishing 'growth centers' in which to encourage industrial development" (Gaventa 127). With more travel routes, even more mountaineers could become "Tennessee wetbacks drifting north in bent and smoking autos" in search of wages (*Suttree* 398). The reasons the Appalachian Regional Commission did not discourage out-migration are several: (1) there have never been enough jobs in Appalachia to employ all the job seekers there, and areas outside Appalachia needed unskilled labor — the auto industry (arguably subsidized in part by the public roads program) and its subsidiaries in the aforementioned Northern cities provided many unskilled labor positions; (2) the Commission and the funds dedicated to it could do more for the people of Appalachia if there were fewer of them; and (3) fewer Appalachian inhabitants would mean less resistance to the development strategies the governmental and corporate authorities wished to pursue.

In the first instance, the difficulties of transportation — few roads, steep mountains, deep valleys, and a proliferation of swiftly moving waterways — have kept Appalachia a difficult place to settle industry; businesses have traditionally built themselves on the periphery of the mountains. Marion Sylder in *The Orchard Keeper* and many of the characters in *Suttree* simply have a difficult time finding gainful employment within the boundaries of the eastern mountains. Clyde B. McCoy and James S. Brown discuss the Appalachian out-migration McCarthy alludes to in *Suttree*: "Southern Appalachia has long been surrounded by areas more highly developed economically, with important cities and metropolitan areas offering many jobs suitable for relatively unskilled and inadequately educated persons. Consequently, for decades Appalachia has been a major, and since immigration from abroad has all but stopped, *the* major labor pool for industrial metropolises, especially in the Midwest" (35). Obviously some roads already connected Appalachia to these cities, but the interstates spoken of at the end of *Suttree* make destinations like Cincinnati, Dayton, Columbus, Cleveland, Akron, and Canton even more popular destinations for the Appalachian "wetbacks." When policy makers saw the writing on the wall and knew that the inhabitants who could move out of their situation most likely would, they made the "determination not to fly in the face of the inexorable, but to face reality and concentrate on the lives of people, preparing them for a better life where they live or, conversely, preparing them to go elsewhere in search of a better life with marketable skills" (Rovetch and Gaskie 9). In fact, the policies put in place by the ARC encouraged people in the rural areas to move to urban centers within Appalachia where, ostensibly, they could be more easily assisted: the policies "placed more and more emphasis on the role of urban places as locations from which public services are delivered and has tried to emphasize the creation of area-serving capabilities in them. At the same time, it was anticipated that there would be a gradual migration of people from the more remote areas toward these urban places" (Newman 51).

This type of movement gets people out of the remote areas where they can more freely engage in commerce and can more readily take advantages of the offered goods and services; as a bonus, the migrating population will not impede the extraction of the resources — coal, timber, oil, and water — when they do not live on top of them. Thus, the last of the three reasons mentioned above best shows how roads have assisted simultaneously in the disciplining of the mountaineer and in the advancing of a capitalist agenda. The people who left Appalachia "were the young couples, with strength and ambitions for themselves and their children.... [T]hey were the better-educated adults who could find in the cities the kind of employment that would enable them to live comfortably.... [T]hey were the leaders who had the skills that were useful in the cities — and would also have been useful in the mountains" (Weller 21). Like their progenitors who took jobs in the coal mines or mill towns, they moved to places where jobs offered them alternatives to agriculture — the cities ripe with the discipline of Fordism: assembly-line employment and compartmentalized housing situations. They endured the specter of regional biases against them. They took jobs at low wages and helped increase industry's profitability. These out-migrants "left behind older people with obsolete skills and the very young who were still in school" (Newman 30). Those who stayed were both the poorest of the poor and the least able to help themselves. They had little social or economic viability and could not combat the potential harm exacted on Appalachia by the various industries advantaged by out-migration in the first place. Again, this is no conspiracy on the part of the government or other entities of authority; it is merely a material situation that advantages those interests. As was the case in the nineteenth century when the indigenous tribes of Appalachia were forcibly moved to reservations west of the Mississippi to make way for Anglo settlers, taking advantage of the resources a region has to offer is easiest when the resistance encountered is minimal. Policy makers claim "the objective is not to force out-migration but to give people a genuine choice consistent with their locational preferences"; however, "they commonly assume that the 'problem' of lagging regions is because people lack education or skills, or live in the wrong places. Consequently, investments are concentrated in people who are potentially most mobile; in skills for urban job markets; and in places *near but not in* lagging regions" (Fowler 93, emphasis mine).

Spatial Placements

The "official" address is a relatively modern development, part of what Foucault might call "a discipline which systematically uses measure, inquiry and examination" (*P/K* 75). In *Outer Dark*, when the squire questions Culla Holme about where he comes from, the answer "down on the Chicken River" is vague. Upon further inquiry, Culla broadens his answer rather than narrowing it. He says, "I come from downstate," to which the squire replies, "And then you come up here. Or down in Johnson County. And now you come up here. What is it?" (46–47). The squire cannot extract an exact answer from Culla, and Culla cannot or will not tell him, "I lived on such-and-such road, just past such-and-such street." A specific address would allow the squire to size up Culla according to certain attributes of place, to "profile" him. As *Outer Dark* relates, Culla's response mirrors an inexact method of direction-giving often characteristic of "old-timers" or people who share a familiarity with a certain area. In antiquity, perhaps because of a lack of roads, locations were identified by landmarks — mountains, rivers, hollows, and geographical oddities. Such places are named, but they require a local knowledge that a specific street address would not. The squire still profiles Culla as an outsider because he is from a different county, but he could know him more efficiently if Holme gave him an address because roads intensify geographical specificity.

Roads stratify culture literally and figuratively. McCarthy's Knoxville is so stratified: the racially mixed neighborhood of McAnally Flats and the adjacent Mechanicsville were west of Henley Street, and south of Western Avenue along Second Creek to the river; Mountain View, the black neighborhood "that President Lyndon Johnson described in 1964 as containing the worst poverty he had ever seen," was east of Gay Street and south of Clinch Avenue along First Creek to the river (McDonald and Wheeler 140). The poorest of Knoxville lived in these areas. The rich folks who lived to the west out Cumberland Avenue and Kingston Pike "belonged to the Cherokee Country Club, played golf and tennis, gave gala parties, drank bonded whiskey, and belonged to St. John's Episcopal Church" (Marius 115–116). Roads provide ways in and out of these places and they denote their spatial situation in relation to the rest of the city. McCarthy's descriptions of Knoxville also coincide with maps in McDonald and Wheeler's *Knoxville, Tennessee: Continuity and Change in an Appalachian City*. As they note, "No native of Knoxville has drawn as vibrant a picture of the city as McCarthy, who portrayed it as a sleazy, gritty collection of disheveled dwellings, shanties, and played-out people whose collective failure was etched into their faces and minds. Poverty, alcoholism, and hopelessness marked McCarthy's Knoxville every bit as much as did the coal dust" (78).

Of course, great portions of Knoxville have been destroyed since the fifties — McAnally Flats and Mechanicsville for the construction of Interstate

40/75 and for the 1982 World's Fair site, and Mountain View for the creation of the downtown interstate spur. *Suttree* shows these roads being built by "Gnostic workmen who would have down this shabby shapeshow that masks the higher world of form ... until nothing stood save rows of doors, some bearing numbers, all nailed to" (*Suttree* 464); such roads promote mobility and opportunity for many, but simultaneously represent dispossession and loss to others. In McAnally, the numbers on the houses did little to arrange the inhabitants spatially: it was a slum. The greater concentration of vagrants ["thieves, derelicts, miscreants, pariahs, poltroons, spalpeens, curmudgeons, clotpolls, murderers, gamblers, bawds, whores, trulls, brigands, topers, tosspots, sots and archsots, lobcocks, smellsmocks, runagates, rakes, and other assorted and felonious debauchees" (457)] and their proximity to one another confused categorization. So who knew who lived where? The perfect example of this is the "death" of Suttree. Concurrently with the ripping down of McAnally, the authorities find a body in Suttree's boathouse. Perhaps they think it is Suttree himself, but the onlooking boys know "Old Suttree aint dead" (*Suttree* 470). The point is that in McAnally Flats, it is difficult to place anyone. That is why Suttree can hide out there from the cops for weeks after he dumps the patrol car in the river. Tearing down the slum reorganizes the local economy and forces the otherwise uncounted residents to seek shelter elsewhere either through private or public social services. Walsh argues that the destruction of the Flats is "another reference in McCarthy to a site of conflict where a proudly independent folk or oppositional culture is eradicated when confronted by the machinations of the state or federal government" (*In the Wake of the Sun* 212); I would maintain that the authorities do not want to eradicate these folk and their culture, but that they want and need to have more efficient ways of monitoring them. The "reorganization" of McAnally allows all the social pariahs therein to be named, categorized, and placed. Of course, the upscale neighborhoods and single-family residences west of downtown Knoxville (between Kingston Pike and the river) remain intact to the present day — those people were already named, categorized and placed on an efficient grid.

Roads here define a literal space, but they also define an ideological space. The Knoxville police cruise the side streets of McAnally Flats and Mountain View more often than four-laned Kingston Pike. Streets signify and watchers watch. The mention of McAnally Flats to any Knoxville resident carries a plethora of connotations even if the resident had never ventured into the neighborhood itself, just as Rodeo Drive in Los Angeles, New York's 42nd Street, or Washington D.C.'s 1600 Pennsylvania Avenue carry with them certain images. They all have become ideological landmarks.

Towns like Knoxville are divided and disciplined by streets. Authorities can have an amped-up presence in places like McAnally Flats where certain types of people coagulate; *Suttree* demonstrates that the police use this type of profiling. McCarthy frequently notes the infiltration of Knoxville's unseemly wards by the police (*Suttree* 29, 83–84, 195–196, 383, 410, 440–443). In most instances, the police drive by in their cars, on the roads of Knoxville — the easiest way for them to make their presence felt. Granted, they do appear on foot, as during Ab Jones's last stand (440). Even then, though, they pass by Ab and Suttree in the "prowlcar," back up, and then get out to assess the situation. Suttree, a temporary denizen of the Flats, finds himself accosted several times by the police (83, 303, 440); when he is drunk and combative like other McAnally residents, they take him to jail; when he is "proper and wellspoke," they leave him alone (383). Regardless, the roads give authority — in this case the Knoxville police — not only the physical ways in and out of their territories, but also a knowledge which allows them to individuate people and categorize them according to place. As a part of a discipline that helps to "eliminate the effects of imprecise distributions," a grid of streets and specific addresses "carve out individual segments and establish operational links; they mark places and indicate values" (*DP* 143; 148).

They also encourage subversion. Marion Sylder's response to the Knoxville police desk clerk shows an attempt at subversion just as Suttree's drunk-tank conversation with the bailbondsman does (*Suttree* 85); furthermore, Sylder's exchange demonstrates a degree of specificity that the squire's examination of Culla Holme lacks:

> Name, he said, gazing at the inkstand with weary boredom.
> Fred Long.
> Marion Paris Sylder. Occupation.
> Iron and Steel...
> None. Married?
> No.
> Married. Address.
> Red Mountain Tennessee.
> Route Nine, Knoxville [*OK* 208–209].

Less specific than the modern address, but more so than Holme's rambling directions, Sylder's address represents a move toward more specificity and shows how such specificity can be used in the service of authority.

When mountaineers inadvertently or purposefully subvert authority — historically, if they joined a union or destroyed industry or government property, or protested government seizure of private lands — they become disciplinary liabilities exposing the gaps in discipline. Roads provide opportunities for authority to extend discipline throughout the social body via the mobility and the spatial relationships roads produce. They serve the interests of both authority and the mountaineer, though perhaps roads benefit one more than the other. Thoroughfares are the sites where the interplay and interchange of authority and the mountaineer have historically taken place; they are territories claimed by both parties, used in both discipline and its subversion. McCarthy's work demonstrates the interactions of authorities and mountaineers on and around the highways and byways of Appalachia.

The Socio-Path, or the Case of Lester Ballard

In *Child of God*, Lester Ballard's business on the roads near Frog Mountain illustrates how one particular mountaineer — one who superlatively embodies mountaineer stereotypes — interacts with authority. Roads play into Ballard's deviance and subversion; the access they provide facilitates his sociopathology; that same accessibility eventually results in his capture and incarceration.

Lester presents a difficult case because he is one of the mountaineers who remains unknowable within the natural environment and unplaceable on a road grid; a vagrant as a result of dispossession at the hands of the county, Lester cannot be consistently located by the authorities. He has no permanent address. They cannot watch him all the time. The roads, nevertheless, bring him into contact with the county authorities.

The opening scene of *Child of God* shows members of the Sevier County community approaching Lester Ballard's homestead "like a caravan of carnival folk ... the truck rocking and pitching in the ruts" of the ill-kept driveway to the farm. Clearly the Ballard place remains beyond the reach of the blacktop and "in the blue shade under the wall of the mountain" (3). Getting there for the auction is a difficult traverse made worse by Ballard's resistance. But get there they do, and Lester's inheritance sells to John Greer, forcing Lester to migrate elsewhere.

Lester finds shelter in the abandoned Waldrop place, a two-room, run-down shack surrounded by "weeds as high as the house eaves." Though closer to a road than his last habitation, this cabin remains off the beaten path and obscured from sight: "From the road a quarter of a mile off travelers could see the gray shake roof and the chimney, nothing more" (14). The authorities know about the house and they know Lester has taken up there, but the space and approach to it remain unknown, as the sheriff proves when he comes to get Lester after the encounter with the naked woman at the turnaround (41). Lester watches Fate Turner "ford the sheer wall of dried briers and weeds at the edge of the road and come on with arms and elbows aloft, treading down brush"; Lester, of course, knows "they's a path if you don't know it" (50–51). The point is that the sheriff *does not* know it. Lester's local knowledge is a form of power. Ballard travels the mountains by the unofficial back ways — the footpaths and the caves — beyond the long arm of the law. Eventually, though, Lester carries out the sorties of his perverse commerce on the roads, which become killing zones where he claims his victims. Lester's sexual deviance first shows itself on the road (*COG* 19); he first turns to necrophilia on the side of the road (88–89). In fact, with the exception of the girl whose "idiot" child Lester torches along with her parents' house, all of his documented murders take place at or near the Frog Mountain turnaround. While the roads enable the community to travel more freely and easily, they also enable Ballard's deviance and his subversion of societal taboos and laws. The roads of McCarthy's Sevier County are marginal places of opportunity and encounter where "things seem to proliferate and amass themselves," while the town of Sevierville, at least in *Child of God*, looks "to these 'Other' places as a source of both nostalgia and threat" (Stewart 42). The forests give Lester solitude and protection; the roads bring him into contact with society and its norms, but he refuses to abide by the basic rules of that society.

The most ambivalent space in *Child of God* remains the center of the novel's action. The Frog Mountain turnaround is one of those "most marginalized, out-of-the-way places that seems to matter most" (42). On a road outside town and in the mountains, the turnaround is a cul-de-sac where those seeking to evade the prying eyes of society travel to commit deviant acts. Like the Green Fly Inn in *The Orchard Keeper*, the Frog Mountain turnaround collects the detritus of the community — both material and human. One only need examine the assortment of abandoned cars, broken bottles and used condoms, and drunk or dead people, to understand this fact. It is a site of power reversals, a space where Lester Ballard, and not Fate Turner, rules. The cul-de-sac might be on the margins, but it is certainly central to Lester's life. Lester discovers the drunken, nearly-naked woman who later accuses him of rape there; he voyeuristically watches and later polices couples parking there; his murderous actions there ultimately lead the authorities to finger him for the disappearances of several people from that very place.

The turnaround persists centrally in the dialectic of the Sevier County authorities too. Among the courthouse "pocketknife society," a deputy of Fate Turner's relates a story about riding with Turner when they caught a couple parking at the turnaround (*COG* 44); later, while investigating the disappearances of several people, the sheriff and his deputy examine the turnaround for evidence of foul play and the sheriff acknowledges the use of the place by the young people of the community who "keep pretty active some of em" (147). In fact, Sheriff Fate Turner and his deputy police the very same places and roads Lester haunts, especially the contested space of the turnaround. While the text demonstrates the sheriff's preoccupation with the turnaround on two occasions (44; 145–148), it shows Lester there four specific times: watching a couple in the car (19), finding the "old whore" (40–43), discovering the dead fornicators (85–91), and policing the young boy and girl whom he wounds and kills, respectively (149–153). This Sevier County road plays an integral part in the power relationship between Turner and Ballard as it does between the mountain and Sevierville communities. It forces each to acknowledge the other's presence. Diane Luce remarks on this relationship:

> Lester explicitly mimics the sheriff when he confronts the young couple on the turnaround, directing the flashlight beam into their eyes and demanding to see the boy's license.... [T]he distinction that Turner's patrolling the road is legally sanctioned is lost on Lester.... [L]ester's fairly precise aping of the sheriff's behaviors in approaching couples suggests that he has secretly witnessed such incidents.... [H]e recognizes little difference between the sheriff's motives and his own ["White Caps" 50].

Both men police the roads in their own ways. In fact, at one point during his investigation into the disappearances, Turner models how authority uses roads to gain access to potential transgressors. He overtakes Ballard on "the road near the top of the mountain" (*COG* 121). Ballard, as always, carries his rifle. It appears that Ballard might be contemplating directly resisting the sheriff when the "sheriff told Ballard to put the rifle down but Ballard didn't move.... [T]he sheriff reached his pistol out the window and cocked it.... [B]oy, you better stick it in the ground, the sheriff said" (121). Ballard wisely obeys, knowing that he is outdone. His open resistance must wait for his attack on John Greer. In the courtroom interactions with Lester that follow, the sheriff and judge are obviously looking for some reason to charge and detain Ballard, but they have no hard evidence and cannot justify holding him on the grounds of nothing more than the sheriff's suspicions. Ballard thereafter continues to use the mountain paths and roads to conduct his commerce with Mr. Fox at the store (124–126) and to sell the watches he has stolen off his collected corpses in a community on the other side of the mountain (127–133). He crisscrosses the roads as he grows increasingly deviant.

The sheriff retains his suspicions and the turnaround is the space where he collects the most evidence. The scene when the sheriff and his deputy find the overturned car in the ravine below the turnaround presents an instance where Ballard has been successful in killing and removing the car's occupants and stealing everything out of it. Turner and the deputy find only a bottle cap in the car and "a jack and a lug wrench and some rags and two empty bottles" in the trunk (146), but Turner's mental wheels move. He knows this is not a wreck situation; he thinks someone shoved the car into the ravine. When the deputy asks him where the occupants went, he replies, "I reckon they've got to wherever that gal got to that was supposed to be with that boy we found up here" (147). He suspects Ballard's involvement and wishes the area on the sides of the turnaround were covered in snow so that he could follow the footprints of the little reprobate. Turner finally gets the evidence he needs to arrest Ballard when Lester shoots a boy in his truck and the boy does not die (149–153). The roads then become dangerous for Ballard. Lester retreats to the woods, away from the mountain thoroughfares, but this retreat only delays his capture.

Once John Greer blows most of his arm off and Ballard recovers from the amputation of the rest of it, a vigilante lynch mob kidnaps him from the hospital. He leads them into the caves and escapes. At this point in the story, however, Ballard's time of subversion is over because he has directly assaulted authority by shooting Greer and leaving the posse members in the caves to die. The community cannot allow him to roam freely any longer. A change has occurred in Ballard too, though. His abjection and the absolute aloneness that results from his isolation in the caves cause in him an epiphany. He can no longer move about freely; he cannot provide for himself. His ability to shoot the rifle was his independence ticket and it is gone. He escapes the caves and wanders the roads where "he'd not got far before a churchbus hove into sight.... [A] small boy was looking out the window.... [Ballard] was trying to fix in his mind where he'd seen the boy when it came to him that the boy looked like himself" (190–191). For Ballard, the entire road complex and how it engages him with the community has changed by this point in the tale. His means of obtaining both subsistence (squirrels and other varmints for food) and commodities (watches, etc., which he could sell for the money it would take to buy other things) has been amputated. He is famished and totally dependent on the charity of the community. Ballard sees that the boy in whom he recognizes himself—perhaps his alter ego had circumstances differed—is a part of a communal activity; he has his place in that social community, even if it is in the back of the bus staring out into the night. Most of Lester's victims were deviants much like himself, people who needed policing, not like the boy. Coming to this realization, Lester understands the alternative. He climbs back onto the road one last time and makes his way to another site of discipline, the hospital, where he turns himself in because, as he says, "I'm supposed to be here" (192). The Sevier County roads directly facilitate his deviance, but they also occasion his capture and submission to discipline. Through the vehicle of the bus and the young boy Lester sees, the roads occasion Lester's self-discipline so that he returns to society.

The Seditionist, or the Case of Arthur Ownby

Arthur Ownby, the titular figure of *The Orchard Keeper*, presents another interesting case. David Paul Ragan calls him "the old man whose traditional lifestyle enables an almost mythical connection to the cycles of nature" (18). Ownby is a relic from a bygone era with his "chambered goat horn slung from his neck" and the staff he cut "of hickory, hewed it octagonal and graced the upper half with hex-carvings — nosed moons, stars, fish of strange and pleistocene aspect" (*OK* 46). Natalie Grant labels Ownby "a shaman defending consecrated ground" whose actions serve a higher purpose (78), and George Guillemin claims "the text establishes Ownby's pastoral status biographically as a progressive immergence into wilderness. This development begins with the failure of his yeoman existence and ends with his retreat into the wilderness" (*Vision* 31). The old man has quite the ambivalent relationship with the roads that mark his territory. Using his cane as a vehicle, Ownby traverses the same roads driven by the olive-clad men whose business at the government installation just beyond the orchard keeps the road busy with their government trucks. These roads bring civilization and all its discontents to the orchard keeper, inevitably facilitating his enclosure in the state hospital.

Ownby's entire existence has become resistance to modernity, the industrial changes occurring in Appalachia, and the discipline thereof as represented by the infringement of the government tank perched on the mountain. Luce sees this facet of the novel as central to its meaning: "The unifying conflict of *The Orchard Keeper* is the contention between traditional mountain culture and the modern, commercial, and technocentric culture of 'mainstream' America, endorsed by the federal government" (*Reading the World* 37). Ownby embodies the traditional culture in the novel and seeks to perpetuate it. However, that was not always the case. As a younger man, Arthur Ownby worked as a member of a railroad crew, blasting its way through the mountains. He relates a story about catching a panther kitten to John Wesley Rattner and Warn Pulliam, beginning, "When I was a younger feller, working on the road crew at that time, I caught [a panther kitten] ... when we was blastin in there" (*OK* 151). He was one of the men clearing the way for the modern development of the mountains, "actually assist[ing] in the destruction of them by working on the railroads," but as he grows older and modernity further encroaches, his attitude towards that modernity changes, despite his continued use of the roads (Walsh, *In the Wake of the Sun* 81). Though it cannot fully explain his rejection of most things modern, surely his wife's abandonment of him for a circuit-riding preacher serves as the touchstone for Ownby's rejection of modernity (*OK* 155–156). His wife's story alludes to a breakdown of traditional sexual mores and gender roles that might be construed as symptomatic of modernity. The bible drummer is, after all, a representative of the ultimate Western authority — the Christian God — and he too experiences the mobility roads enable. Perhaps he was connected with some Appalachian benevolence organization. At the very least, like many historical mountaineers, Ownby feels betrayed by the people who encroach from outside the mountains, of whom the wife-seducing preacher was one.

The government is yet another group of outsiders who invade Ownby's natural environment; his attitude resembles that of the historical mountaineer who "finds it difficult to understand the bureaucracies of business and government. He has a certain fear of them, as if those who run them were out to get him or were interested only in doing things to their own advantage and at his expense" (Weller 56). The roads themselves do not present a problem to Ownby; he uses them as he uses his cane and other mountain paths — as inanimate means to help him get from one place to another (*OK* 88–92; 157–158). What bothers the old man is how other people use the roads, especially when those people want to use those roads exclusively. Natalie Grant believes the tank, and the government installation on which it stands, "scars the landscape of Red Mountain and deeply offends Ownby" (78). Grant calls the installation a "storage facility for the Oak Ridge nuclear laboratory nearby" (78). The TVA did begin developing Appalachia in the early thirties, and as K. Wesley Berry notes, "The cheap power generated by hydroelectric plants attracted other industries, notably the nuclear facility at Oak Ridge, built in 1943 to produce enriched uranium for the making of the atomic bomb" (49–50). In all actuality, however, *what* the facility near the orchard contains is much less important than what it represents — the coming of modernity and the discipline required to exist in this brave new world. The tank is a machine in Ownby's garden, placed there by the same people who chained off the entrance to the orchard road. The people who built the installation ruined the space for anyone else's use, making it "a barren spot, bright in the moonwash, mercurial and luminescent as the sea, the pits from which the trees had been wrenched dark on the naked bulb of the mountain as moon craters" (*OK* 93); they have torn the mountain apart and they have enclosed it in a chain-link fence where "the great dome stood complacent, huge, seeming older than the very dirt, the rocks, as if it had spawned them of itself and stood surveying the work, clean and coldly gleaming and capable of infinite contempt" (93).

Luce maintains that "the contempt is that of the now-dominant machine culture, arrogant to the point of claiming sovereignty and even precedence over the materials of nature from which it rests its being" (*Reading the World* 45). This contempt, this exclusivity, and this inability to incorporate any possibility of plural use offends the orchard keeper. The old man sees this encroachment and its impulse "to impose stability, order and reason upon the fluid reality of existence at Red Branch" as the most serious threat to his world (Grammer 34).

Ownby has always been able to inhabit a world ripe with pluralism and ambivalence. When the ex-slave woman "felt the movements and significations" in Tuckaleechee, the young Ownby does not fear her despite the fact that his mother thereafter "held the cross of Jesus against his forehead and prayed long and fervently" over him (*OK* 59–60). His mother has no room in her world-view for the "movements and significations," but Ownby himself does; the government has no room in its world-view for the pastoral lifestyle of Ownby. Post-cuckolding, Ownby's un-anthropocentric footprint on the earth barely scratches its surface, while the government "wrenches" up trees and encloses the mountain so much that the natural world around the tower seems to have sprung up from it and not the other way around. In many ways, roads do the same thing — they clear out nature to create anthropocentric lines of demarcation, but they remain open for a plethora of uses.

The road that leads past the orchard and the insecticide spray-pit and up to the government tank "on high legs [with] a fence around it with red signs" is gated and the signs undoubtedly read "Keep Out"; this road presents the perfect demonstration of how roads are contentious sites between Ownby and the authorities (51). The signs and the gate show that the government wants this mountain space for its exclusive use, yet Arthur Ownby wanders this road in his seven-year vigil over the body of Kenneth Rattner, a vigil that itself resists the discipline of law and culture.[3] With the spray-pit crypt as a backdrop, the agents of the government come and go about their business. Kenneth Rattner receives no burial; his wife and child get no closure to his disappearance. Modern practice would dictate a proper burial and the pursuit of justice, but justice never occurs because for seven years the old man cuts "a cedar to serve for a wreath and covering" (90). Ownby's vigil subversively undercuts the law in favor of "tradition"; a murder has been committed and the evidence is just under the authorities' noses. This vigil, however, does not directly contest authority because the conflict between the murdered man and his murderer was mountaineer-on-mountaineer violence and the revenge John Wesley swears to execute would be the same. However, the open hostility Ownby exhibits when he shoots his mark on the tower cannot be pushed to the side of the road and ignored. Ownby has a reason for his actions: "He commits this act out of a sense of confederation with and responsibility to the people of the older order, all the inheritors of the mountain traditions who are being disinherited by the machinery of the modern world," just as he guards Rattner's body in the spray pit (*Reading the World* 45). The difference is that while guarding the body was under authority's nose, this act of rebellion is a slap in the face that gets their attention.

The authorities react to Ownby's violence: "They came three times for the old man" and each time they use the road (185). Each time his resistance becomes more violent, so they bring more men: "The second time they pulled up in the curve of the road with three deputies and a county officer" (185). A shoot-out, with policemen getting shot, one of whom "was dressed in khakis and looked like an ATU agent," results (187). Figuring that the authorities will not give up, the old man leaves and heads for the "Harrykin" wilderness before the authorities can come for him the third time (187–195). Even in this late instance he piles his belongings on a sledge and sets out with his dog "south along the road, until they were faint and pale shapes in the rain" (188). Soon, though, Ownby exits the roads for the woods and goes to a place with no roads where "a woodhen called from the timber on the mountain and to that sound of all summer days of seclusion and peace the old man slept" (195). He retreats deeper into the hills and hollows to a place unmarred by the paved grid of modernity, confident that the authorities will not follow him there. But authorities are patient.

Chris Walsh claims, "Ownby himself is a bastion of a pastoral and communal order that he sees disappearing before his eyes, a character who acts as a conduit for other ways of knowing and understanding the world that are at odds with the rigid modernistic forces" (32). These ways of knowing are ritualistic, seemingly random, and dependent on an inscrutable methodology; they are neither scientific nor decipherable to the agents of modernity. Unlike the local authorities that shoot up Ownby's dilapidated cottage, the (federal?) government agent exhibits a resigned, passive confidence. As the bureaucratic representative of the new order, the government man, "dressed in clean gray chinos" and "a neat felt hat tipped back on his head" (*OK* 196), has nothing better to do than sit there eating "a box of soda crackers and some cheese" and a Moon Pie (198). That is his job. The agent represents "modernistic" forces and he does not understand Ownby. No episode in the novel better illustrates how Ownby's "older set of values and its connection with a new order, represented by the city and the laws of centralized government, make up the central action of the novel" (Brickman 123) than the interaction between the old man and this cookie-cutter government man in "a plain black

Ford, a late model" (*OK* 196). Throughout *The Orchard Keeper* the roads of the county have played an integral part in bringing the government and its representatives to Red Branch, so setting the encounter between Ownby and the agent at the store in the fork of Twin Forks Road brings the conflict between this mountaineer and the authorities to an appropriate conclusion — one where the discipline of modernity encloses Ownby's mountaineer individualism.

The agent has tidbits of information about Ownby and he uses them to extract more from the store clerk Huffaker. He wants to know if the old man trades there and if so, what he buys, and "Huffaker informs the agent about Ownby's antiquated trading and purchasing practices that lay outside of the cash nexus" (Walsh, *In the Wake of the Sun* 57). The agent is making a case out of Ownby, classifying him as a mountaineer type. Ownby trades what many mountaineer families did, according to Laurel Shackelford and Bill Weinberg: "Whole families scoured the hills for ginseng, sent dried herbs to export firms, and were rewarded — often for the first times in their lives — with cash money" (91–92). Like the historical mountaineer, Ownby is not exclusively a subsistence agrarian; he must trade for some things like "backer [tobacco] and a sack of cornmeal. Little sidemeat," so he trades ginseng at Huffaker's store (*OK* 197). Unlike those mountaineer families Shackelford and Weinberg chronicle, however, Ownby refuses the exchange of money — notes sanctioned by the government. Huffaker says, "He's a right funny old feller, don't have no money at all I don't reckon" (197). Shackelford and Weinberg note, "In some respects trading among mountain people was — and is — a way of meeting needs without the stigma of charity" (97). Ownby's trading seems to have more to do with his desire to remain free of the taint of monetary exchange than with his status as a charity case. The trading does, however, bring him back to the roads, and there the government agent waits dutifully for seven days until Ownby appears "on the bridge with the crudely carved staff, carrying a small paper bag in his hand, a moldy crokersack tied at his waist in front like an immense and disreputable sporran, and the wreckage of dog padding at his heels" (*OK* 201–202).

The agent confronts the old man on the store porch, arrests him, and puts him in his car. The cane and the car serve similar functions in the lives of the two men who possess them. They give each man more efficient mobility. The difference between the two, however, is that one is a commodity and the other is not. The one-of-a-kind, homemade staff, with its crude hand-carved symbols, has helped the old man move from place to place for years. The car, mass-produced and homogenized, black like so many others, the very emblem of the new social order of the twentieth century that both enabled and demanded the betterment of mountain roads, is a late-model Ford produced on a Detroit assembly line. When the agent slams the door on Ownby, "the old man's cane was hanging over the runningboard and in mutual defeat the door rocked open again as the cane cracked" (203). The staff resists the metal machine, but it is cracked and damaged and Ownby draws it in to himself. The agent again slams the door on Ownby, enclosing him in the car.

In Ownby's cultural view people take care of their own — witness his diligence over Rattner's body — so his insistence on bringing his dog Scout surprises no one but the agent, who tells him, "I ain't no dog catcher and this ain't no kennel" (204). Despite the fact that the old hound cannot fend for itself, the government representative has no compassion and leaves "the dog still standing there like some atavistic symbol or brute herald of all questions ever pressed upon humanity and beyond understanding" (205). Scout is in fact both an atavistic symbol and a brute herald, as is Ownby. They are representatives of an older age whose time has passed. Scout meets his fate at the hands of Legwater, another uncompassionate, bureaucratic representative of modern authority, who shoots him down. Deputy Jefferson Gifford "spun and saw the dog lurch forward, still holding up its head, slew sideways and fold up in the dust of the road" as the blast of Legwater's shotgun echoes in his ear (242). Modernity has no use for the symbols of the old order and Scout ends up like so many others in this novel, as "myth, legend, dust" in the roadside spaces (246). And Scout might fare better than Ownby.

The old orchard keeper "cannot reconcile the technological advances of the modern age to his naturalistic world view and is undone by the resulting collision of universes" (Grant 82). The severity of his undoing, however, is a direct result of his resistance to the modern forces of authority. Had he not shot the holes in the government tank, he most likely would have pined away in relative obscurity, left as the crazy old man up the road. But he does not pine away and his resistance must be transformed back into a useful thing. He is "misrelegated to a state mental hospital" where he is studied, categorized, made subject to discipline "at the hands of well-meaning representatives of the social order" (Bell 9). When the social worker asks Ownby his present address, Ownby responds, "I did live on Forked Creek—Twin Fork Road, but I moved up to the mountains" (*OK* 220). He first gives the address as he would describe it — Forked Creek, a space not defined by the grid of roads — but then he translates it to a road address that the man will understand because the man tells him, "We have to have an address, Mr. Ownby" (220). Ownby must be fitted into the modern grid. Ownby resists the questions of the social worker with vicious mountaineer suspicion when he says, "Where *you* from, heh? You talk like a Goddamned yankee. What you do for a livin? Ast questions?" (221). The social worker, as one of the "conformist agents [who] represent[s] the points of contact between the citizen and the institutions of government" (Luce, *Reading the World* 48), who does in fact ask questions for a living, comes away from the interview musing, "definitely an anomic type" (222). He labels Ownby a rootless vagrant, someone who does not stick to the roads. Like many historical mountaineers, Ownby does not move to a city or become gainfully employed, so the only way to bring him into the fold of discipline is to enclose him in an institution — the insane asylum. There, like Lester Ballard, Arthur Ownby's existence becomes regimented; he is "caught up and situated within a hierarchy," "fixed in definite relations of domination" (*DP* 291). He can no longer wander the roads subverting authority, shooting up government tanks, and influencing young boys with his tales of bygone days, but must wait in small rooms for "the attendant to lead him away" (*OK* 231).

The Bootlegger, or the Case of Marion Sylder

By 1920, the roads that facilitated the extractive industries also enabled freer movement by the mountaineer, not all of it legal or licensed. Meanwhile, the thirteen-year national experiment known as "Prohibition" only exacerbated the conflicts over liquor distribution. Former President William Howard Taft saw the writing on the wall when he noted "the business of manufacturing alcohol, liquor, and beer will go out of the hands of law-abiding members of the community and will be transferred to the quasi-criminal classes" (qtd. in Behr 80). Behr details the life and times of Cincinnati's George Remus, who bought up whiskey certificates and became the largest distillery owner in America: "within a few months of Prohibition, he was depositing tens of thousands of dollars a day into various bank accounts" (96–97). His story demonstrates the hypocrisy of Prohibition. He bought and sold booze under the nose of the authorities while "thousands of mountaineers were arrested, tried and convicted in the Federal courts, and hundreds of them were sent in chartered railroad cars to the Federal penitentiaries at Atlanta and Leavenworth" (Caudill 153–154). Mountaineers did not have the cash on hand to purchase certificates, so they had to resort to illegality, often adapting barely one step ahead of the authorities. Again roads facilitated adaptation: souped-up cars with stiffer rear leaf-springs to carry heavier loads and stronger engines to pull them — all after-market additions — appeared, as did men who could drive them on the tight curves of the mountains while being chased by the police. The mountaineer developed these new areas of expertise. Marion Sylder drives such a car quite well; the men in Knoxville unload it with "the car creaking and rising bit by bit until they had finished and it stood with its rear end high in the air like a cat in heat" (*OK* 165). The sturdier leaf springs stabilize the car's handling by both distributing the weight more efficiently and keeping the back end of the vehicle off the wheels. When the car carries a load, it rides like a normal car (a bonus for disguise), but when unloaded the stiffer leaf springs push the car's back end up in the air. Blockaders like the fictional Sylder and real-life Junior Johnson drove the authorities around the bend with their racing prowess — prowess Johnson would later use as one of the first hillbilly NASCAR drivers.

As Prohibition wore on and wore out, roads continued to improve, and the throats of American consumers remained dry. The value of distilled spirits only increased as the enforcement of Prohibition hardened. Historian Durwood Dunn notes the mountaineer's attraction to making whiskey and the resulting animosity between revenuers and mountaineers: "National prohibition in 1919 suddenly highlighted the advantages of the cove's geographic isolation for distilling illicit whiskey. Distilling had always occupied a small fraction of the community before, but by 1920 many mainstream, respectable citizens turned to moonshining in desperation as farm prices continued to fall" (qtd. in Berry 50–51). The decline of agriculture, exacerbated by the failure of the oft-abused, oft-maligned Appalachian mountain soil, heightened the pull of bootlegging. Additionally, a government who asked the mountaineer to fight a stalemate in Europe now told him that he could no longer make one of the staples of his economic livelihood in his own mountain backyard. He might have resented the hypocrisy. Such a confluence of events created an environment where the mountaineers had few alternatives. Bootlegging became easy money, the only caveat being that the authorities had to be avoided.

McCarthy employs a rather circuitous route to introduce Marion Sylder's occupational proclivities. His prior and soon-to-be-current involvement with bootlegging slowly appears via community innuendo and insinuation well before the scenes in which he evades the revenuers, but his violent delinquency appears much earlier, as does his habit of running the roads. McCarthy chronicles Sylder's movements to "the mountains to join what crowds marshaled there beyond the dominion of laws either civil or spiritual" (*OK* 16). He drives his Ford coupe up there when the bars of Knoxville close; he buys drinks for the locals; he takes advantage of the naivety of country girls he finds walking the roads to Knoxville (17–20). To clear his head after he loses his job at the fertilizer factory, he jumps in the coupe and hits the road. On this trip he encounters another delinquent mountaineer from Blount County — Kenneth Rattner, whose activities on a road "deserted, white, and scorching" open the main body of the novel and who, like Sylder, sees the road as an opportunity for making money illicitly (7). As is evidenced by a skinned elbow and torn shin received from "a low strand of barbed wire" while fleeing the scene of some crime, the hitchhiking Rattner makes his living robbing people who give him a ride (15). Rattner identifies Sylder as from the Maryville, Tennessee, area so quickly that one thinks he might have used this tactic on other drivers. When he tries to rob Sylder, however, he has met his match. On the side of the road, Rattner breaks Sylder's shoulder with a tire jack but Sylder slams Rattner's head into the pavement repeatedly and then strangles him dead, "flat backward in the road" (39). The mountain roads provide both men economic opportunity; they eventually bring the two mountaineer delinquents together and the stronger one wins the ensuing conflict.

While Lester Ballard and Arthur Ownby's stories demonstrate how roads remain ambivalent spaces utilized by both authority and its subversion, no plotline in McCarthy better shows this relationship than the case of Marion Sylder. The counterpoised activities of the government men and the "swaggering renegade ... [who] thrives upon taunting and thwarting the law" (Bell 22) along the road to the government installation reveal yet another classic relationship between authority and the mountaineer:

> There was a gate across the orchard road since the installation had been set up on the mountain and only official carriers were permitted access — olive-painted trucks with gold emblems on the doors, passing in and out of the gate, the men in drab fatigues locking and unlocking the chain sedulously. With like diligence Sylder bolted and unbolted the ring-plate that held the chain on his comings and goings in the old Plymouth. But the two parties using the road kept different hours and they never met [*OK* 96].

The government men use a key, Sylder a wrench; the government men drive the road only in daylight hours, Sylder only at night; no one knows the business of the government men, everyone knows Sylder is a whiskey runner. Twin Forks Road serves dual purposes: the government men traverse it in "an olivecolored truck, the driver and other man in the cab looking serious and official, but somewhat sleepy and not in any particular hurry"; Sylder, on the other hand, drives his souped-up Plymouth, "genial, unofficial and awake" (98). Authority uses the road for "official" purposes (those licensed by the authorities), perhaps carrying something out to the metal tank for storage, while Sylder subverts authority by running Hobie's unbonded, bootlegged liquor in an enclosed metal compartment from Red Branch down to McAnally Flats in Knoxville by the very same Twin Forks Road.

When he leaves Red Branch in September of 1929 for a life of vagrancy, Sylder heads south to the Gulf of Mexico, where he becomes a rum-runner, making tremendous amounts of money and losing his big toe in the process (*OK* 12, 161–162). He attempts to get honest work upon his return to Red Branch because he thinks "Louisiana or anywhere else, his job had gone off the market December fifth 1933," the day of Prohibition's repeal (32). However, his job subverting the law remains viable on the mountain roads. The action of *The Orchard Keeper* takes place after the repeal of Prohibition, so the dynamic between authority and whiskey runners like Sylder differs slightly from what it would have been, had liquor been totally illegal. The problem with bootlegged liquor post–Prohibition and in *The Orchard Keeper* is that its makers and distributors hold no government-issued licenses; like many distillers of the Whiskey Rebellion era, they do not pay taxes on it. The whiskey is *unbonded*. The isolation of the mountains made them a good place for making whiskey; the independence of the mountaineer, his mistrust of the government's motives, and his predilection for making whiskey put him in the perfect position to fill a market need. Harry Caudill sees the hypocrisy of the government's Prohibition enforcement as having a huge effect on the mountaineer's perception of that government: "Realizing that he was being pilloried by society for manufacturing a product which that same society demanded and highly prized, he developed an abiding distrust of officials at all levels. He became deeply suspicious of the motives of government, both state and Federal, and cynical of its purposes in every field" (164). Sylder detests Jefferson Giffords before he threatens John Wesley Rattner. The Hobies of Red Branch in *The Orchard Keeper* "were a whiskey making family before whiskey making was illegal, their family history mythical, preliterate and legendary," and they all have run-ins with the authorities (95). Ef Hobie spends time in "Petros — Brushy Mountain — eighteen months, illegal possession of liquor" (21) during Prohibition. After its repeal, the Hobies' seventy-eight-year-old mother gets carted off to jail, leaving only Garland Hobie to run the business. Everyone in the area knows they are in the whiskey-making business, including the boys Warn Pulliam and John Wesley Rattner; everyone in the area either fears or respects them (144). When Jack the Runner gets caught and sent to Brushy Mountain, the Hobies need another runner to take their wares to market.

Enter Marion Sylder.

Sylder has a fairly complex understanding of the relationship between a bootlegger and the authorities. A proliferation of subversive activities usually means that authority can move about as it pleases because the illegality legitimates the infiltration of a space by authorities who hope to control the illegality. If the existence of delinquency and crime in a community justifies the presence of the police, as Foucault suggests, then Sylder's re-entrance into the community occasions "Gifford's entrance into the community as well" (Ragan 21). Ragan maintains that

> the overbearing constable Gifford, the ludicrous humane officer Legwater and the nameless men who attend the mysterious government tank on the mountaintop represent the intrusion of institutional and bureaucratic authority upon age-old lifestyles. The values those figures project are faceless, exploitive and aligned with powers accountable to neither individual responsibility nor community standards [21].

These representatives of authority use the roads to enter the Red Branch community, but Sylder's illegality prompts their intrusion. Guillemin actually *blames* Sylder for this intrusion: "If anything, it is [Sylder] who encroaches upon the city with his untaxed liquor and his outlaw morality, he who introduces urban commodities and customs to the village of Red Branch, his machine that invades the garden" (*Vision* 22). Like the officials who chase him down, Sylder uses the country lanes to the tucked-away places, especially Henderson Valley Road and Twin Forks Road. Marion Sylder is not some naïve dolt used by Garland Hobie to do his dirty work; Sylder is a seasoned professional. The way he drives a car to escape police and his knowledge of the local roads give him advantages (*OK* 74–76). When Sylder wrecks — a result of a blown tire and not human error — Deputy Gifford says, "I sure never heard of nobody hauling whiskey in a Plymouth" (113); he is amazed that Sylder could maneuver a Plymouth full of sixty gallons of whiskey.

In fact, the incident where Sylder wrecks is the one that eventually brings the authorities to him. When Sylder wrecks in the creek, he meets John Wesley Rattner, a mountain boy engaged in unlicensed mink trapping. Sylder and the boy have to use Henderson Valley Road in their escape from the crime scene, and Marion warns the boy, "We got to stay off this road.... [The authorities] might have found [the whiskey] by now what with the light and all" (104). Sylder readily recognizes his relationship to authority; he understands their mutual use of the roads; he understands his position as a *subversivo*. Sylder knows that his use of the road depends on darkness, his vehicle, and the absence of the authorities. Jefferson Gifford uses John Wesley's unlicensed trapping as a way to question him about his involvement with Sylder. John Wesley says Gifford "said he was goin to take me to jail for trapping without license and bettin criminals" (159). Marion's activities bring Gifford to John Wesley's illegality. Gifford then threatens John Wesley in order to pressure him to rat out his bootlegging mentor. Given that he "knowed [John Wesley] didn't have no daddy, nobody to take up for" him (161), Gifford "was counting on John Wesley's weakness as an individual without clan support" to make him turn a witness for the authorities (Brickman 128). Of course, John Wesley has already developed the classic mountaineer obstinacy and mistrust of authority, and he tells the constable he "didn't know nothing bout some criminals" (*OK* 159). Nevertheless, John Wesley's encounter on the road with Gifford and Legwater—beginning at the bridge where the boy has set his traps and ending when the two policemen "turned me loose at the forks, the store"—serves its purpose for the authorities (160). With all the delinquency running rampant in the mountains, Gifford and Legwater *need* to be there. Gifford's abuse of his power in his confrontation with John Wesley verifies Sylder's judgment of authority, so Sylder directly engages Gifford after his interrogation of John Wesley. He breaks into Gifford's house and catches him sleeping. Gifford seems to rise to meet Marion's "shut fist rocketing down out of the blackness and into [Gifford's] face with a pulpy sound like a thrown melon bursting" (167). Tit for tat. Resistance gets the best of authority this time.

Inevitably, though, Sylder gets caught "in the middle of the Henley Street Bridge," crossing into Knoxville (211). As with the wreck in the creek, a mechanical failure—Mr. Eller's watery gas—and not Sylder's incompetence gets him busted. The bridge seems not to be an accidental setting. Sylder traverses the byways between the two worlds: mountains on one hand and the modern city on the other. The Henley Street Bridge is the physical connection between the two areas: the eastern side heads to Sevier and Blount Counties and the mountain topography; the western side ends in downtown Knoxville. Mountaineers have traveled that route to town for years. And Sylder is apprehended between the two worlds. The authorities take Sylder to jail, where he remains uncooperative and gets "booked on illegal possession—*untaxed*" (208–210, emphasis added).

Later, when John Wesley comes to see him in jail after Gifford has roughed him up, Sylder explains, "I had a little disagreement with these fellers ... as to whether a man can haul untaxed whiskey over tax-kept roads or whether by not payin the whiskey tax he forfeits the privilege of drivin over the roads the whiskey don't keep up that ain't taxed or if it was would be illegal anyway" (210). Sylder understands *exactly* why he is in jail. He subverted the tax code. John Wesley wants revenge on Gifford, but Sylder explains the relationship between bootleggers, revenuers, and economics. He warns John Wesley:

Me and Gif are square.
The boy looked at him curiously.
Yes, he said. I busted him and he busted me. That's fair, ain't it?
The boy was still silent, calmly incredulous.
No, Sylder went on, I ain't forgotten about jail. You think because he arrested me that throws it off again I reckon? I don't. It's his job. It's what he gets paid for. To arrest people that break the law. And I didn't jest break the law, I made a

livin at it. He leaned forward and looked the boy in the face. More money in three hours than a working man makes in a week. Why is that? Because it's harder work? No, because a man who makes a livin doin something that has to get him in jail sooner or later has to be paid for the jail, has to be paid in advance not jest for his time breakin the law but for the time he has to build when he gets caught at it. So I been paid. Gifford's been paid. Nobody owes nobody [213–214].

Sylder's understanding of the interdependency of authority and its subversion is a truly perceptive interpretation of the way that crime, the penal system, and the economic system are intertwined. Jail itself is planted firmly within the overall economic scheme of things. Roads give Sylder economic opportunity, but in doing so, they essentially create both authority and its subversion.

The connections between Sylder and authority via the subversive actions of bootlegging shed light on the way authority can manipulate illegality for its own ends. Foucault states that power "depends on a multiplicity of points of resistance: these play the role of adversary, target, support, or handle in power relations" (*HS* 95). Sylder himself acknowledges the codependency he shares with Gifford. To make the most money, bootlegging must be illegal; to justify the infiltration of the mountaineer population, authority needs bootlegging and other deviant behaviors. Sweet symbiosis. Authority does not want to eliminate illegality, it wants to use it. One particular conversation in *The Orchard Keeper* reveals both this relationship and the players' consciousness of it. Sylder has delivered his load of whiskey to Knoxville, and as he and Tiny unload it, they discuss the car:

> How's the new car? [Tiny] asked.
> All right.
> Ward says it come out of Crosby.
> Could be.
> Ward says it's plenty fast. Says they blockaded the feller on the Newport highway is the only way they ever come to catch him at all.... [D]on't she sound sweet though, [Tiny] said.
> Sylder looked up at him. That what Ward says?
> Tiny grinned. Naw, he said. Seems to me that's what McCrary said. When Ward lent him the money to buy it.
> Tell Ward good car cost good money. Even at a government auction. Or even if you done paid for em oncet [*OK* 165].

The coupe Sylder drives has been seized by the authorities once already in a blockade on the Newport highway. This car, with its hefty motor and reinforced leaf springs is specially modified for one purpose — hauling booze. And the authorities knowingly sell it back to the very lawbreakers they claim to be trying to stop.

Historically, this happened fairly frequently in Appalachia. In *The Wildest Ride: A History of NASCAR (or How a Bunch of Good Ol' Boys Built a Billion-Dollar Industry out of Wrecking Cars),* Joe Menzer claims:

> Local sheriffs, at least the ones who weren't paid off by the bootleggers in advance, wanted to help revenuers catch the whiskey runners not so much so they could bust them for making illegal liquor that otherwise went untaxed, but because they stood to make a bundle [of money] if they impounded a bootlegger's souped-up ride. Sheriffs typically sold such automobiles at auctions and pocketed half or more of the money themselves. They weren't above selling the cars back to the very folks they had impounded them from, *which would then get the cycle rolling again* [61, emphasis added].

Clearly the historical precedent exists, and clearly the authorities knew exactly what they were doing when they seized these cars and resold them. They needed that cycle. In both this historical and textual instance, as in so many others in Appalachia, authority allows deviant behavior to continue because it solidifies their presence in the community. The authorities know who runs the whiskey; they know that the economy of contraband will continue to attract certain denizens, so they police it. This "milieu of delinquents, loyal to one another," can be and is actively watched as Gifford watches Sylder (*DP* 267).

Sylder, despite being "the freewheeling highlander who courageously breaks certain laws based on his and his culture's assessments of their merits," also gives Gifford reason to watch normal, law-abiding citizens, like those in Mr. Eller's store who go silent when Gifford and Legwater enter to question them about the upturned Plymouth in the creek (Luce, *Reading the World* 50). Mr. Eller and his patrons tolerate the presence of these constables because of miscreants like Sylder, but they just barely tolerate them (*OK* 115–118). They know injustice even when it hides behind a badge, perhaps especially when it hides behind a badge. When Gifford threatens to pester Mrs. Rattner with the truth about her late husband, "Mr. Eller turned on the constable. No, he said, I doubt she has [heard about Kenneth Rattner's criminality]. I don't reckon she needs any sech…. [O]r the boy either" (235). The discipline of modernity and the mistrust of authority coexist on the side of the road in the context of Mr. Eller's store, which is situated at the fork in Twin Forks Road. These Appalachian roads bring together subversives, authorities, and normative citizens alike; the roads place them all under discipline, but authority cannot eliminate subversion. It does not want to.

When John Wesley leaves the jail, Sylder thinks: "*It was a damn lie ever word.* [Gifford's] *a rogue and outlaw himself…. [H]e's a traitor to boot…. [H]e sells his own neighbors out for money and it's few lie that deep in the pit, that far beyond the pale*" (214–215). He knows that his occupation depends on its illegality, but like his mountaineer predecessors, taxes and laws and those who enforce them remain objects of disdain. Sylder has come to "the deep-seated conviction that he is governed not by just laws but by corrupt and venal men — men who would betray him when it was to their purpose and reward him when it was to their gain" (Caudill 164). He understands his relationship to authority but feels betrayed by Gifford, an individual who as a fellow mountaineer should understand his plight. Perhaps Mr. Eller and his patrons feel the same way. They do not go out of their way to be hospitable to Gifford and Legwater.

Opportunity and Limitation

The Orchard Keeper laments the passing of a "vanquished race [that] includes failed subsistence farmers and descendants of farmers, hunters, and moonshiners — those whose ancestors were once independent of 'outside' sources of sustenance and entertainment but who are now locked into the broader world of commerce connected with the outroads of Appalachia" (Berry 55). In fact, all of McCarthy's Appalachian works share this lament. Men like Arthur Ownby, Lester Ballard, Gene Harrogate, and Marion Sylder — mountaineers all — meet authority headlong on the roads of Appalachia. They subvert that authority in different ways, but they cannot escape discipline. Ownby and Ballard find themselves in the crazy house, Harrogate and Sylder in prison. Before they became targets of the law, the men had alternatives. They might have taken a job in a coal camp or at a cotton mill; they might have moved to an industrial city in the region or to the north like so many other mountaineer brethren, but they chose another route: they chose wholesale resistance. In the end they are disciplined anyway. They become the Appalachian stereotypes — the mountain feudist protecting his land against intrusion (Ownby), the "backward" hillbilly rapist-murderer (Ballard), the dumb hillbilly-come-to-town (Harrogate), and the opportunistic bootlegger running from the law (Sylder). These stereotypes are as institutionalized in literature as these characters are at the ends of their respective novels. And as I will discuss in Chapter Four, these stereotypes help to discipline the mountaineers who choose to stay home, those who have no other choice. Cornelius Suttree exits the Appalachian scene as McCarthy himself did. Suttree, too, directly affronts the law and decides to leave Knoxville, but only Suttree escapes, and an argument can be made that because of his upper-middle-class status and his lifelong habitation in the city of Knoxville, Suttree is no true mountaineer.

The roads that take Sylder "to Brushy. Three years. For runnin whiskey" are the same ones that take Ballard and Ownby to state-sponsored hospitals, and take John Wesley Rattner west (*OK* 226; 246). Since the year is about 1941 at John Wesley's departure from Red Branch, it is entirely possible that he joins the military — yet another disciplinary site — for World War II. They also provide Suttree a way out of Knoxville after he sinks the patrol car in the Tennessee River. Knowing that he could join the Gene Harrogates and Marion Sylders of society in the state penitentiary for such a crime, Suttree decides to leave town. Suttree's whole existence in McAnally has been one of resistance to the discipline of bourgeois normalcy. In his "'Ruder Forms Survive,' or Slumming for Subjectivity: Self-Marginalization in *Suttree*," Daniel S. Traber comments about the late 1970s era in which *Suttree* was published, and his commentary applies equally to the 1950s setting of the novel; he says that in the late '70s (as in the late '50s) "the ascendancy of the individual over society was entrenched in policies that favored moneyed interests over the needs of the underclasses, and forms of national resistance to this system were weakened and forced into atomized acts of rebellion" (34). Suttree's sinking of the patrol car is just such an act, as is his rejection of his bourgeois roots, and his departure from Knoxville. The policies of road building in the late '50s benefited people like Suttree — people with the wherewithal and resources to get out of difficult socioeconomic situations.

On the flip side of the coin is a hillbilly like Gene Harrogate. Gene's final get-rich-quick scheme has him stealing from the telephone company. He gets caught, of course, and Suttree advises, "Maybe you ought to get out of town for a while" (*Suttree* 435). In the conversation that follows, Gene gives a glimpse into the limited world of many mountaineers, showing why road development remains ambivalent to the most disenfranchised and why it is the silver bullet for development but not for "uplift":

> Harrogate looked at him vaguely. Out of town? he said.
> If you stay here they'll nail your ass.
> Hell, Sut. I aint never been out of town. I wouldn't know where to go. I wouldn't know which way to start.
> Just get on a bus and go. What difference does it make? You've scuffled in this town for three years, hell, you could make it somewhere else.
> I dont have no friends somewhere else.
> You dont have any here.
> Harrogate shook his head. Shit, he said. Bus? I aint never even been on a goddamned bus.
> All you do is get a ticket and get on.
> Yeah yeah, sure sure. I'd get on the wrong damned bus or something.
> There's not any wrong bus. Not for you.
> Well how the hell would I know where to get off at? And where would I be when I did?
> They'd tell you.

He looked at the ground. Naw, he said. I'd never make it. I'd get lost and never would get home again ever. He shook his head [436].

Harrogate's discussion with Suttree sounds much like an encounter Kathleen Stewart details between a West Virginia mountaineer named Hollie Smith, "a member of the worst trash family up Devil's Fork holler," and an occupational counselor she takes Hollie to see (Stewart 135). Despite the good intentions of Stewart and the counselor who both want to help Hollie, just as Sut wants to help Gene, the counselor's inquiry "enclosed Hollie in a finished symbolic order of personal and cultural deficiencies that read like a textbook on 'Appalachian culture'— he lacked schooling, he lacked money, and in the end he lacked the will" (136). Harrogate hems in himself in similar ways: Harrogate is not equipped to just light out; it is beyond the scope of his imagination and his comprehension. I do not mean to suggest that all mountaineers fit the mold of a Gene Harrogate or a Hollie Smith, but so many factors contribute to the attitudes and difficulties of the mountaineers that for policy makers to suggest that road building will solve the "problems" of the mountaineers is simply naïve.

Suttree, though, has the resources to move on. An undisciplined criminal himself, Suttree hitchhikes like Kenneth Rattner:

Traffic was slow along the road and he was there a long time.... [A]cross the road a construction gang was at work and he watched them. A backhoe was dragging out a ditch and a caterpillar was going along the banks with mounds of clay shaling across its canted blade. Carpenters were hammering up forms and a cement truck waited on with its drum slowly clanking. Suttree watched this industry accomplish itself in the hot afternoon [*Suttree* 470].

Road building does provide economic opportunity in this instance. The carpenters and cement workers and construction gang all have gainful employment. Unlike Harrogate or Ballard or Ownby or Sylder, these "Gnostic workmen" have entered into the economy in ways that fit the norms and they have been rewarded; they do not need the discipline of the state hospital or penitentiary because they have joined in the development of modernity. They have moved to the larger regional city and they work, punching the time clock on (in this particular case) the government's dime. *Suttree* ends in a space on the side of the road.

When the roads of Appalachia are sites of encounter, of conflict, of discipline, and of resistance, resistance will always coexist with power and discipline, just as Gifford and Sylder depend on one another for legitimacy. Suttree will continue to employ his "strategy of atomization" and he will continue to be "caught in a double-bind ... of both transgression and complicity" (Traber 34). While Suttree quietly slips out of Knoxville, Ownby and Sylder openly resist authority on the roads of Appalachia. The authorities have decided that a particular mountaintop piece of real estate will serve their purposes exclusively, so Ownby's crime subverts the will of authority. Likewise, Marion Sylder cannot be allowed to break into Jefferson Gifford's house and punch him in the face while he sleeps; such a direct challenge to authority makes Sylder dangerous. The same could be said for Suttree's sinking of the patrol car. At that point, his resistance ceases to be subversion and becomes an attack on the representatives of authority. Unlike Harrogate, who lacks both the desire and the means to relocate, Suttree can and does remove himself from the purview of the local authorities. John Wesley's wish to exact revenge on Gifford for Sylder's imprisonment validates the authorities' desires to quell Ownby's and Sylder's personal insurrections just as Suttree's actions make him the target of the law.

David Paul Ragan claims that with Ownby in the asylum and Sylder in jail, John Wesley Rattner "is now clearly identified as an avatar of earlier values" in *The Orchard Keeper* (25). I would say, rather, that like Suttree, he is an avatar of resistance. A "complex action — one imparting both hope and heavy loss — occurs near the end of the novel, when John Wesley returns a dead hawk bounty he had collected on it to the Knox County courthouse and announces, 'I cain't take no dollar. I made a mistake, he wadn't for sale'" (Berry 57). This marks *his* conscious rejection of modern values (commodity exchange, for instance), his valuing of nature, and his identification with his two surrogate fathers — Ownby and Sylder; it marks his rejection of modernity and its discipline. John Wesley converses with the woman to whom he previously gave the hawk when she suggests that the county has destroyed it:

> Burn em? He said. They burn em?
> I believe so, she said.
>   He looked about him vaguely, back to her, still not leaning on or touching the counter. And thow people in jail and beat up on em.
> What? She said, leaning forward.
> And old men in the crazy house [*OK* 233].

He rejects authority and all the things that he perceives they do; he becomes yet another Tennessee wetback and leaves the region just as Suttree does. When he later returns "and visits his old house, the close attention he pays to the details of building and landscape recalls Uncle Ather's careful observations.... [A]nd the young man's removal of his shoes to check for dampness parallels a characteristic gesture of Sylder's" (Ragan 26). But, like Suttree, John Wesley resists authority only on an atomized level. Rather than punching some deputy in the face or busting up government property, John Wesley does what

Gene Harrogate cannot — he moves on. Gifford continues to look for him despite Mr. Eller's admonitions, but John Wesley is nowhere to be found.

The opening scene of *The Orchard Keeper* is perplexing. Two men are sawing a fallen tree when a young man — John Wesley Rattner, as it turns out — approaches to see why they have stopped:

> *Here, said the man. Look sideways here. See? He looked. All the way up here? He said. Yep, the man said. He took hold of the twisted wrought-iron, the mangled fragment of the fence and shook it. It didn't shake. It's growed all through the tree, the man said. We cain't cut no more on it. Damned old elum's bad enough on a saw* [*OK* 3].

Perhaps one might interpret the metaphor this way: the trappings of modernity — industrialization, commodification, discipline — the wrought iron, have thoroughly infiltrated the tree — the Appalachian region and the lives of those who live there. No matter the angle of the woodman's cut, there is no separating the two. Roads are part of that modernization, they have "growed all up" in Appalachia (3). The roads of Appalachia help the mountaineers of the region seek and find economic opportunities not previously available to them, but authority can more efficiently police the mountain populace via those roads. Yet they cannot eliminate the subversion of their authority altogether. Every road John Wesley might take leads him to another form of discipline, but none of them can totally cut down his subversion. He will always carry Sylder and Ownby with him. And so it is with the mountaineer.

Two

Modernizing Discipline
MILL VILLAGES, METROPOLISES AND MOUNTAINEERS

When the economic difficulties spurred by the Civil War hit the Appalachian Mountains, the mountaineer found himself hemmed in by bureaucracies he could not possibly comprehend and surrounded by entities he could not possibly combat; mountaineers, who had little land available to them in the first place, increasingly had less and less. Wilma Dunnaway contends, "In Tennessee merchant capitalists, land companies, and distant planters amassed more than two-thirds of the Appalachian lands"; she adds: "One-quarter of the eastern Tennessee and eastern Kentucky families monopolized more than three-quarters of all acres titled to residents" (54, 62). Begun by the earliest American capitalists, this trend accelerated between 1880 and 1920, when railroads opened Appalachia to industrial development. With nowhere to live and no land to farm, the mountaineer took the same roads out of the hollows and hills that would soon bring the industries into those hollows and hills; mountaineers began moving out of the mountains to chase employment opportunity elsewhere.

During Reconstruction and immediately thereafter, the mountain people moved to cotton mill towns and regional cities. While some found work in the timber camps, many became coal miners or millhands, forsaking their traditional practices of agriculture. As Paul Salstrom notes, "Had agriculturally productive land been as expandable as the labor supply, wage labor need never have grown common in Appalachia. The increasing paucity of available land forced labor to leave self-employment and enter the market" (52). Unfortunately for them, the mountain people owned no greater percentage of the Appalachian land in the late nineteenth century than they did in the late eighteenth century.

The advent of better highways in the twentieth century exacerbated this "hillbilly diaspora." The President's Appalachian Regional Commission (PARC) report of the 1960s claimed that "a place specific program was devised and a conscious policy of encouraging massive out-migration was rejected," but by the 1960s, the die already had been cast (*Appalachian Experiment* 20). Moving by gradation, the diaspora rippled forward as eddies of employment cropped up throughout the mountain region and beyond its boundaries. The diaspora increased steadily until it reached its apex in the years between 1930 and 1970. What began in the 1860s accelerated until "the net loss through migration from the Southern Appalachians was more than three million persons during the three decades between 1940 and 1970" (McCoy and Brown 35). John Alexander Williams explains how "the connection between official policies and the Appalachian diaspora was obvious in the cases of those expelled from their homes to make way for TVA lakes or national parks or the secret military reservation that the government built near Oak Ridge, Tennessee, during the Second World War," but there need not have been a concerted effort to remove the mountaineer on the part of the government or industry because "the great majority of migrants left home voluntarily, under no compulsion save their own circumstances" (J. Williams 313). The mountaineers moved from areas of lesser employment concentration to areas of greater employment concentration — a kind of reverse occupational osmosis; they felt pushed by landowners and industries that wanted them out and pulled by the opportunities afforded elsewhere.

When the mountain inhabitants remained on the land, they often impeded the progress of industry, particularly the extractive industries — timber, coal, and to a lesser extent oil and natural gas; these mountaineers were broadly dispersed throughout the region, but they remained in the way nonetheless because the resources were also broadly located. The real problem with the mountaineers in relation to the modern economy as represented by the extractive industries is twofold: (a) self-sufficient agriculture is inefficient — farmers produce only for themselves, not for the market, and they do not broadly purchase from the market; to be proper members of the modern American economy, they needed to be made into both consumers and producers; an (b) the mountain people needed to be removed from the hills so that industry might have free reign to extract as they pleased. Precourt further notes that in order to circumnavigate the needs and desires of a population "most often, the rationale is that, because the exploited peoples are culturally or biologically inferior, they must be 'saved' or 'modernized'" (101). This occurred in the Appalachian Mountains first with the Native Americans (culminating in Native American removal along the Trail of Tears) and then later with the mountaineer; it occurred because both groups of people occupied lands needed for the advancement of modern industry. With the advent of industry, mountain agriculture, though not purely subsistence as both Wilma Dunaway and Dwight Billings and Kathleen Blee have proved,[4] became a comparatively inefficient use of the mountain land. Since first settling in the mountains, when pushed, the mountaineer settled deeper into them, further up into the hollows to the poorer land unwanted by those who occupied the tracts in the fertile valleys. But these "unwanted" hills and hollows had become fertile in a different way. Someone found bituminous bones under the mountains' skin and outsiders came for them with iron scalpels — orthopedic geologists with picks and axes and shovels who cared little about how their methods of extraction affected the viability of the mountaineer's way of life.

The surge of modernizing industry exposed the fallacy of continued limited agriculture; absentee landowners, multinational corporations, and the government itself collected massive tracts of Appalachian land, and the farmer felt the squeeze of capitalism's invisible hand. The mountaineer needed to join the "forward" progress; the mountaineer needed discipline. For those people to be disciplined effectively, "the effects of imprecise distributions, the uncontrolled disappearance of individuals, their diffuse circulation, their unusable and dangerous coagulation" needed to be eliminated (*DP* 143). From the standpoint of modernity, mountaineers have always been too diffuse, too unpredictable, too unknowable, and too inefficient. Industry needed the mountaineer to move out of his isolation and the mountaineer needed new economic options.

The hillbilly diaspora, a continuing movement of mountain people out of the mountains that started after the Civil War, would potentially solve several Appalachian problems simultaneously: (1) undisciplined mountaineers would be brought into disciplinary situations that could make them more adapted members of a capitalist society; (2) the vast expanses of Appalachia could be further opened to industry with lessened resistance from inhabitants who were on their way out of the hinterland; and (3) the new industrial aspirations of the region and country could find realization with an influx of cheap labor. Industry, specifically the coal and textile producers, were more than happy to oblige the migrating mountaineers with low-paying jobs in areas of greater population concentration. The redistribution of the mountaineer as he came down from the mountains into the cotton-mill villages and into towns like Knoxville, Tennessee, hastened his integration into the capitalist economy, quickened his assimilation into modern discipline, and removed him from the path of the large-scale industrial extractive processes on the lands he once occupied.

One of the mountaineer's initial encounters with wage labor — logging — grew enormously in the nineteenth century, transforming a winter tree-harvesting habit of mountain farmers into an industry dominated by corporate lumbering interests. Thousands of mountaineers left their farm plots for the lumber camps. These camps gradually accustomed some mountaineers to more urban conditions, and more importantly, they made the workers more dependent on the wage and less on the farm: "Thus, when logging declined in the early decades of the twentieth century, many of these wage-dependent workers formed a ready labor pool for the newly opened coal mines and textile mills of the southeast" (Billings and Blee 268–269). The mountaineer, once watched over by only the wind and weather, learned to labor under the ever-watchful eyes of managers and overseers whose jobs existed to ensure his efficiency in the mines and mills.

Compared to the vast expanses of the Appalachian terrain — the backcountry hills and hollows — the enclosed spaces of lumber and coal camps, cotton mill villages, and regional towns represent clearly demarcated spatial relationships. Lumber camps, coal mill towns, and mill villages shared similar spatial arrangements in housing and in mechanized patterns of labor, even though "no comparative studies of coal and textile communities ha[d] been made" (Walls and Billings 48). The similarities between coal town and cotton mill villages can be seen in how the employers controlled all aspects of their employees' lives. In both labor situations, housing for the workers was supplied. Mill village owners, like mine operators, built houses from a similar pattern because "the uniformity in size of dwelling does have a decided compensating attraction to the tenants, for [workers] need have no sense of inferiority about their homes. They are as large as the other homes in the community" (Simpson 23). While the uniformity of housing might have eliminated potential jealousies among the operatives, it also gave operators certain advantages. Companies arranged workers' housing spatially, giving workers specific houses and exact addresses. This spatial arrangement formed disciplinary controls. As Harriet Herring notes in her interviews with mill managers, "The majority of mill managers and superintendents are thoroughly convinced that mill housing and control is necessary and best for all concerned. Many remarked on the advantages of being able to get rid of a family which is undesirable from a community and social point of view as well as from the point of view of mill work" (*Welfare Work* 270). Given this type of discipline, it should come as no surprise that the mountain and Piedmont regions saw "*operators* seize the initiative — by shepherding miners [and mill workers] into company towns where union organizing could be outlawed under property-owners' prerogatives." Harriet Herring maintains that as far as "controls as related to morals, absence of freedom of occupational choice, [and] separatism of the village as a breeding ground of class and caste" were concerned, "the southern mill village became far better known than its prototypes in other industries.... [T]he lumber towns were usually far worse physically, but they were thought of as temporary. The coal mining towns were controlled with an iron hand, but they were out of sight in the hills, and, besides, their people were often immigrants and not the 'purest Anglo-Saxon blood in America'" (*Passing of the Mill Village* 4–5). In many of these cases, the housing arrangements often bettered the situation for the employees. Herring gives one possible reason Appalachian migrants so readily took to company-provided housing: "Its housing compared favorably with much in any specific area" (*Passing of the Mill Village* 69). Further, she notes that to the mill operative, "life in the 'four room cottages' is not more monotonous or colorless or more lacking in drama — that it could hardly be!— than in the dull, unpainted little farm tenant houses, on the one hand, or in the homes of village Main Streets, on the other" (*Welfare Work* 3). Ben Lemert says, "After riding and walking through village after village in North Carolina, South Carolina, Georgia, and Alabama ... the writer found [mill houses] far superior to the hundreds of mountain cabins he had seen while driving as far as possible up the dirt roads leading out from the main highways" (70). Mountaineers accepted these living arrangements, including the lessened personal privacy and increased oversight, because they were more desirable and pleasant than their previous arrangements. Nevertheless, the meticulously ordered mill villages definitely advantaged the operators:

> Workers lived, shopped, socialized, and worshipped in tightly clustered villages owned and operated by the same company that determined their employment and wages, 92 percent of the southern mill workers lived in company mill towns ... [where the company] not only regulated the daily affairs, but "controls everything, and to a large extent controls everybody in the village." The villages were fed by Southern Appalachians, as hill folk and mountaineers yielded to the increasingly difficult realities of subsistence farming [Biggers 148–149].

The mountaineer gave up the freedoms and difficulties of the subsistence farm for the discipline and difficulties of the mine and the mill.

Not all mountaineers left farms for coal camps and mill towns. The roads of Appalachia also pointed toward regional cities. In the twentieth century the Appalachian diaspora spread to large northern cities where they were "*the major labor pool for industrial metropolises, especially in the Midwest*" (McCoy and Brown 35). Movement to regional cities, however, has been a mountaineer alternative since the first mountaineer came out of the hollow looking for a job. Knoxville, Tennessee, one such destination, has seen its mountain migrants accused of many of the same characteristics as the people moving to the "Little Kentuckys" and "Little West Virginias" of many midwestern metropolises. Gradually, beginning during Reconstruction and continuing unabated through the 1940s and 1950s, Appalachian mountain towns like Knoxville filled with "*countrymen come for miles with the earth clinging to their shoes ... lean Aryans with their abrogate semitic chapbook reenacting the dramas and parables therein and mindless and pale with a longing that nothing save dark's total restitution could appease*" (*Suttree* 3–4). Perhaps McCarthy overstates both the ignorance and the backwardness the mountaineers brought to the city, but perhaps not. If Thomas R. Ford can claim that "the fierce independence and proud self-reliance of the highlander, a heritage of frontier life, were viewed with mixed feelings even by so sympathetic an observer as [John C.] Campbell," a mountaineer educator and apologist, then McCarthy's might be no exaggeration about the mountaineer and the attitudes toward him (Ford 12). The new migrants were undoubtedly resented everywhere they settled. According to Harry Caudill, "In larger northern cities, outmigration from the Appalachians created 'Little Kentuckys'— areas overrun with expatriate mountaineers who clannishly stuck together and perpetuated the ingrained habits to which they were accustomed back home" (228). These same habits perpetuated in Knoxville's slum areas like Mechanicsville and McAnally Flats. Life in the city was new to the mountaineers, and locals saw them as threatening usurpers there to steal jobs, produce numerous tow-headed children, and start drunken brawls. McCoy and Watkins discuss the attitudes toward and stereotypes placed on Appalachian migrants in the form of the jokes about them in their article "Stereotypes of Appalachian Migrants." In many instances, these jokes follow patterns present in off-color jests about other migrant populations (105). Such joking demonstrates a nervous resentment on the part of urban inhabitants at the thought of new migrant populations swarming their cities. The actual adjustment of the Appalachian migrants to urban life, though, "is more remarkable when one considers the lack of support from outside sources, either in the mountains or in the cities (unless the controversial support of the Appalachian Regional Commission is considered, and their expenditure of millions of dollars, at a late date, mostly for highways and other projects unrelated to support for individuals)" (McCoy and Watkins 105).

The Appalachian Regional Commission (ARC) came about in the 1960s, somewhat late to help smooth the mountaineers' transition from the country to the city. In the preceding decades, the mountaineer relied on kinship networks when he moved to town. Like many ethnic minorities, mountaineers congregated in areas where the people seemed most like themselves. They came to town poor — had they been rich there would have been little need to move — and poverty often breeds criminality and delinquency, just as it always encounters contempt from the more fortunate. So the reception for the mountaineer was unenthusiastic at best. And the mountaineers were rarely quick to assimilate to the urban environment, given that they surrounded themselves with things they knew.

In the mountains, they conducted themselves as they saw fit and no "authority" was there to tell them otherwise. Given their isolation, their actions infringed little on the rights of those around them. Further, if what Cratis Williams says is true, if "the general attitude of the mountain people is not one conducive to progress, for they have been victimized through exploitation of the natural resources around them and quaint journalism," then their resistance to assimilation and authority and benevolence should be unsurprising (C. Williams 58). Of course, the mountaineers' habitat changed in the confining environs of the city. Proximity to their neighbors exposed their quaint "hillbilly" habits and "Appalachian" mores. Such attitudes and mores, even if they were nothing more than unjustified stereotypes, could be used by city authorities to justify the presence of disciplinary mechanisms that helped to regulate the mountaineer populace and keep the urban peace.

In Knoxville, specifically, mountain in-migrants gravitated toward Mechanicsville and McAnally Flats, where they fit in culturally and where rents remained cheap; these two areas became known for their delinquency and criminality and for their subsequent police presence. John Lewis Longley Jr. calls McAnally Flats the "slum area of Knoxville, Tennessee, in the early 1950s" (80). His personal experience with the area confirms McCarthy's assessment of it. In a footnote in his "Suttree and the Metaphysics of Death," he says, "The present writer, for his sins, used to cross McAnally Flats on foot each midnight and morning, for several years, coming to and from his place of employment" (80). McCarthy walks the reader through the same McAnally with which Longley was familiar, "past corrugated warehouse walls down sandy streets where blownout autos sulk on pedestals of cinderblock. Through these warrens of sumac and pokeweed and withered honeysuckle giving onto the scored banks of the railway.... [A] steamshovel reared in solitary abandonment against the night sky" (*Suttree* 3). Knoxville, in the 1950s setting of *Suttree*, like the rusty steamshovel McCarthy describes, is a place of decay, past its prime, yet still clawing at the earthen margins of civilization. McAnally Flats sits on the margins of Knoxville.

While the similarities between the coal mining towns and the mill villages abound, and while the Appalachian migrations to northern and midwestern cities have outnumbered migrations to Appalachian regional centers historically, the rest of this chapter will concentrate on cotton mill villages and the regional town of Knoxville because McCarthy's works describe both in detail. Coal mining presents a demonstration of Foucauldian discipline, as John Gaventa's work suggests, but in actuality, a "higher proportion of millhands lived in company housing than coal miners in coal camps, and although most mill villages were located near larger, more diversified towns, psychological and social factors rendered them nearly as isolated as coal camps were in the preautomobile age" (J. Williams 275). The main reason for my concentration on textile mill villages, of course, presents itself in McCarthy's examination of the mills in *The Gardener's Son*. Likewise, his attention to the details of the relationships of power and the mountaineer in *Suttree* presents the perfect connection to Knoxville. McCarthy's forays into both of these social situations demonstrate Foucauldian power relations to a great extent, and his teleplay and novel both deal with quintessential mountain characters.

"Ask Not for Whom the Bell Tolls..."

The prehistory of Southern cotton mills is essentially a story of labor relations. Historians have claimed that in Appalachia as well as in the broader South, "slavery unified capital and labor and thus forestalled *class* struggle, considered the most dangerous and corrosive of sociopolitical antagonisms" (Fox-Genovese and Genovese 11, emphasis added). In some of the earliest civic unrest in the Appalachian region, poor white involvement existed. The Whiskey Rebellion in Pennsylvania is certainly an example of yeoman rebellion and "major urban slave revolts, such as that in New York City in 1741 and Gabriel's Rebellion in Richmond in 1800 included white participants. In early Virginia revolts, such limited support was said to come from the 'very poor' whites" (Roediger 25). However, with the exception of Bacon's Rebellion, the wholesale collusion of poor whites and blacks, free or enslaved, seems to have been truncated by the social identification of poor whites with upper class whites, especially in the both the South and Appalachia. Charles Bolton claims:

> In the more "settled" areas of the South that had both a sizable free black population and a recognizable group of permanent and dependant landless whites, the line between white independence and black dependence could become quite blurred. Numerous factors, however, including white racism, kinship ties, religion, education, and mobility, helped keep racial barriers high enough to militate strongly against the development of any political alliance between landless whites and enslaved or free blacks [9].

An uneasy alliance of wealthy and poor whites existed because "status and privileges conferred by race could be used to make up for alienating and exploitive class relationships.... [W]hite workers could, and did, define and accept their class status positions by fashioning identities as 'not slaves' and as 'not Blacks'" (Roediger 13). The idea of "white privilege" has been "effective in unifying coalitions of disparate groups of people. It has generally been much more successful than class in uniting people across national cultural differences and against their best interests" (Dyer 19). Thus, there were few revolts in antebellum Appalachia in which both poor blacks and poor whites participated.

Often the white industrial elite fostered the racial connection they shared with poor whites; the effects of such fostering helped to solidify the poor white labor pool as a buffer between the elite and poor black laborers. The development of the textile industry in the Carolina Piedmont "after the War of 1812," when industrial capitalists "transported their textile machinery in wagons from Charleston over unimproved roads for over 200 miles," shows a concerted effort of the white Southern elite to provide poor whites—both Piedmont tenant farmers and Appalachian mountaineers—with economic opportunities so as to create the illusion of their enfranchisement (Simpson 12–13). Bolton claims "these economic 'losers' constituted a sizable part of the southern population, which, if united in opposition to the South's ruling class, could have posed a formidable danger" (43). Broadus Mitchell sees the poor white as having interiorized an oft-cultivated negative attitude toward blacks that would predispose him to cooperate with the white elite to the exclusion of blacks; simultaneously, the specter of black laborers as potential competition kept poor whites in line: "The Poor Whites had always hated the Negroes rather than their owners, and the trials of Reconstruction had wiped out lingering enmities. Therefore, as Whites and as Southerners and as injured and poor men, all were partners in enterprise" (*Industrial Revolution* 32).

Regardless of whether or not the elite consciously sought to use the fracture between poor whites and blacks, the fact remains that it was exploited: "Because whiteness carries such rewards and privileges, the sense of a border that might be crossed and a hierarchy that might be climbed has produced a dynamic that had enthralled people who have had any chance of participating in it" (Dyer 20). The possibility that the poor white might one day be an unmitigated member of the ruling elite has always carried a certain allure. The elite simply took advantage of existing circumstances. As Charles Bolton notes,

> Central Piedmont blacks and poor whites never mounted a united opposition to slavery for many reasons. White racism certainly played a pivotal role in driving a wedge between poor whites and blacks, but other factors were equally impor-

tant. Kinship ties and shared religious and educational experiences helped link many poor whites to the landed population of the central Piedmont. These connections helped blur the readily apparent economic disparities that separated landless and landed whites and lessened the dangers — real and perceived — that a class of dependant whites might see their interests as similar to those of enslaved or free blacks [65].

After the Civil War, the idea of white privilege became even more important and even easier to promote because poor blacks and whites competed for employment. The paternalism of the Southern aristocrat toward his poor white brother continued with hiring practices in the textile industry; mill owners wanted poor white women and children because of the dexterity of their smaller hands and the fact that they worked for lower wages, and they wanted a segregated work force to perpetuate a system that would decrease the chances of white/black labor solidarity. As has been suggested already, living and working conditions in the cotton mill village represented an upgrade from the farm and tenant shack, so the mountaineer and the Piedmont poor white carried his or her labor potential there.

When Charleston, South Carolina, merchant-capitalist William Gregg founded his antebellum Graniteville, South Carolina, cotton mill in 1846, he was one of the first entrepreneurs to build a large cotton mill that utilized the location of the Carolina Piedmont for its energy *and* labor source. The machinery of the textile industry required a great deal of power for operation, and the Piedmont, just on the eastern side of the Appalachian fall line with its various watersheds, provided a ready source of hydro-power. In *Habits of Industry*, Allen Tullos comments on the perfect placement of the Carolina Piedmont for textile manufacturing endeavors: "Crossing the rivers and streams of the Carolinas at a distance between 100 and 150 miles from and running parallel to the Atlantic coastline is the belt of waterfalls and rapids known as the fall line. The fall line divides ancient residual Appalachian soils from recently surfaced (measured in the eons of geological time) ocean bottom" (43). The rapids and waterfalls of the rivers flowing down out of the mountains toward the Atlantic made the generation of hydro-power possible because "the break between the Appalachian Blue Ridge chain and the westward edge of the Piedmont is sharp, with the elevation falling as much as three thousand feet across a dozen miles" (Tullos 45). In the years that followed the Civil War, many industrialists followed the antebellum lead of William Gregg by locating their mills on these streams and rivers where both the power and the labor remained economically desirable.

The problem with these locations remained that they were nowhere near the urban centers of the day, so there was little housing for the mill employees.

Therefore, "the manufacturers established their own building sites, usually where water power was available, and built villages around them for the housing and accommodations of their employees. The cotton mill village originated therefore as a social and economic necessity" (Simpson 21–22). This arrangement became the norm for the industry. Harriet Herring comments that "the company-owned village has been a conspicuous adjunct of the cotton mill whenever and wherever this branch of textiles has sprung up" because "operatives brought or attracted from elsewhere had no means with which to build homes" (*Passing of the Mill Village* 3). The mill operators owned all aspects of the mill village; they determined the pay scale, dictated the social rules, provided health care, and even established extracurricular activities for their employees — schools with teachers (*Welfare Work* 32); churches (86); baseball teams (137); instrumental bands (141). *The Gardener's Son* mirrors the mill operators' absolute control over mill life; in fact, as Diane Luce notes, "the reiteration of tolling bells" connects the mills and the mill village churches, implying "enforced conformity not only in the villagers' workaday lives but in their spiritual lives as well (*Reading the World* 180).

William Gregg, like others who followed his lead, hired hands for his mill exclusively from the white population; his was, according to Herring, both a paternalistic philanthropy and capitalistic venture. She quotes him as saying, "Unless our poor [white] people can be brought together *in villages* and some means of employment afforded them, it will be an utterly hopeless effort to undertake to educate them" (quoted in Herring, *Welfare Work* 370, emphasis added). Broadus Mitchell, in a fairly laudatory and one-sided tract, claims that "William Gregg, the builder of the Graniteville Factory in South Carolina, was the father, in the sense that he was the anticipator, of a new economic life for the South" (*Rise of the Cotton Mills* 168). Gregg took a keen interest in the plight of the Southern poor white, and though few followed his lead into the cotton industry in the antebellum period, his example provided a template for post-bellum mill industry. While Simpson decries the suggestion of paternalism on the part of the operators and Herring sees it as a natural development of the industry, Mitchell takes a more pragmatic view: "What at first had been a necessity of mill building, and a perfectly natural expression of the traditional responsibility of the master for his dependants, now became, on the part of many, a studied tactical pose" (*Industrial Revolution* 11). Gregg's mill town served as a model for many of those that followed, and most of what McCarthy writes in *The Gardener's Son* about the elder Gregg and his methodology is historically founded. As the industrial elite discovered, the mill village itself had multiple advantages in the training of mill personnel, a traditionally nonindustrial, undisciplined population.

William Gregg and those who followed found that the training of mill operatives required attention to specific spatial arrangements. Industrial spaces intensify discipline for efficient industrial production. Subsistence farming, on the other hand, "is characterized by periods of productive labor with alternate periods of inactivity" (Precourt 100). On the farm, work periods were divided into times of the year, not hours of the day. The mountaineer awakened and slept with the cycles of the sun, he planted and harvested by the cycles of the moon. Industry, on the other hand, required daily, regimented input. The mountaineer-turned-millhand's work situation once depended on the whims of the seasons, not on the tolls of the mill bell; so "there were hardships for those who migrated from worn-out farms and nonproductive mountain sections. It was a psychological hardship to exchange farm or mountain isolation for village living. Moreover, it was hardship to exchange 'do-as-one-pleases' living style for that of the mill bell, which said 'come and do it now' and until the bell rings to quit" (Andrews 15). Jack Weller claims that the attitudes the mountaineer developed over the long period he spent in isolation served as an impediment to his assimilation in a modern industrial environment. He says that the mountaineer's "independence-turned-individualism, a corruption of the virtue which was once the foundation stone of the mountain man's way of life, now proves to be a great stumbling block to his finding a place in our increasingly complex and cooperative society" (Weller 32). The mill village helped the highlander assimilate to the industrial environment — a "complex and cooperative society."

The cotton mills mirrored the factories of the early-nineteenth-century North and eighteenth-century Europe where "the principle of individualizing partitioning became more complicated. It was a question of distributing individuals in a space in which one might isolate and map them; but also of articulating this distribution on a production machinery that had its own requirements" (*DP* 144). A mill operative spent a certain number of hours at one machine and this spatial situation itself compartmentalized the work, so that

> [b]y walking up and down the central isle of the workshop, it was possible to carry out a supervision that was both general and individual: to observe the worker's presence and application, and the quality of [her] work; to compare workers with one another, to classify them according to skill and speed; to follow successive stages of progress. All these serializations formed a permanent grid: confusion was eliminated [145].

Every movement was predetermined for the mountaineers who came from the hills to the mills; "every process was awkward to them. Continuous hours of close attention to machinery contrasted with the variety and simplicity of old familiar habit in the country. They were not accustomed to coordination of effort, or to receiving directions" (Mitchell, *Industrial Revolution* 240). The disciplinary spatial arrangement inside of the mill itself helped to train the new operatives to the new economic order.

The compartmentalization evident in the mills themselves was mirrored in the village housing situation: "The cotton mill village was like one big white family closed off to the external world. Rows and rows of white clapboard houses lined dirt roads leading to the mill" (Byerly 12). This metaphor of "family" obscures the workings of discipline. The mill villages resembled Foucault's "perfect camp" where "all power would be exercised solely through exact observation; each gaze would form a part of the overall functioning of power" (*DP* 171). William Gregg's mill was seen "as a model factory, where due attention is paid to the comforts, education, and morals of the operatives"; a mill village based on Gregg's Graniteville became "a 'temperance town, with no liquor sold, and if anyone is known to bring any into the place, he is expelled, driven off in disgrace'" (*Welfare Work* 369–370). Mill overseers could know which operative lived in which house on which row and could also see how each operative conducted him- or herself— did he or she keep a clean residence? who visited the house and when? what were the operatives' domestic relations like? Ever-watchful neighbors could know the comings and goings of every other millhand. As James Cobb notes, "The configuration of the housing in the early mill village was more reminiscent of the slave quarters," built in rows and tightly situated close together; "the mill village would have allowed little enough privacy even without the snooping practiced by some mill officials" (71). The villages themselves became "disciplinary institutions" which "secreted a machinery of control that functioned like a microscope of conduct; the fine, analytical divisions that they created formed around men an apparatus of observation, recording and training" (*DP* 173). The entire arrangement of the mill workspace and the mill village established a situation "subject to a whole micro-penalty of time (lateness, absences, interruptions of tasks), of activity (inattention, negligence, lack of zeal), of behavior (impoliteness, disobedience) of speech (idle chatter, insolence), of the body ('incorrect' attitudes, irregular gestures, lack of cleanliness), of sexuality (impurity, indecency)" (178). The mill did not erect guard towers or post gunmen at the village gates to control the operatives; they merely set the space up "without any physical instrument other than architecture and geometry" (206). The rows of machines and the rows of houses manufactured a relationship where "disciplinary power became an 'integrated' system, linked from the inside to the economy and to the aims of the mechanism in which it was practiced" (176).

What began as a necessity evolved into a machinery of control: "The mill village system was meant to control all aspects of the workers' lives — from church to education to the welfare system" (Byerly 14). So when the operatives misbehaved and threatened the social equilibrium, they could be expelled from the community. Allen Tullos cites Gerald W. Johnson's biography of mill owner Simpson Billbo Tanner, which says that Tanner

> "regulated not merely working conditions, but the private lives of his operatives."... [C]ompany police enforced prohibitions against drinking, "rowdiness," and "sexual misbehavior." Tanner acted as the ultimate judge. Although biographer Johnson finds his regime authoritarian by "modern" standards, he defends Tanner's rule as *"discipline, not mere domination"* by insisting that it was necessary for the transforming of rural whites into town dwellers and *efficient* factory "operatives" [Tullos 12; emphasis added].

Accounts at mill stores further hastened the mountaineer's progression towards becoming the compliant operative, tightening the strands of the disciplinary web; the relationship between the operative and the mill stores was couched as "for the convenience of the employees, as well as for the sake of monetary gain." Often "the company stores [were] owned by the mills, and the managers and clerks [were] employees of the mills. Under this system the collection of store debts [was] facilitated by pay-roll deductions" (Simpson 68).

All of these threads intersected with the others to weave the fabric of the workers' lives. The mill village served as a laboratory of panoptic power which arranged "things in such a way that the exercise of power is not added on from the outside, like a rigid, heavy constraint, to the functions it invests, but is so subtly present in them as to increase their efficiency by itself increasing its own points of contact" (*DP* 206). Proof that this spatial arrangement worked resides in how the operatives themselves became the enforcers of the community mores. As Herring suggests, "The villagers themselves are among the first to protest against any undesirable person"; for example, "if a girl gets a bad reputation [the mill executives] have a talk with her parents and warn them that they must exercise better control or move; some quietly get rid of the family — but the people all know why the action is taken" (*Welfare Work* 270–271).

The mill village presented no mere habitat of oppression, however; it presented the mountaineer with an alternative to vagabondage and shrinking Appalachian farm acreage: "With only their labor to invest and in numbers that exceeded the region's capacity to support its population through agriculture, forestry, and mining, most Appalachian migrants had little choice but to go wherever work could be found" (J. Williams 312). Billings and Blee confirm Williams's assessment of the mountaineers' attraction to the stability of the cotton mill village when they write that "limits on agricultural capacity contributed to the development of an underemployed labor pool that could be utilized cheaply in railroad, timber, and mining industries" as well as in cotton mills (207). The subsistence agriculture of the Appalachian folk could no longer support them because "there is not enough land to go around as the families increase" (Lemert 8). So moving to a planned town with the accouterments of modern society was attractive to many former agrarians: when the textile mills promised both work and shelter, "dirt farmers jumped at the chance to be engaged in wage labor" (Byerly 11). Speaking of villages in the years prior to 1933, Ben Lemert says operatives "are free from the unsanitary conditions of crowded cities, rents are lower and more space can be obtained, the employee can have his lawn and his garden where he and his family can work and play" (11). Broadus Mitchell echoes Lemert's assessment, believing "the pertinence of recent accounts of the poorer mountain and tenant whites in their native surroundings is illustrated by the fact that the mills very recently [1921] were receiving families in just as destitute condition as those which first entered the factory communities" (*Rise of the Cotton Mills* 167). No one forced the mountaineer into the villages; they were nudged out by divestment and pulled in by opportunity. For the mountaineer of the late nineteenth and early twentieth century, the mill became a viable alternative to the farm and to the city.

Village Life

Cormac McCarthy's *The Gardener's Son* evidences all of these facets of mill life. The teleplay deconstructs the myth of the cotton mill and the benevolence of its operator. McCarthy exposes the relationships between the powerful mill-owning Gregg family and the luckless McEvoys — couched as typical mill operatives — who have come down from Pickens, South Carolina, for the same reasons so many mountaineers left the mountains for the mills: economic opportunity. In his *Habits of Industry*, Allen Tullos tells the story of the D.W. League family from near Greenville, South Carolina. The patriarch, Commodore Butler League, moved the family to the Poe mill in order to supplement his farming income, taking a job as a carpenter. The family cultivated a garden and "kept its ties to the country through regular trips to the Simpsonville farm" (175–177). Financially pressed like the Leagues, Patrick McEvoy gives the lawyer Whipper the reason that he moved his family to the mill: "We come here nine year ago. We tried to stay on at home after the [Civil] war but they wasnt no way. I wanted the children to have something" (*GS*

67–68). Like so many mountaineers, the McEvoys journey to the mills out of economic necessity: "As entire families moved to the villages, they often arrived with some sense of failure and with a strong determination to return to farming as soon as they could save enough money to buy the land. Neither factory wages nor agricultural conditions, however, favored a return to the land" (Tullos 19). D.W. League's parents went back to Simpsonville, but the McEvoys suffer a different fate, as Martha relates how her father "always said we'd save up and go back to Greenville ... but we never done it" (*GS* 92). Compared to the worn-out land from which the McEvoys tried to extract a living and in relation to the urban areas they knew so little about, the textile mill village presents them and many other mountaineers with a living situation that, while considerably different from their experience, could be adjusted to over time; therefore, perhaps unsurprisingly, "when it was known that a factory was to be erected, mountaineers and poor tenants began to inquire eagerly for employment, and to make plans for moving their families to the new village" (*Industrial Revolution* 251).

William Gregg believed it was his responsibility to educate his workers and their children; he once said, "our company are determined to spare no means which will be necessary to school the children of Graniteville" (quoted in Herring, *Welfare Work* 370). While the elder Gregg seems to have been genuinely concerned with the welfare of his employees, "Many mill men of course justified the expense of welfare activities to themselves and their boards of directors by adding that such things paid" (296). Like so many other mill owners of his generation, he knew that the education of the people of the mill would benefit his endeavors as well as the workers themselves. In *The Gardener's Son*, the speaker at his funeral eulogizes him with thanks from the community for his benevolence: "There are many among us today who can remember what life held in the way of promise before this man came among us ... to see what he has wrought, the neat homes, the churches and schools, the gardens and the lovely grounds" (*GS* 19). The founder of the Graniteville mill "practiced a paternalistic despotism toward his employees, preaching piety and requiring attendance at the school that he built in the mill village" (Cobb 6). Gregg's operatives "were for the most part recruited from an economically underprivileged rural class who had little or no education, whose children did not attend the poor little district schools that were available, who, far from wanting education, had rather a prejudice against it, and who had little vision to lead them in the right direction" (*Welfare Work* 32).

Yet Gregg's support of schools or other extracurricular activities was by no means a completely altruistic enterprise. Certainly education helped the individual workers—expanding their minds and interests—but it also *strengthened their efficiency.* If the mill controlled the purse strings of the school, then it controlled the curriculum, and the operatives' children learned just what the mill owners wanted them to learn, including obedience to authority, the deprecation of one's roots, and acceptance of one's social position. Una Mae Lange Reck and George G. Reck expose how schools have often benefited authority in Appalachia generally: "Historically, schools ... have been a major institutional arm of the colonialization of Appalachia, participating in the denigration of regional lifestyles, perpetuating external control through discrimination, and helping to insure the continued powerlessness of Appalachian rural people" (284). Schools in the mill villages were no different, and like the layout of the mill, became disciplinary mechanisms, as Foucault shows and Gregg as recognized. Gregg's welfare work and "paternalistic despotism" toward his operatives did not stop at education but extended to other forms of social uplift. He forbade the consumption of alcohol by the operatives on his property and insisted on their punctuality and cleanliness; he demanded that they assimilate to *his* sense of propriety.

William Gregg presents one ownership type, but his son James exposes another. The Timekeeper makes a distinction between the two Greggs: "The old man they say was just a pistol. James was a different cut. He was alright, but the blood runs thin" (*GS* 4). Broadus Mitchell maintains that second-generation mill owners did not hold with the same philanthropic ideals as their forebears. Philanthropy was more of a ruse for them. Writing in the late nineteen-teens and early nineteen-twenties, he says that the second generation of Southern industrialists

> are not subject to the restraints of their fathers. They do not have an emotional attitude toward their workers. They are not burdened with a sense of noblesse oblige. They are not aristocrats, but bourgeois.... Qualities which in their fathers were spontaneous and meaningful, they have laid claim to and adapted to their uses ... there is some good in all of this, and in particular instances it is mostly good will, but generally speaking the welfare program is prosecuted because it pays [*Industrial Revolution* 33].

In fact, James does not even pretend to continue the philosophy of his father. Chris Walsh claims that James "may actually be less of a hypocrite in that he abandoned any philanthropic pretensions in exchange for profits and commercial advancement" (*In the Wake of the Sun* 331). His paternalism is devoid of philanthropy. He is more like mill operator Lee Love, who "brought the technical tools of cost accounting and efficiency analysis into his mills, never adopted the institutions of village 'welfare work,' scattered factories throughout the region in order to make union organizing more difficult, and integrated his company's production and advertising into the constantly changing style demanded of national and international textile marketing" (Tullos 116). Like the younger Gregg, Love focused only on the products and the profits and how the mill would benefit himself. The "Third Man" in one scene recognizes James's concerns: "Thing about James. He never did want to put the jam on the lower shelf where the little man could get some" (*GS* 50).

Patrick McEvoy's capacity as a gardener demonstrates the "tradition among the cotton mills of the South that each house shall have its garden space ... to supply their tables when and where the markets were poor" (*Welfare Work* 207). Yet this too changes with the change in management. As the Old Man tells Bobby McEvoy when he returns looking for his father after his mother's death, "Not big on gardens here no more. Gardens is always the first thing to go" (*GS* 41). James himself confirms this attitude when he tells Robert McEvoy that his father is no longer the gardener but "works in the mill. This company is in the textile business. We have stockholders to answer to. We're not in the flower business" (53).

One of the more telling scenes of the teleplay comes when James Gregg turns away the family that has traveled down from the mountains hunting jobs (21–24). After the mills sprang up and the mill villages spoked outward from the factory, the mills needed workers; so "labor agents were employed by the mills to comb the highlands of neighboring states or counties to induce the unemployed or poor nonlanded whites to move to the mill villages where they could enjoy the advantages of village life and a cash payroll" (Andrews 14). The family in the text has been shown a "dodger" that advertised jobs in the mill; according to Herring, such tactics were commonplace when a mill wanted to attract new workers. She notes, "Labor scouts sent to the country around and to the mountains enticed families with rather too glowing pictures. They told of wages amounting to cash far beyond anything these families had ever handled" (*Welfare Work* 21). The crew that the Ragged Man brings with him are "*a band of filthy and ragged people with bales of bedding and sorry household effects, nearly all barefooted, some appearing to be albinos, a couple of emaciated hound dogs, a few crates of chickens,*" according to McCarthy's directions (*GS* 22–23). They are stereotypical mountaineers. Robert McEvoy looks on as James Gregg turns them away, saying "The last bill we put out was four years ago" (24). For Bobby, whose leg was broken "fallin off the gravel train" (4), James Gregg's lack of sympathy for these unfortunates echoes the callousness Gregg's mother demonstrated when she insisted that the doctor be allowed to remove Bobby's gangrenous appendage. He feels like the Greggs are at least partially to blame for the ostracism he has experienced due to his handicap. Bobby obviously identifies more readily with the mountain family than with Gregg because the McEvoys likewise came to the mill from upstate as victims of hard times. Bobby realizes that had James been in charge of the mill when the McEvoys came down from Pickens rather than William Gregg, they too likely would have been turned away. Gregg, of course, does not care where these undesirables go, as long as they get out of his mill village. His words betray his lack of compassion: of them he says, "Some of God's seed has fallen on barren ground" (24). That Robert McEvoy watches these proceedings becomes increasingly important as the teleplay moves along. He has a chip on his shoulder and a general disrespect for authority, and perhaps James Gregg's nonchalance toward the plight of the job-hunting mountaineers affirms his notions.

The attitude of the doctor toward the respective parties reveals the less than subtle differences in class. Robert McEvoy understands these social stratifications perhaps better than anyone else in the teleplay, and his lack of respect for the mill's elite makes him problematic within the confines of the mill's environment. When the doctor — who conflates class, ignorance, and contagion — confronts Bobby about removing his rotting leg, McEvoy exclaims, "No, damn you!"— clearly a disrespectful response not lost on the doctor, who tells Mrs. Gregg, "He swore at me" (13–14). The doctor implies that the McEvoy house is, perhaps because they are poor mountain people, a "flyway" for germs: "I'm sorry to be so blunt but *you people* will not seem to understand" (14, emphasis added). He does not show the McEvoys any more respect than the Greggs do. Robert's conversation with Mrs. Gregg — who poses as a philanthropist with Bobby's best interests at heart — reveals his contempt for his social "betters," and for God, the "ultimate authority." Bobby essentially blames God for his condition when he charges, "If God put the rot in it then let it rot off" (15). Given that he disrespects the deity, it should come as no surprise then that Robert shows no respect to the timekeeper, his boss:

TIMEKEEPER: McEvoy. That it? McEvoy?
ROBERT: That's it.
TIMEKEEPER: That's it? Did they not learn you to sir at your home?
ROBERT: Sir.
TIMEKEEPER: If Mr. Gregg was to hear that he'd flop in his grave like a fish, God rest his soul. Good manners are never out of place. What he used to say [20].

Regardless of whether or not Robert has a legitimate predilection for disrespect, he presents a problem for the mill authorities because he recognizes that they use the labor of the operatives and offer limited wages and zero social equality in return. The housing is just a show, yet another control. When Maryellen says that she wishes they lived in a better house, Patrick

McEvoy quotes Bobby as saying, "That wouldnt make you no better than you are" (29). Some of what Robert has reportedly said implies that the family would be better off had they stayed in Pickens, that at least there they had their independence and equality. He sees their dependence on the mill and how it degrades them. He tells Martha, "The good book says all men are brothers but it dont seem to cut no ice, does it?" (39). They are not all brothers at the mill.

Robert recognizes James Gregg's disregard for the mill operatives, and he in turn sees Bobby's insolence. Gregg's dealings with the Ragged Man and his family reveal his true feelings of contempt toward his mountaineer workers. Bobby exposes the hypocrisy of the mill's disciplinary environment, and his resistance to it merely proves the need for it. Mr. Giles reminds Patrick McEvoy that Bobby "aint supposed to stay on at company house if he aint employed by the company. Old as he is. I mean it's company policy" (32). If an employee will not work or causes problems on the job as Robert McEvoy does, or if he questions the authority of the mill operators, he loses his housing privileges. Had Bobby not already left the mill, the mill administrators would have kicked him out.

Bobby's relationship to the mill exposes the class conflicts inherent in an endeavor where "the company village furnished workers to the mills and housing to the workers. In the achievement of these essential needs the social by-product was communities with conflicting values: mobility versus controls; physical and community facilities usually beyond what the people themselves could have established, but created and operated outside the democratic process" (*Passing of the Mill Village* 6). Dissent could not be tolerated in Graniteville. Besides, neither James Gregg nor his mother holds with William Gregg's original project. Their own words betray their true feelings toward their employees. When James tells Robert McEvoy, "We don't need *your kind* here," he talks not about his handicap or even his attitude, but about his social status, his vagrancy, and what Gregg perceives as his latent criminality (*GS* 54; emphasis added). For Gregg, Bobby embodies the stereotypes that paint the mountaineer/millhand as slovenly, rebellious, and unwilling to work. When Martha attempts to save Bobby by pleading with Mrs. Gregg, Mrs. Gregg confirms James's condescension by placing Martha in the same social category as Bobby: "My son was right about *you people* ... the poor and the downtrodden," her words dripping sarcasm (76, emphasis added). Whereas William Gregg saw his endeavors as an opportunity to make money and help the local people, the conflicts between the owners and the operatives — conflicts stemming from class difference — have colored the attitudes of both sides. James and his mother become the stereotypical uncaring mill owners, and Bobby and Martha become mountain trash. The attitude passes down to later generations too. The Young Man says to the timekeeper "I guess if you hire *these people* you have to take the consequences" (4, emphasis added).

Robert McEvoy's incident with the mill ownership demonstrates the need for and the subsequent effectiveness of the disciplinary controls as they function in the mill village environment. While he does murder Gregg, the solitary event does not precipitate a full-scale class revolt. When his resistance crosses the threshold of acceptability, he meets with harsh justice. Bobby's resistance presents the mill-owning bourgeoisie with one of the "series of illegalities [which] was inscribed in struggles in which those struggling knew that they were confronting both the law and the class that had imposed it" (*DP* 274); his *cognizance* gives him power. His attack on one of the elite illuminates a class conflict with potentially serious social repercussions. Robert McEvoy's identification of James Gregg and his mill-owning cohorts as the underlying force that keeps the millhand in wage slavery provides a real challenge to the mill-owning elite. While killing one of that elite's members was what got Robert hanged, the real crime was exposing the inequality of the system and the abuse of power on James Gregg's part, as evidenced by his attempt to "buy" Martha with a ten-dollar coin (*GS* 26–28). As a character, Robert McEvoy allows McCarthy to deconstruct the relationships between the elite and their mountain-turned-millhand operatives; Herring, Simpson, Lemert, and Mitchell — all writing in the heyday of the southern cotton mills — posit the development of these relationships as a natural occurrence, as positive for the mountaineer and good for the industry, as *progress* towards modernization. Bobby McEvoy bucks these assumptions; *The Gardener's Son* indicts this *progress*. McCarthy gives no overt moral judgment, he sides with neither Gregg nor McEvoy, but his portrayal of the story complicates the interpretations of history; it deconstructs the historical record, or as Christopher Walsh puts it: "On a more profoundly philosophical level [the teleplay] can also be read as McCarthy's attempt to rescue all of the Robert McEvoys who are absented from historical discourses" (*In the Wake of the Sun* 330). McCarthy gives them voice. His text recontextualizes this murder case and "takes into account the possibility that both history and justice are owned by the more powerful and that fiction may be used to subvert this cultural hegemony" (Cant 139). *The Gardener's Son* demonstrates that progress may be desirable, but there are always casualties along the way.

The mill-owning elite have no desire to see Robert McEvoy become a working-class hero, so they make him a pariah, an example to the other operatives. Diane Luce notes, "The elite of [South Carolina] saw the shooting of

James Gregg as a threatening escalation of violence in that section" ("McCarthy's First Screenplay" 85). She maintains that historically, the elite saw this incident as an opportunity to manifest their control over the poor whites of the area. In that they have the support of the legal system: the country lawyer Jordan tells Patrick McEvoy, "We wont get anywhere in an attempt to blacken the Gregg name," so the lawyers have "agreed with Mrs. Gregg to call no female witnesses" (*GS* 61). Tullos notes "the prerogatives of Piedmont mill owners were supported by municipal and state police power" (188); clearly the collusion between Mrs. Gregg and the McEvoys' lawyer truncates justice in this case. This seems to be nothing unusual historically. One of the coal camp operatives that Laurel Shackelford and Bill Weinberg interview makes this accusation, one that holds water in the case of James Gregg's murder: "Justice in the courts wasn't too good at that time: the judge could be bought; the lawyers was crooked most of the time ... back then the 'will of the people' was the man that had the money, that big operator" (222). The collusion of the defending attorney and the Gregg family in McEvoy's trial certainly leads one to believe Cant's assertion that the courts are bought. Robert McEvoy is not allowed to take the stand because he might tell the jury the real reason he killed Gregg—James's personal peccadilloes with various millgirls and the various injustices he committed toward Martha and others. These revelations, were they taken to heart by the mill operatives, might cause more civic unrest.

So the courts of both justice and public opinion, influenced by the money and power of the Greggs, paint Bobby as crazy. Patrick McEvoy's comment to Whipper—"I know my boy done wrong. But he aint like they're tryin to make him out"—reveals that the prosecution, rather than just making him a murderer, wants a psychopath, a vagabond, a social anomaly whose inherent criminality betrays all the mill village society holds dear—respect for authority, hard work, and discipline (*GS* 65). Bobby becomes the stereotypical degenerate, ornery, violent hillbilly in the hands of the elite and their denizens. The Gregg murder is one "of the assaults allegedly committed by poor whites in the central Piedmont [that] involved battles that crossed class lines" (Bolton 60). The elite had to make Robert out to be a monster in order to quell any idea that they might be mistreating the poorer classes; therefore, "the punishment of landless people involved in violent confrontations with members of their own social group essentially represented an opportunity for central Piedmont leaders to reaffirm publicly existing power relations" (60). Thus the death penalty for Bobby. The photographer wants extra pictures to sell (*GS* 78) for the same reason that Martha is afraid the doctors will come dig Bobby up, crack open his skull and examine his brain: people want to know what makes someone so rebellious in spite of all the "charity" he has been shown by his social "betters" (91). People want to know how one can take the boy out of the hills and fail to take the hills out of the boy.

Bobby McEvoy's murder of James Gregg exposes the working of discipline — the spatial divisions of the village, the compartmentalization of time by the mill bell's toll, the watching of one operative over another. McEvoy enters the mill itself, "*clumping down the aisle past the machinery and the workers. They watch him but he doesnt watch back*" (52). The discipline of the mill village is subtle; it "tends to increase aptitudes, speeds, output and therefore profits; it still exerts a moral influence over behavior, but more it treats actions in terms of their results, introduces bodies into machinery, forces into an economy" (*DP* 210). After Bobby shoots Gregg and Gregg stumbles out of the mill's door onto the village street, Bobby shoots again and "the clatter of machinery in the background suddenly comes to a halt. There is an immense silence" (*GS* 57). The gunshot disturbs the peace and shuts the mill down for a short time. However, none of the workers identifies with McEvoy. They surely know of James Gregg's behavior towards the girls of the mill, but their jobs depend on their discretion. While they might think Gregg got what he deserved, they dare not indicate it. Conversely, Bobby's action of murder produces telling reactions on the part of other mill operatives. His resistance colors his whole family. The First Jailor assumes Patrick McEvoy, not known for drinking, to be drunk despite McEvoy's protestation to the contrary (83); Mrs. Gregg assumes Martha is "loose" despite all evidence to the contrary (75–76). As he goes to see his son, Patrick McEvoy says to a fellow worker, "Mornin Louis," but the man "glances his way and looks away again as if he hadnt seen him" (79). The rest of the mill folk seem to buy into this system; they enforce the discipline. The social ostracism of the McEvoy family has begun. Torn by the grief over his son's rapid demise, Patrick neglects his wife's decomposing body, and the Constable tells him, "Mr. McEvoy you got to see to your affairs at home sir.... I dont want to get a court order, but those people are entitled to some consideration. They can detect her four houses down" (61–62). As Patrick returns to his house after the trial, his neighbors demand that he bury his wife. One says, "It's an outrage is what it is. A damned outrage" (69). The close quarters of the mill village make very personal affairs like a funeral community business. The other mill workers chastise McEvoy for his infringement on their olfactories rather than consoling him on the death of his wife and the imminent death of his son. The juxtaposition of chastising and consolation stems from the fact that Bobby has betrayed the mill's hierarchy. And the disciplinary web is exposed.

The mill workers want to know less about the inequalities and abuses of power in the mills than the operators do. They have allowed them to continue because their jobs depend on the benevolence of the Gregg family and any deconstruction of that system calls into question the very foundation of their lives. So rather than questioning the system, rather than holding the feet of the elite to the fire, they comply; they side with the elite, and they isolate the McEvoys. The mill operatives choose to identify with the mill operators, whom they recognize as having control of the situation and whom they understand are watching for their reactions. In both the factory and village, the operative "is seen, but he does not see; he is the object of information, never a subject of communication. The arrangement ... imposes on him an axial visibility but ... impl[ies] a lateral invisibility. And this invisibility is a guarantee of order" (*DP* 200). The literal inability to see another factory worker and the knowledge that the operators are always watching becomes a metaphorical inability for one operative to identify with another's plight. The panoptic spatial arrangement affects the desired discipline. Perhaps fearing for their jobs (as Gaventa or Herring might suggest), or perhaps feeling the claustrophobia induced in close quarters by a rotting body four houses down the road, the mill village ostracizes Patrick.

Despite his enormous misfortunes, the elder McEvoy becomes, not a welcomed member with whom the mill community empathizes, but an outcast just like his murdering son. Like the inmates of Benthum's Panopticon, the millhands internalize discipline. Herring notes,

> the mill village has been ingrained in its life rather than its houses. The people are all of the same stock, the same cultural background with closely similar religions, of about the same educational attainments and economic level. They all work on the same product at tasks all comprehend and many are experienced in. They are all subject to the ups and downs of the same erratic market and of the same company. The policies of the same management irritate or satisfy them *en masse*. It is homogeneity run riot [*Passing of the Mill Village* 114–115].

The McEvoys become an abnormality against which the rest of the community is defined.

Regardless of the seemingly negative aspects of discipline, the dream of many mountaineers who moved to the mills was that their children would not have to work those same mills, and that dream *did* come true. The efficiency created by discipline helps ensure the realization of such dreams as well as ensuring industrial survival for the mill. In *The Gardener's Son*, Harvey (the Timekeeper) is one of those workers who, as Tullos says, "worked their way up to skilled mill jobs" (173). He abides by the mill's mores and advances as a result. At the end of the teleplay, Martha McEvoy says, "[Harvey] had a son that's a district court judge. He had five children and they wasnt one of em ever worked the first day in that mill" (*GS* 89). According to Foucault, one of the things power constructs is the "modern subject"— the figure who wants to be recognized as an individual and who wishes to be assimilated to the modern economy. The discipline of the mill thereby works to the advantage of the *operator and the operative* in many cases. The toll of the mill bell and the schedule it demarcates helps the mountaineer acclimate to modern industrial society; the education and other opportunities provided in the mill villages bettered the lives of the operatives. The mountaineer learned bourgeois values in the mills: ownership, work ethic, and time management—all things necessary for assimilation in a modern society.

Once, the individualistic mountaineer rebelled against these values. Jack Weller thinks this rebellion is simply part of the mountaineer psyche; he says, "Although most [mountaineers] were interested in cooperative programs, they were not willing to support them by local taxes. Here again the mountaineer's individualism comes to the fore" (Weller 33). Harriet Herring shows, however, that after years spent in millwork the disciplined mountaineer-turned-millhand changed his attitude. For example, the mountaineers' "response to so unaccustomed and unpleasant a subject as property taxes is perhaps sort of an index" of their acculturation; one county tax official whom Harriet Herring interviewed "was indignant at the question as to [the mountaineers'] relative standing in this respect: 'Of course they pay their taxes. They are just as responsible citizens as anybody else'" (*Passing of the Mill Village* 65). The supposition evident here is that mountaineers did not act as modern subjects until they came to the mills. The discipline of the mill town worked.

Later developments in mill villages demonstrate the mountaineers' cultural assimilation. In the twentieth century the cotton manufacturers began selling off their mill villages as a method of reducing their costs. Most of them gave mill operatives the first opportunity to purchase their houses. This is a further reach of discipline: "American people believe so firmly in home ownership as a foundation for good citizenship that when observers are asked to appraise the effects of the sales on the community they almost unanimously say that it has been good: 'Naturally makes them more interested'; 'they feel more responsible'; 'more permanent'; and so on" (Herring, *Passing of the Mill Village* 89). Home ownership ties them even more intimately to the mill and to the capitalist economy as mortgage holders who participate in finance capitalism; they go into monetary debt when they purchase houses and the strings attaching them to culture tighten. Herring continues, "The sale of a mill village changes the way of life for the people. They must make decisions which they had very likely never thought would be necessary. They have new responsibilities and, in times of rising values, new temptations" (65). They are no longer "unknowable" mountaineers, but have become members of a modern economic society.

Thus, when the mills began selling off their villages, the real advantage again was for the operators. Mill managers, according to Herring, "accept as a by-product of the new order the fact that they will not be able to 'control' any labor in the economic sense" once they relinquish the deeds to the housing (*Passing of the Mill Village* 112). Nevertheless, the trade-off was good for business, the managers felt. It "(1) stopped the subsidy on the house and released funds from that investment; (2) allowed full attention to manufacturing; (3) rid [the managers] of a source of annoyance; (4) proved fairer to employees owning or paying high rent outside the village; (5) and *converted workers into better citizens and more responsible members of the community*" (81, emphasis added). This last characteristic (5) demonstrates the assimilation of the mountaineer to bourgeois property-ownership ideals and shows how the management understood the importance of such a development. Property owners ultimately make more responsible citizens because they have more at stake in the social and economic system. Therefore, the mills were no longer in the philanthropy business because they did not have to be. The mountaineer accepted his role in their economic system. Once trained in the mill, he aspired to the bourgeois ideal. The discipline of the mill village became arcane. Herring argues that the discipline of home ownership binds the millhand to the capitalist program even more solidly than the village itself had; but this too is a gradual result of the disciplining of the mountaineer.

Labor leaders' opposition to the selling of the mill village reveals their knowledge of the way the village has historically disciplined the millhand: "Labor leaders believed in home ownership in principle, [but] they shared the doubts of social economists after the depression, whether it was wise for low income, mass production workers.... [T]hey feared that owning a house so handy to the mill would tie a worker to it more securely than the village institution had done" (Herring, *Passing of the Mill Village* 69). This development in the mill village saga, facilitated by economics and a disciplined work force, puts the mill ownership in a position the latter-generation Gregg would have appreciated.

The undisciplined way of life fades for the mountaineer when he leaves the mountains. Patrick McEvoy moves from independent yeoman farmer, to wage-earning gardener, to underappreciated millhand on the fluctuations of the economy and the whims of mill ownership. His mountaineer-turned-millhand neighbors do not sympathize with his plight; they do not help him bury his dead, but turn on him when he and his son demonstrate a lack of adherence to community norms. He and his family became the negative example of and for the millhand, the example of "this is what happens to you when you refuse the discipline of the mill village."

Regional Metropolises

The mill village served as a quintessential laboratory of disciplinary power for the mountaineer, but not the only one. It pulled mountaineers into its residences as the encroaching industries repossessed the mountains and pushed the mountaineers out. Mountaineers migrated to cotton mill villages where they labored over company machines and lived in company housing; people who had once awakened in the night to the "dread 'painter' ... whose wailing cry so chilled the occupants of lonely cabins that the folk memory of it had assumed supernatural overtones" heard only the wail of the time bell, morning and night (Caudill 22).

Regional urban centers also attracted mountaineers. The draw of cities has always existed for the mountaineer because "Appalachia has long been surrounded by areas more highly developed economically, with important cities and metropolitan areas offering many jobs suitable for relatively unskilled and inadequately educated persons" (McCoy and Brown 35). The mountaineer, vocationally unskilled and intellectually uneducated, moved to the cities more quickly as the land deteriorated, as coal and textile jobs fluctuated with the market, and as advances in transportation made such moves more possible.

The mountaineer chose cities for the same reason he chose the coal camps and the cotton mill villages: he could work and support his family. Gary Fowler says, "Contrary to conventional wisdom, migrants from the rural South to the urban North significantly increase[d] their personal incomes and, at the same time, reduce[d] their chances of being poor and aid-dependant" (90). The same was the case in regional urban areas or the mountaineer would not have moved there in such numbers. If he could have eked out a living on the family farm, the mountain man would have stayed put. Ultimately, however, cities and towns provided him with better opportunities.

Regional cities always experienced an influx of mountain migrants, but during the height of the "hillbilly diaspora" many migrants headed to the North or the Midwest. Specifically, as David Lilienthal, one of the first directors of the Tennessee Valley Authority, concludes, "During the heyday of prosperity, [Appalachian migrants] went north — to Detroit, Pontiac, Cleveland, Cincinnati, Columbus, and to other cities" (quoted in Morgan 157). The tides of migrants and opportunities floated on the currents of the national economy. The Great Depression sent many mountaineers back to the hills, but World War II and the subsequent economic boom provided employment in the nation's larger metropolises. The mountain people headed to Northern and Midwestern urban centers looking for work again. Toward the middle of the twentieth century, the influx of Appalachian migrants became such a difficulty for Midwestern cities that policy makers attempted to redirect the migration to regional urban centers like Asheville, Greenville, and Knoxville, and greater highway access made such policies implementable: "Since 1920, with the expansion of highways through the Appalachian area and the increasing importance of motor transportation, the growth of cities *in the Region* has been greatly enhanced" (Belcher 42, emphasis added).

Knoxville, Tennessee, is one such Appalachian regional town. James S. Brown and George A. Hillary claim, "The growth of the Knoxville area in the 1940s was due primarily to the development of the Atomic Energy Commission plants at Oak Ridge," but the mountaineers' movement to Knoxville began long before that (61). Sensing that they could not stem the tide of out-migration, policy makers accepted that "while migration from the most isolated areas was expected to continue, it was hoped that this flow would be redirected to 'growth areas' within each major subregion, and that the highway system could stimulate development in these areas" (*Appalachian Experiment* 67). Given its geographical placement and cultural history, as a regional destination for Appalachian migrants, and its factories and textile mills, Knoxville became one of these regional centers; as in other places, the expansion of interstate highways (I-40 and I-75) through Knoxville — as alluded to at the end of *Suttree*— helped this growth, as did the construction of the government's nuclear facility at Oak Ridge.

In the early days of its settlement, Knoxville had many things going for it. The Tennessee River, flowing from the confluence of several smaller rivers in the headwaters east of the city, ran deep enough on Knoxville's southern border to permit the passage of moderately large vessels. The city stood at the western foot of the southeastern band of the Appalachian Mountains and eventually became a hub on the north-south railroad lines that hugged the western border of those mountains. In examining the development of Knoxville, Michael J. McDonald and William Bruce Wheeler discuss its respectable growth as a regional destination by the time of the Civil War: "Knoxville was a modest town that had served successfully as a speculative venture, a seat of government, a way-station through which travelers heading west would pass, a small commercial center, and (by the time of the Civil War) one of several towns on the railroad lines that linked the South to the more dynamic regions to the north and west" (11). As the nineteenth century progressed into the twentieth, timber and coal companies extracted products from the surrounding countryside while subsistence farming declined. When their farms and orchards and fields played out, these agrarians came to Knoxville. The areas around Knoxville experienced an agricultural decline, especially after 1900 and during World War I. So, "true to historical conditions, [McCarthy's] *The Orchard Keeper* reveals this agricultural decline through such details as the wrecked orchard and farms of Red Branch.... [T]he fictional abandoned farms evoke the historic mass migrations of the yeomanry into towns to claim factory jobs" (Berry 51).

After the Civil War, and well into the 1900s, "the white in-migrants [to Knoxville] were only marginally skilled and hence took low-wage jobs in the factories, wholesale houses and shops of the mushrooming city" (McDonald and Wheeler 19); "because the city was a major railroad hub, Knoxville's primary industry became light manufacturing, which drew on the surrounding mountain population for its labor force, rather than the black 'industrial reserve' of the Black Belt" (R. Lewis 33). These mountaineers also found work where "cloth mills and furniture factories sprang up and prospered" (McDonald and Wheeler 21). Given their economic straits and their marginal social status, they settled where they could, often with people of similar backgrounds and occupational possibilities, so that "by the 1880s Knoxville's commercial center (the 'downtown') was ringed on the northern and northwestern fringe by a collection of mill villages (Mechanicsville, Brookside Village) that continued to maintain characteristics of individual neighborhoods long after they had grown together as one city" (21). McAnally Flats, adjacent to Mechanicsville, was one such marginal area settled by the economically challenged from the countryside; like many of their poor white kinsmen from the broader South, the Appalachian mountaineers who came to Knoxville showed how "one viable response to feelings of being marginalized is to *build* on the margins," to take what is given to them and make the best of it (Gray 69). They brought with them the hunger for work and for advancement just like any other migrants; but they could not apostatize from their Appalachian mores, "their rough-and-tumble democratic politics, their fundamentalist religions, or their suspicion of their economic betters"; in McAnally Flats and Mechnicsville, "violence was widespread, taverns still far outnumbered churches, and homicide was a regular feature of the city's life" (McDonald and Wheeler 19). Gay Street with its department stores, theaters, and general mercantiles separated the slums of McAnally from Mountain View, the poor mostly-black area. By the 1950s, bus lines gradually replaced the trolley system and urban flight took Knoxville's wealthier citizens to the western suburbs. The University of Tennessee began experiencing growing pains as the number of students outstripped the facilities and the university began acquiring more land for expansion west of Second Creek.

This is the world of *Suttree*, McCarthy's world, "the world of Knoxville and its environs, one of, if not the most economically, culturally, and imaginatively dispossessed areas within a larger region that has historically reveled in these factors" (Walsh, "There's NO Place Like Holme" 32). McCarthy's Knoxville is a world of violence and mayhem, drunkenness and debauchery: "The inhabitants of McAnally Flats form a grotesque community of exiles and escapees from the modern social order" whose legality and criminality push and pull each other constantly (Cawelti 167). Like the mill village, this is a world needing surveillance and discipline.

The concentrated lawlessness of McAnally Flats both in *Suttree* and in historical reality stems from a century of settlement by peoples who were disenfranchised and displaced. The volatile miscellany of poor blacks and mountain whites made this slum of Knoxville "a high crime area, with more than its share of blind pigs, aggravated assaults and bootlegging" (Longley Jr. 80). Mountain whites brought with them "the fierce independence and proud self-reliance of the highlander.... [O]n the one hand they symbolized the courage and resourcefulness of the pioneer — qualities to be valued in any age. On the other hand, independence carried to its extreme became a major obstacle to the establishment of law and order necessary for the functioning of a more complex society" (Ford 12). They brought with them a cultural naivety and inexperience. McCarthy shows an exaggerated instance of this inexperience when Gene Harrogate encounters the shower at the workhouse. Asked if he has never taken a shower before, he answers, "I aint never seen one" (*Suttree* 37). Before the "moonlight melonmounter" takes his place on his individual bunk within the confines of the workhouse, he must first be subjected to the discipline of hygiene. Not only do the guards force him to shower, after he finishes, a fellow inmate sprays him down for "bugs" and "crotch crickets" (38).

Like Harrogate, the mountain people brought with them old habits from the mountains where "each family had its own dump over the river bank in front of its house. Heaps of stinking refuse, old cans, bottles, bedsprings, and cartons made the banks of every stream look like a continuous trash heap" (Weller 98). Suttree watches as the river moves past his houseboat "bearing along garbage and rafted trash, bottles of suncured glass wherein corollas of mauve and gold lie exploded, orangepeels ambered with age. A dead sow pink and bloated and jars and crates ... one day a dead baby. Bloated, pulpy rotted eyes in a bulbous skull" (*Suttree* 306–307). The poorer reaches of Knoxville exhibited all the idiosyncrasies of the mountain experience in a more concentrated form because the people, once widely dispersed throughout the mountains, came together on the streets of McAnally Flats. The disgusting litany of river detritus demonstrates the fact that for the mountaineers' personal landfills, "the high waters of spring were the only collection system. As the waters rose to the tops of the banks, the junk was washed away, along with the topsoil of the hillsides" (Weller 99).

McCarthy's Knoxville "bears the clear mark of its pioneer ancestry, upon whom the entitlements of socialization — commerce, institutionalized government, law and order — still sit somewhat uneasily" (Young 98). To prevent chaos, the authorities of the city must control the populace. One tool in their arsenal of manipulations is discipline. Foucault describes the double edges of discipline:

> The enclosed institution, established on the edges of a society, turned inwards towards negative functions: arresting evil, breaking communications, suspending time. At the other extreme, with panopticism, is the discipline-mechanism: a functional mechanism that must improve the exercise of power by making it lighter, more rapid, more effective, a design of subtle coercion [*DP* 209].

Foucault further maintains that throughout the seventeenth and eighteenth centuries, societies moved "from a schema of exceptional discipline to one of generalized surveillance" via a "gradual extension of the mechanisms of discipline ... throughout the whole social body" (*DP* 209). In the Knoxville of *Suttree*, both schemes work. McAnally Flats, though not completely cut off from the rest of Knoxville, was an enclosed area, physically, economically, and socially; a circulation between McAnally and the rest of the city existed, but often the inhabitants of this slum area were known generally for their deviance and delinquency.

At times maintaining power in those streets mandated oppression. Therefore, policemen had to "be found who could maintain order on streets whose lusty population was certain to be quick with gun and knife and fist" (Caudill 101). Caudill talks here about coal camps, but as has been noted, the environment of coal camps, mill villages, and towns like Knoxville are similar, especially in a working-class enclave, or in this case an economically destitute area like McAnally Flats. They are rough-and-tumble places where the police must keep an ever-watchful eye on the population. Nevertheless, criminality in Knoxville, especially of this enclosed variety, became too useful for authority "to dream of anything as crazy — or ultimately as dangerous — as a society without crime" (*P/K* 47). How else could authority infiltrate an uncooperative populace? In *Suttree*'s McAnally, Tarzan Quinn, "swinging his billyclub by its thong to and fro onto and out of his enormous hand," fits right in among the beggars and thieves (301). Certainly, he can meet their resistance with an equal physical force, arresting when, where, and whom he sees fit; but the physical expression of Quinn's power — when he smashes up Ab Jones or some other perpetrator — is oppressive. Furthermore, it remains inefficient. Despite his physical prowess, Quinn cannot take on all of the criminals of McAnally at once. However, his *position* as the eye of authority does facilitate a disciplinary mechanism. He and his ilk hang over McAnally like a fine mist, and *the threat of their continual presence* is an effective reducer of crime. Such a presence helps the delinquents of McAnally interiorize the panoptic gaze of authority. It makes Suttree dread interaction with the authorities (383); it occasions Hooper's revelation to Suttree that he is not safe (365); it induces Ab Jones's admonition to Suttree about avoiding the police (202–204). In fact, Ab Jones himself has interiorized the presence of Quinn; this adversarial policeman preoccupies Jones's mind so intensely that he wants Mother She to curse him (278–281).

One factor aiding in the administering of discipline to the mountain population of McCarthy's Knoxville is, of course, its spatial arrangement, for "it is spaces that provide fixed positions and permit circulation; they carve out individual segments and establish operational links" (*DP* 148). The collection of mill villages surrounding the downtown area about which McDonald and Wheeler speak enclosed the Appalachian poor in specific areas like McAnally Flats; these mountain migrants had spaces apportioned to them, not by legal limitations or city declarations, but by habits and circumstances. They sought out people like themselves and places whose characteristics they recognized. Too, the price of shelter fit their limited means. Authority could and did take advantage of such spatial arrangements in much the same way as in cotton mill villages elsewhere. Such spaces facilitate a certain profiling of their inhabitants. Mechanicsville and McAnally Flats thereby became a "*world within a world ... alien reaches, these maugre sinks and interstitial wastes that the righteous see from carriage and car another life dreams*" where the "*ill-shapen or black or deranged, fugitive of all order, strangers in everyland*" congregated (*Suttree* 4). In the valley cut through the city by Second Creek, the rooftops of McAnally could be seen from the higher parts of the city, and the roads that cut through it, though they remained difficult to traverse, made it possible for the authorities to maintain a presence.

In *Suttree*, Knoxville's Finest, the eyes of social order, profile both behavior and locality. The constant threat of McAnally's concentrated delinquency justifies the constant gaze of the appointed agents of authority. When Suttree walks downtown on Gay Street, "a police cruiser passed slowly. He moved on, from out of his eyecorner *watching them watch*," but they do not take him in (29, emphasis added). However, when the police find him drunk in

McAnally on Grand Street, having just spoken to Jim and Junior Long's mother, the police call the paddywagon and haul him to the drunk tank (82–86). Public drunkenness is a crime of delinquency and though Suttree does not truly belong to the disenfranchised class, his physical location within the city makes him subject to the pervasive gaze of the police. Likewise, it is interesting to note that the entire italicized opening sequence of *Suttree* is panoptic in nature. An unnamed, godlike voice flies above the streets and spaces of Knoxville describing the panorama below. This opening scene establishes an awareness for the novel that calls attention to the act of watching.

McAnally is a world apart from Knoxville's "proper" society or Suttree would not have chosen to live there in the first place. Like other McAnally residents, Suttree's penchant for drunkenness, for visiting illicit booze establishments, and for other illegalities, paints a bull's-eye on his back. Foucault says "the existence of legal prohibition creates around it a field of illegal practices, which one manages to supervise.... [T]his organization is an instrument for administering and exploiting illegalities" (*DP* 280). His happens in *Suttree*. Richard Marius maintains that in historical Knoxville "bootleggers and Baptist preachers combined forces to keep the town legally dry" (114). In this case, bootlegged liquor occasions policing. Ab Jones's joint is illicit, but its existence gives the authorities the opportunity to infiltrate McAnally Flats in order to check on all the delinquents who loiter there and in other similar dives throughout the slums. They arrest the drunks, throw them in the paddywagon, and then into the drunk tank, but they never shut Jones down; they want his joint there. Police play such an important role in this civic administration in *Suttree* because "the organization of an isolated illegality, enclosed in delinquency, would not have been possible without the development of police supervision" (*DP* 280). McAnally Flats is such an enclosed illegality. The authorities know where these "felonious debauchees" all live—McAnally. Supervision, the watchful presence of the police, keeps a lid on criminality as often as a billyclub oppresses it.

One of the most ingenious facets of this panoptic style of disciplinary control comes from how easily and efficiently it can be applied in the social apparatus and facilitated by addresses. When the driver from the workhouse drops Gene Harrogate in Knoxville, Gene tries to get him to let him out anywhere, but the driver says, "You got to have an address, peckerhead" (91). As with the cotton mill village, the dispersal of individuals in such a regimented fashion in one section of Knoxville narrows the focus of panoptic power. Harrogate first suggests he be let off at "the Smokey Mountain Market," but the county's driver replies, "It's got to be where people lives," because as an agent of the county, the driver has to place Harrogate in an appropriate space (*Suttree*

91). The inhabitants of McAnally may not all have exact addresses, but the authorities can easily identify them by place; the existence of an area like McAnally Flats allows for a certain profiling, as the arrests of Jim and Junior Long, Suttree, Ab Jones, Michael and others demonstrate. Daniel Traber claims that the people of McAnally "create their own social system, a subclass living and moving beneath the conventional super- and infrastructures of society. Their objectives are contrary to the trivial desires of the aspiring middle class, and they have mastered life within the system which subtly exploits the exploiters" (37). Christopher Walsh maintains that "one of the central narrative threads in the novel concerns the counter-hegemonic and oppositional exploits of the residents of McAnally and the manner in which they resist the embourgeoisement of American society" (*In the Wake of the Sun* 203). I would argue something quite different. Within the enclosed space of McAnally Flats, the "hustlers and criminals" Traber speaks of serve a purpose for the overall community: they necessitate police presence and the subsequent observation of both delinquents and "normal" citizens; they also remind the affluent community that if they do not toe the line culturally, economically, and socially, they too might slip into the gutter of society like the pariahs of this multi-ethnic slum.

Suttree remains a book about class. While the literal margins might be a viable place for social "lessers" to build, as Richard Gray suggests, economic marginalization always presents problems for the social "betters." The socially mobile label those who have limited opportunities "monsters" because they act out their frustrations through violence — fighting, robbing, and stealing. Douglas Canfield, on the other hand, gives the "monster" moniker to the elite themselves. He concludes, "The monster is the capitalist system that both produces and condemns the underclass" (675). Canfield's essentially Marxist-Freudian interpretation of the novel further claims that the social and economic elite "represented by Suttree's absent patrician father, who sees meaning only in the institutions — law, business, government — that run the system, that enforce its divisive privileges," use that class-based divisiveness to maintain their privileged positions (675). The old man tells his son, "There is nothing occurring in the streets. Nothing but a dumbshow composed of the helpless and the impotent" (*Suttree* 14). The "helpless and the impotent" are the marginalized characters — the poor blacks, the indigent, the sexually perverse, the unemployed, *the mountaineers*— who inhabit McAnally, and who, as "much they try to carve out a life ... are always already doomed, in McCarthy's world, never to be able to rise above the materiality of their circumstances. However heroic their cruelties and violations, they are usually inert and passive objects with little or no control" (Buttersworth 132). They are the "dumbshow" props whose seemingly futile resistance nonetheless warrants surveillance. Their "enclosed illegality" becomes advantageous for the elite like Suttree's father because, in McAnally Flats, "for the vague swarming mass of a population practicing occasionally illegality ... is substituted a relatively small and enclosed group of individuals on whom a constant surveillance may be kept" (*DP* 278). Even in McAnally Flats everyone has his place: the ragpicker his viaduct, Harvey his junkyard, Daddy Watson his caboose, Gene his First Creek viaduct, and Suttree his houseboat. Thus, in keeping their eyes on these people, "the ubiquitous police with their constant surveillance of the vagrants and derelicts" perform a necessary function for the upholding of the system (Canfield 676).

The gaze of authority focuses on the potential subversion of McAnally Flats. The miscreants or "petty criminals who are more interested in drinking and senseless brawling than submitting to the systems of work, family, and responsible civic duty" have to be kept in check (Traber 36). Crime, therefore, becomes a useful part of the economy. Suttree himself, of course, has the advantage of his bourgeois social position and education, so when he is accosted by the police, he can disarm the situation verbally, using this tool from his educated arsenal. He does so on at least one occasion (*Suttree* 383). His rejection of bourgeois mores shows that he has studied society and that he therefore recognizes that the best way to deal with the agents of authority is to avoid them altogether, to sneak under the radar, to go unnoticed, unseen. Though Suttree leaps into this underclass social situation, he is an imposter, a bourgeois slummer whose presence in the Flats calls attention to the dynamics of power. As Frank Shelton says, Suttree "has turned his back on his past and his southern white [privileged] background and is thus alienated by his own choice, not by irresistible social or economic forces as are most of the other residents of McAnally Flats" (73). Sutree's ability to shift back into his bourgeois shape, depending on his situation or the level of alcohol in his bloodstream, exposes the inequalities inherent in the system; he, because of his bloodline, has advantages unavailable to other McAnally residents.

In *Suttree*, one mountaineer seems willing enough to fill the delinquent role. The true mountaineer representative in *Suttree*, Gene Harrogate — whose story proves particularly illuminative of the power relations present in the novel — demonstrates how the mountaineer can be disciplined when he finds a city to inhabit. Callahan, Daddy Watson, the ragpicker, Leonard, and the Reeses flank him in the novel. None of these characters abides by bourgeois mores. They inhabit the social margins. Some are habitual drunks who remain disinclined toward a bourgeois work ethic; some are vagrants whose lack of respect for the bourgeois sense of property continually gets them in trouble with authority. All of them display stereotypical mountaineer/hillbilly behavior, including the "shiftlessness" and "laziness" that designates the workhouse and the subsequent recidivist delinquency as the appropriate institutions for their disciplining.

The Moonlight Melonmounter

Gene Harrogate, "sly, ratfaced, a convicted pervert of a botanical bent," represents the exemplary case of the mountaineer-come-to-town (*Suttree* 54). With his outsized clothes, simpleton's goofy smile, and country naivety, Harrogate brings to mind a dimwitted version of Harris's Sut Lovingood. George Guillemin aptly notes, "Along with the idiomatic banter, roughhousing, and tall tales, the humor of [Harrogate's] picaresque story line constitutes a counter-discourse to the existential gloom of the novel's bulk" (*Vision* 5). He is the court jester without the wisdom, the mountaineer simpleton archetype. Like many a mountaineer, Harrogate's outlook is "formed from the dire economic and social/familial conditions he has come from" (Traber 41). Harrogate and other migrants who move to the city experience heightened economic potential, but they also find themselves in more confined spaces, subject to the prying eyes of neighbors, employers, and the police. Gene, who is first recognized by the farmer's prying eyes, carries some of the same traits McDonald and Wheeler attribute to the mountain whites who moved into Knoxville and took jobs in the mills there, such as a penchant for racism (McDonald and Wheeler 24). When Harrogate first comes to the city after being released from the workhouse, he peruses Knoxville looking for a place to live and comes to the conclusion "he'd not be put to living next door to niggers leastways" (*Suttree* 98). This racist attitude does not hold long, however, as Gene eventually shows when he tells the "tawny freckled halfbreed" when Suttree enters Mrs. Rufus's place, "He's cool man, he's cool ... having fallen easily into the way of things" (176–177). He is adaptable to circumstances.

Unlike many of Knoxville's mountaineers, Harrogate's path to the city comes via the county workhouse, a penal environment where it was hoped "that, compelled to work, convicts may come in the end to like it; when they have reaped the reward, they will acquire the habit, the taste, the need for occupation" (*DP* 234). He has been arrested because he has exhibited a lack of respect for the property of others. Ideally, the discipline experienced in the workhouse would carry over with Harrogate when he re-enters society because it is not "an external respect for the law or fear of punishment alone that will act upon the convict but the workings of the conscience itself. A profound submission, rather than a superficial training; a change of 'morality,' rather than of attitude" (238–239). The desired result of the workhouse in *Suttree*, according to Foucault, would be to make "a machine whose convict-workers are both the cogs and the products ... if, in the final analysis, the work of the prison has an economic effect, it is by producing individuals mechanized according to the general norms of an industrial society" (*DP* 242). Of course, the workhouse meets with no such success. Paradoxically, then, such institutions, while they are supposed to provide disciplined workers, often produce "useful" delinquents, of whom Harrogate is one—"linked to his offence[s] by a whole bundle of complex threads (instincts, drives, tendencies, character)" (253). In *Suttree*, the workhouse is a school for crime.

Billy Ray Callahan serves as a more violent, grown-up mirror for Gene's childish naivety. When he first enters the workhouse, Gene asks Billy Ray, "How long you been in here Mr. Callahan?" with the professional respect owed to one of Callahan's stature. Suttree replies for Billy Ray, "He's been in and out" (48). He is the recidivist Suttree warns Harrogate he will become. Callahan is a workhouse bootlegger, a McAnally brawler, and a petty thief. His "julep" gets Harrogate in trouble, though Gene drinks it without his permission, Callahan's brawl with Slusser having landed him in solitary confinement. Just before Suttree nearly meets his maker by way of the floorbuffer in the roadhouse, he sees "Callahan go by, one eye blue shiny, smiling, his teeth in a grout of blood. His busy freckled fists ferrying folks to sleep" (186). The authorities should keep an eye on him. Eventually Billy Ray's exploits—the "thousand brawls and stoven jaws, the clubbings and the broken bottles and the little knives that come from nowhere" (375–376)—catch up to him "on the Clinton Highway at the Moonlite Diner," where the barman shoots him in the face while his "freckled fists" remain in his pockets and his last words "came out lie" (375). Suttree sits up with his grieving mother. Callahan's social origins remain unknown. Is he a mountaineer-come-to-town? Possibly. Probably. He certainly possesses the stereotypical independence, impudence, and lack of respect for authority. He likes to drink, he does not shy away from a fight, and he cannot hold a steady job (374). Callahan is a man Harrogate admires; his is a station to which Harrogate aspires, but Gene does not have Callahan's physical prowess and Billy Ray lacks Gene's congenial naivety. They, however, share a lack of respect for other people's personal property. Billy Ray steals other peoples' drinks and money and violates their personal space by punching them in the face. Harrogate steals other folks' pigs and money and violates their watermelons.

The real crime of Harrogate's watermelon escapades is not his sexual perversion—that alone is not enough. He is brought to the workhouse for crime against property—theft, one might assume. According to the farmer whose crop has been violated, his watermelons are now worthless because Harrogate has "damn near screwed the whole patch" (33). He lands in the workhouse because he has broken the bourgeois rules that govern personal property. There, theoretically, he should learn the values of work, respect for others and authority, and temperance — all characteristics important in modern society — but he learns none of these things. When the guards assign him to washing dishes, the best job in the joint according to Suttree and Callahan, he complains, "I dont want to be no goddamned dishwarsher. I got to get up at four oclock in the morning" (47). Really, he just deplores "normal" work, the difficult physical labor and all of the surrounding requirements that "normal" people endure. He works hard at his schemes, but none of them are socially acceptable.

Gene respects neither the wishes nor the possessions of others. Despite the irritation it causes his fellow inmates, he continues shaping a coin into his "jailhouse ring" (53). The fight between Slusser and Callahan does not convince him to stop; the complaints of his fellow inmates and the admonitions of the guards fail; only Suttree's plaintive request that he "knock off that goddamn clicking" gets Gene to temporarily consider the desires of the workhouse community (54). Gene later steals Callahan's "julep" and drinks himself stupid, putting himself and the other men in jeopardy as "they covered for him in line, holding him erect, shielding him from the guards" (57). He shows his gratitude by vomiting on Wilson's shoe. Callahan was in solitary so Gene just stole what he wanted.

While in the workhouse, Suttree warns Harrogate not to attempt an escape because he knows that "if you run off from here [Gene] you'll wind up like Slusser ... in and out of institutions for the rest of your life," consigned to recidivism (59). And that is exactly what happens. The workhouse turns Gene from a deviant into "an institutional product" (*DP* 301). Harrogate becomes, along with "Mr. Callahan" and others, members "of a milieu of delinquents, loyal to one another, hierarchized, ready to aid and abet any future criminal act" (267). It might be noted that many of the eventual inhabitants of McAnally — Suttree and Billy Ray Callahan included — have spent time in the workhouse. Like Gene, their work there does not induce a change in attitude or morality. Quite the opposite. It makes them Foucauldian delinquents all. It is a school for crime. These former inmates congregate in the billiard rooms and illicit beer halls of McAnally Flats. They get drunk at five o'clock in the morning and pick fights in the local dives where, as McCulley tells Suttree, "If [a guy] aint from McAnally bust him" (*Suttree* 186). They create camaraderie and a solidarity that only the aspirations of respectability can disrupt. Of course, few of them aspire to respectability. They inhabit

McAnally as a delinquent milieu and as one distinct focus of disciplinary power, and Harrogate is among them.

Like his McAnally compadres, Harrogate has not learned the rudiments of "civilized" society before he lands in the workhouse. He possesses no work ethic, he lacks the common morality, and if even he knows any taboos, he ignores them, as his moonlight capers prove. Before he ever comes to the city, Harrogate exhibits a disregard for all things work-related. His sister struggles with the weekly wash while Gene looks on. He will not attend to his mother, and when Josie suggests he weed the tomatoes, he just stares across the yard with a finger in his ear (30). He is slovenly and opportunistic. Later in the novel, while talking to Suttree after his release from the workhouse, Gene relates a story about how he burned down an old woman's house just out of meanness, and when Suttree asks him if he was sorry he replies, "Sorry I got caught" (145). He feels no remorse at having nearly killed the woman. He feels none of the sensibilities society disciplines into its members, none of the social or economic responsibilities. He wants to get rich quick without having to work for it — not exactly a bourgeois value — and is willing to take from others in the process.

The workhouse, despite being designed to reintegrate a deviant into society, fails to inculcate bourgeois values within Gene. Once he gets out, he still has no respect for authority or personal property, and he is still a vagrant. When he checks out the old trains looking for a place to settle, fellow vagrant (and potential "crazy") Daddy Watson, the old railroader who eventually ends up in the asylum with Suttree's aunt Alice, chases him away (93). Daddy Watson lives in a caboose that undoubtedly technically remains the property of the railroad company; he seems to be in the habit of chasing potential vandalizers away from the cars. While obviously no longer an employee of the railroad, Daddy Watson retains a ritualistic connection to the property of the company. Agents of the company might be the ones who come to get Daddy Watson and take him to the crazy-house, or it might be the police or government social workers. Suttree asks the ragpicker who took Watson. "Was it the police?" he asks, and Hooper replies, "It might be any of em. I reckon I'll be next. You aint safe" (365). The implication is that the authorities are "cleaning up" the homeless in preparation for the building of the interstate system which takes place at novel's end, and that the marginal members of Knoxville's "blighted areas" need be wary of the authorities. Plans for this project certainly started in the decade prior to the setting of *Suttree*, historically. McDonald and Wheeler note "by 1949 the survey, 'a study of Knoxville's blighted areas,' was completed and plans for urban redevelopment produced ... 'expressway construction was coordinated, to a degree, with redevelopment.

The two activities together resulted in radical alterations in Knoxville's appearance, its population, and the functions of its urban systems'" (71). Since discipline is a web of institutions, Suttree, Gene, Daddy Watson, the ragpicker, and many other McAnally inhabitants might find themselves under increased scrutiny as the authorities designate areas destined for "improvment."

However, before this particular threat arises, Gene makes Knoxville his stomping grounds, bringing his disregard for the welfare of others in from the country with him. Walking the streets of Knoxville, newly released Harrogate opportunistically steals a peach from a vendor (and receives a mealscoop to the head for it) and then uses a glob of chewing gum that sticks to his shoe to rob money from Blind Richard's panhandling box. The fact that he stands there watching the people around him to see if they will notice the robbery proves not that he has moral compunction, but that he does not want to suffer the consequences of getting caught. His interactions with Rufus once he has killed the shoat further prove both Harrogate's continued lack of respect for the property rights of others and his unabashed lack of remorse once Rufus apprehends him. Rufus demands payment for the hog, and since Gene has no money, Rufus forces him to work off the debt; he tells Gene, "Work. It's how most folks get they livin. Them that ain't prowlin other folks' hogpens" (142). Harrogate reluctantly capitulates when Rufus threatens to "law" him. Stepping well beyond hog-thievery, Harrogate tries to blow a hole in what he thinks is a bank vault. He tries to steal other people's hard-earned savings, but ruptures a sewer main instead. This last incident literalizes both his immersion in the scatological and his position as the waste of society. Had Suttree not saved him, he would have perished. Yet his delinquency continues.

Whereas Suttree comes to McAnally looking to escape his bourgeois existence, Harrogate comes looking to better his economic station: "Gene is excited by the prospect of city living" (Traber 40); the aptly labeled "country mouse turned city rat, is life at its lowest denominator. Half-crazy but also half-shrewd with his many money-making schemes, Harrogate is completely oblivious to any concern other than prospering in the city" (Shelton 76). The mountaineer eked out an existence on the most substandard, difficultly cultivated land; likewise, Harrogate turns a small space under a viaduct into his city-rat Shangri-La. When first looking for a place to live, he checks out the train cars; then he cases the ragpicker's viaduct and the old "ragged troll" runs him off (*Suttree* 96–97), but the old vagabond's lair gives him an idea. Harrogate finds his space and takes up residence on city property below the First Street viaduct, thinking "livin uptown like this you can find pret near anything you need" (118). He constructs his home from the castoff refuse he finds, "some crates ... a firepit of old bricks ... a mattress from a lounge on a houseporch" (116). Like the mountaineers before him, Harrogate "improves" this small plot on which he squats. Before long his home is more accommodating than even the ragpicker's: Gene devises an electric line that kills pigeons for his supper.

When Suttree comes to visit the city-rat's new abode, he warns him to steer clear of the agents of authority and notes that the parking meters in his viaduct living quarters could present trouble for Gene. Those meters represent vehicles of official taxation — they are the connectors between authority and drivers — and their theft is the usurpation of authority. The refusal to pay taxes or the destruction of the vehicles of their payment is an undisguised affront to authority in *Suttree* just as it was when the western Pennsylvania whiskey rebels tarred and feathered revenue collectors. Cheating the state is a theme in *Suttree*; Gene tries it, and Leonard, the "pale and pimpled part-time catamite," seeks Suttree's help in getting out of a similar jam (241). He and his mother have been cheating the state out of his father's medical and unemployment benefits for months after the old man dies. And with Suttree's help sinking him in the river, they will continue to do so for many more months. Leonard's father eventually floats to the river's surface "draggin all them chains with him," to which Suttree wryly replies, "fathers will do that" (417). Suttree knows something neither Harrogate nor Leonard understands, that cheating the authorities will rise up to haunt them; he guesses rightly that Leonard will never get away with his scheme. In Gene's case, Suttree knows exactly what those meters mean to the authorities and how seriously they would take the theft of them, so even though he knows Gene did not steal them, he warns him twice: "You better get rid of those parking meters" (117). But, unlike Leonard or Gene, Suttree possesses a bourgeois sensibility: one of his boldest acts — stealing the police car and pushing it into the river — presents a similar affront to authority. Notably, Suttree has to stay out of sight for a long time thereafter and he's both aware enough and disciplined enough to do so (*Suttree* 441–442). Discipline creates many opportunities for its subversion and many of the delinquent characters in *Suttree* almost turn discipline to their advantage; however, they lack one thing that Suttree himself possesses — knowledge of the system — and that disadvantages them immensely.

Gene's ingenious schemes (including making the "jerry-built" boat and using a slingshot to ensnare and poison dozens of bats for the rabies reward — despite the fact that none of them have rabies) are often attempts on his part to make discipline pay; like his adaptive living quarters, they evidence his mountaineer's adaptive ability to take the circumstances handed to him and make the best of them. This and the other schemes he undertakes fail, not because of a fatal flaw in design or even in execution, but because of a failure to understand the boundaries of social acceptability. The people in positions of authority will not appease him. As the doctor says: "Mr. Harrogate, the city is offering a reward for any dead bats found in the streets. We have what could become a critical situation here with rabies. That's the purpose of the reward. We have not authorized the wholesale slaughter of bats" (218). Harrogate tries to cheat the county, and the county does not pay him a dollar for every bat. In Gene's mind, they change the rules. However, this vignette further sheds light on the mountaineer's relationship with agents of authority: like Harrogate, the mountaineer fears "the bureaucracies of business and government ... as if those who run them were out to get him" (Weller 56). The ways of the country are different from the ways of the city. Harrogate's response to the doctor typifies his undimmed optimism. When the doctor apologizes for his efforts coming to naught, he replies, "Maybe a dollar and a quarter aint nothing to you but it is to me" (*Suttree* 219). His efforts and ingenuity go into these outlandish get-rich-quick episodes. Never does getting a real job cross his mind.

Paddling his boat down the river, Gene encounters fellow migrants to the city—the Reeses. Their shanty house has conveniently come to rest on the banks of the Tennessee just past the bridge in Knoxville. Gene first sees them "going along Blount Avenue Sunday morning. They wore outfits all cut from the same bolt of cloth," so he decides to introduce himself (313). Mr. Reese, with his mussel brailing scheme and the way he takes advantage of Suttree's ambivalence, reminds the reader of a more knowledgeable and cunning Harrogate. Like Gene, he has a get-rich-quick scheme and he has no desire to get a real job. Reese seems to be a man disinclined to abide by a schedule. However, Reese does not appear to be afraid of hard work, if he works half as hard at brailing as Suttree does. Also unlike Gene, the Reeses come to Knoxville via an accident—if Reese's story about the vengeful Tong opponent is believed—and by the literal transience of low-income housing. Furthermore, as soon as Suttree signs on to help them with the mussel brailing, the Reeses leave "the crazy looking shanty in Knoxville and [go back upriver] by bus with their bedding and household goods baled up," looking probably much like the group of mountaineers James Gregg casts out of his cotton mill village (316). The Reeses are mountaineer stereotypes: the drunken father, the old-before-her-time crone of a mother, the lazy, degenerate son, and the one pristine "mountain lass" who ensnares the novel's protagonist and then meets an untimely end at the hands of a *deus ex machina* so that the protagonist can be free of her influence. The demise of their family (Wanda dies and Willard runs off), their unsuccessful business scheme, and their return to Jefferson County might indicate that if they had stayed in Knoxville, then maybe

Reese would not have had to ask Suttree, "Did you ever know anybody to be so bad about luck?" (372). Regardless, Reese honestly pays Suttree his share of the profits from the musseling and exits his life as abruptly as he entered it, again unlike Harrogate.

While Reese ensnares Suttree in an ultimately tragic moneymaking scheme, Suttree learns to steer clear of Gene's shenanigans. The scheme that lands Harrogate in the most trouble has nothing to do with Suttree; in fact, Gene's final affront to bourgeois decency parodies the capitalist enterprise of every young aspiring entrepreneur — the paper route. Gene has his "routes," stealing coins out of pay telephones. Harrogate's transgression is yet again an economic one. He steals money from the pay phone users. This crime takes him out of the enclosed confines of McAnally because the telephone system presents a literal network of lines and nodes stretching all across the countryside. It is a web of communication and surveillance and yet another encounter with discipline in *Suttree*. Harrogate has "half the telephones in Knoxville plugged up," and as he says, it "takes me all day to run em. I put on a few new ones ever day. You get away from uptown they's a lot of hard sidewalk tween telephones. I done worn out two pair of brand new Thom McAn shoes" (419). His efforts often parody bourgeois mores, but in this case he also parodies criminality itself. The clothes he wears and the stance he takes make him look like a wannabe gangster (Walsh, *In the Wake of the Sun* 207), or at least like the image of one he might have seen at the movies or on television: "With a cigar between his teeth ... he had grown a wispy [undoubtedly pencil-thin] mustache. He wore a corduroy hat a helping larger than his head size and a black gabardine shirt with slacks to match. His shoes were black and sharply pointed, his socks were yellow" (418). Harrogate embraces his delinquent criminality, but he cannot escape the panoptic "discipline-mechanism" (*DP* 209).

Apprehended by the "telephone heat" whose foot he stomps on, but whose face he never sees, Gene refuses to make himself scarce, as Suttree admonishes him to do; he declines to remove himself from the gaze of authority (*Suttree* 436). He has not learned to shun the focus of the authorities as Suttree has. In criminal desperation, Harrogate gets caught in his first robbery; his incompetence gets him sentenced to three to five years in Petros at Brushy Mountain, an enclosed penal environment ripe with even more discipline than McAnally Flats. He has continually broken the rules of capitalist engagement, so the authorities incarcerate him. Suttree has told him this might happen, warning, "They have these coal mines up there for you to work in," but as has been the case all along, Gene will not listen; he will not leave town (420). When Harrogate usurps the generalized discipline of Knoxville, he has to be corralled. All along he has refused to engage in "productive" work; he has refused to learn from his mistakes. He is unrepentant; he has refused discipline. He will now get to try again at Brushy Mountain.

Workhorse: A Metaphor for the Mountaineer

And so, perhaps ironically, we come full circle. The story of the most recognizable mountaineer character in *Suttree* ends with him on a train heading back to the mountains to a penitentiary famous for its coal mines, "his pinched face watching him back from the cold glass" of the car (439). He has moved from the farm to the workhouse to the city to the penitentiary — all gradations of discipline — but he never fully adapts to his environment. Gene Harrogate's story and that of the mountaineers' disciplining is mirrored in the allegory of Captain the horse.

McCarthy uses this same reminiscence in *Suttree* and *The Gardener's Son*. In the former, Suttree's Aunt Alice, whose geriatric situation resembles Martha McEvoy's, relates the story to Cornelius. She and Martha are both old maids in a state hospital in an industrial (and a college) town — Martha in Columbia, South Carolina, and Aunt Alice in Knoxville, Tennessee; both tell the story to a young man of a later generation. That McCarthy uses this scene twice is probably not incidental. He was putting the final touches on *Suttree* in the late 1970s while writing *The Gardener's Son* teleplay. But the metaphor, as I see it, is a fascinating one in relation to the movement of the mountaineer from the mountains to the mill village or to the city. It also metaphorically displays the subsequent discipline therein.

Aunt Alice tells her visitor:

> Daddy kept this store you know, and we had this horse his name was Captain and he used to pull the wagon delivered the groceries and he was my pet. He'd foller me around, just foller me around like a dog would. We lived in Sweetwater then. And they was hard times then and we had to sell the store and Daddy had to sell Captain. And they took me up to Nanny's because the man was comin to take him, you see. I was just a little thing. Years later when I was a young girl I was in Knoxville one Saturday and I seen this horse standin in front of a feed store hitched to a wagon and it was Captain. I run over to him and thowed my arms around him and I reckon everbody thought I was crazy, me about full growed standin there in the street huggin a old horse and just a bawlin to beat the band [*Suttree* 433–434][5].

The horse, representative of an unmechanized, pastoral, older order in its own right, stands in for the mountaineer's old way of life, isolated and dependent on what it can forage for the energy to do its work (as opposed to the automobile, which needs gasoline, a host of other fluids, and often a mechanic, to keep it running). Captain, while on the farm, retains this independence. He can graze for himself and subsist on his own; he is a pet too, though, cared for and loved by Martha/Alice apart from his status as an animated farm implement. Captain is a domesticated pet with utilitarian value until economic hardship causes the family to sell him. His life on the farm consisted of long stretches of leisure punctuated by moments of intense exertion. Like the mountaineer who is rousted out of his supposed pastoral utopia, straitened circumstances force Captain to journey to the city where he stands monotonously in the traces until his driver puts him to work pulling the cart; he becomes a cog used in a specific economic transaction. When the old maid of either story looks back at herself as a girl who loved the animal and who found him at his work in the city (both Knoxville and Columbia doubled as cotton mill towns), all she can do is hug and kiss him in the street; all she can do is reminisce — he is no longer her pet, she cannot take him back again. In his new position, he *only* works, disciplined in the traces.

Three

A Case of the Superlative
LESTER BALLARD, MOUNTAINEERS, CHILDREN OF GOD AND MEN

> "...a man at the barn door. He is small, unclean, unshaven. He moves in the dry chaff among the dust and slats of sunlight with constrained truculence. Saxon and Celtic bloods. A child of God much like yourself perhaps."

In the geographical demarcation used by the Appalachian Regional Commission, "Appalachia ... is a 195,000-square-mile region that follows the spine of the Appalachian Mountains from southern New York to Northern Mississippi. It includes all of West Virginia and parts of twelve other states: Alabama, Georgia, Kentucky, Maryland, New York, North Carolina, Ohio, Pennsylvania, South Carolina and Tennessee" (*Appalachian Regional Commission* 1). Sevier County, Tennessee, the setting of *Child of God*, sits well within the geographical boundaries of Appalachia's eastern Tennessee confines. Like much of the Appalachian geographical region, the mountains in Sevier County give it a "high relief relative to the areas surrounding it" (Raitz and Ulack 11). Today this "high relief," cut through by creeks and rivers and gorges, insulates the white-trash meccas of Pigeon Forge and Gatlinburg, where the consumers of "hillbilly" culture can buy NASCAR trinkets just down the road from Dolly Parton's mountaineer theme park Dollywood. By the 1980s, some hillbillies had figured out how to cash in on their own objectification. The historical framework of *Child of God*, however, does not include this recently developed hillbilly shtick dotting the southern Appalachian mountain environment because even in the late 1960s and early 1970s when McCarthy wrote this novel, many inhabitants of Sevier County remained tucked away in mountain and valley enclaves—topographical idiosyncrasies which shielded the people from the blatant commercialism gestating just over the next ridge. Lester Ballard's homestead stands "in the blue shade under the wall of the mountain," in just such an enclave (*COG* 3).

While the self-promoting commercialism of the latter half of the twentieth century has not yet encroached upon life in *Child of God*, the industrialization about which Harry Caudill, Ronald Eller, John Gaventa and many others speak has made its mark on the world of Lester Ballard. The fact that the old hardwoods have been harvested from his property indicates a connection between McCarthy's novel and the historical Appalachian environment: timber harvesting had been occurring in the region for two hundred or more years. K. Wesley Berry concludes that the Appalachian environment was, even in Ballard's day, "a place both beautiful and ruined, a land of scant patches of virgin woodlands juxtaposed with the scars of more than two centuries of pioneering" (47). The fact that the local government evicts him from that property places Ballard, his community, and *Child of God* squarely within the historical context of late nineteenth and early twentieth century Appalachian industrialization. The Great Depression, while particularly difficult for the poorer quarters of the entire country, hit poor mountaineers especially hard, often resulting in the loss of the family homestead and the increase of mountaineer antipathy toward authority. John Cant writes, "The loss of farms due to the inability to pay taxes was a commonplace of rural America during the Depressions" (Cant 95), and more specifically, as Ronald Eller notes, "During the 1930s, the government's acquisition of large numbers of small farms sold at sheriff's auctions for non-payment of taxes seemed to support ... feelings of suspicion, hostility, and despair" (*Miners* 120). Absentee land speculation, timber extraction, the infiltration of Appalachia by commercial interests, and government intervention — all of which have historically taken resources *out* of Appalachia without returning the reaped benefits — provide the canvas on which McCarthy paints *Child of God*. In his *The Appalachian Regional Commission: Twenty-five Years of Government Policy,* Michael Bradshaw looks at the role the government has played in the construction of Appalachia. He claims that industrial interests, absentee landowners and even the government have worked separately to disenfranchise the mountaineer. Bradshaw makes no claims that this disenfranchising was a result of collusion — it does not have to be; rather, he suggests that the practices of the landowners and extractive industries alongside the policies of the government have combined to reduce the economic, social, and cultural viability of the Appalachian people. Bradshaw demonstrates how government policies on soil erosion and cheap electrical power "were paralleled by other federal programs directed more toward conserving resources than to helping people: they developed areas of southern Appalachia as national forests and national parks, despite the fact that this policy often turned farmers off their land" (22). Like Caudill, Eller, Gaventa and others before him who examine the impact of industry on Appalachia, Bradshaw concludes that the Federal government's policies only exacerbated the difficulties of Appalachia's poor-white inhabitants; furthermore, like these other scholars, he makes the distinction between perception and reality of Appalachia, saying, "By the 1950s ... the term 'Appalachian' had become a rude name, implying not only poverty but also blame for descending to that condition within a predominantly prosperous nation" (20). *Child of God* takes place within this time frame after the advent of the extractive industries and the government: land has been monopolized and people have been ostracized.

Though not monolithically, the people depicted in McCarthy's Sevier County exhibit all of the pejorative and complimentary attributes typically associated with the mountaineer whose "bloodlines carry the traits of hillbilly agency — orneriness, meanness," and shiftlessness, as well as peculiarity, independence and stubbornness (Stewart 46). While the inhabitants of Sevier County might reveal "the apparent disparity between mountain life and the 'normal' life of Americans elsewhere" (Shapiro, *Appalachia on Our Mind* 63), Lester Ballard, however, takes the characterization of the mountaineer to the superlative; even within his disenfranchised culture, he epitomizes the literary and historical mountaineer who has been left at the bottom of the cup as the economic dregs of society. He "is emblematic of the society from which he arises" (Luce, *Reading the World* 161). His land repossessed and sold to someone else like that of so many mountaineers of history and literature, Lester stands in a position of alterity in relation to the economically, politically, and socially secure mainstream of his community and of American society at large; like his real-life mountaineer counterparts, for McCarthy and his readership, and for the people of Sevier County within the novel, Lester *becomes the signifier* "of a culture that [is] irredeemably white, poor, rural, male, racist, illiterate, fundamentalist, inbred, alcoholic, violent, and given to all forms of excess, degradation, and decay" (Stewart 119). If, however, as the comparative speculations of the "pocketknife society" suggest (*COG* 48), Ballard is the "wacko" who exists — in McCarthy's own words— *beyond the pale*, then all else within the pale can be rationalized and hierarchized through these comparisons. Lester Ballard becomes a discursive strategy, a central figure that assumes an important role in the ratification and continuation of the hegemonic culture through the collective storytelling of this novel's community. Through these stories, and through the legend Ballard becomes, the community tries to rationalize the role it has played in the construction of Ballard as the perverse delinquent.

So, what course of events causes Ballard to become the counter-hegemonic sociopath who can be manipulated by the authorities of his community? Several aspects of Lester's personality and situation converge to place him in this role: (a) his dispossession by the county turns him into a vagrant — a social position inherently on the periphery and one often occupied by the historical mountaineer; (b) his dispossession results in his blaming the community for his vagrancy despite the fact that he himself did not pay the taxes on his land — ultimately this characteristic manifests itself in Ballard's preoccupation with, and eventual attempted murder of John Greer, a somewhat liminal figure himself within the society, but one who readily accepts the tenets of bourgeois land ownership; and (c) his sexual ineptitude — a trait which preludes his eventual descent into necrophilia.

Lester represents one disciplinary mechanism through which the hegemonic subject position exercises its power throughout the populace. As the superlative of inherent meanness, uncontrolled violence, genetic degradation, human squalor, and sexual deviance, Ballard helps arrange the cacophony of social discourse, including the resisting voices, into units that can be used by the hegemony in a couple of ways: (a) he physically polices the out-of-the-way spaces frequented by social deviants, providing severe consequences for their deviant actions (as his escapades at the Frog Mountain turnaround show); and (b) both literally and rhetorically he becomes a mythical "boogie man," an example of degeneracy through which other members of society can be categorized and ordered.

Society uses individuals like Ballard, just as it has used the figure of the mountaineer. Lester's story "engages with the issues of impoverished whites, [but] does not, for example, alleviate class oppression, or even necessarily challenge the status quo" (Sandell 214) because Ballard's resistance, like most resistances to social norms, can be manipulated by the social hegemony. Figures like Lester perform a myriad of purposes: they serve as rhetorical "others" against whom society can mobilize. The "pocketknife society," whittling and conversing and loitering around the county courthouse — the seat of county authority — uses Ballard's story to define the outer limits of social deviance (*COG* 22; 36; 80–81). The courthouse talkers define other potential violations of social norms via the superlative nature of Ballard's tale. Ultimately, too, Ballard's delinquency legitimates the infiltration of his world by chosen authority figures. It even seems as though the "pocketknife society" understand how the Ballards of the world necessitate the Sheriff Fates, for they relate stories of the two opposing ends of the social spectrum within the same conversational confines. When one man says, "Fate's all right. He's plain spoken but I like him," it could be in response to another man's questioning of the sheriff's motives and actions (44–45). The man then relates a story about Turner's fairness in dealing with the Frog Mountain parkers. One way or another, "the community consistently tries to explain Lester's evil acts in such a way as to prove his constitutional difference from them, that he is *other*" (Luce, "Cave of Oblivion" 185). When another man of the community sings "the chickenshit blues" at his wife's burial, the people think it odd; yet in a conversation about that event on the courthouse lawn, the people listening come to the same conclusion that the storyteller does, that Gresham "wasn't a patch on Lester Ballard for crazy" (*COG* 22). Despite this judgment, Ballard's society, like American society in general, "gives suck to the maimed and crazed, [it] wants their wrong blood in its history and will have it" (156). Flannery O'Connor knew this, as did William Faulkner and Erskine Caldwell and George Washington Harris. The Ballards of the world are useful indeed.

Ballard the Mountaineer

With the story set in rural Sevier County, Tennessee, and with Lester Ballard living almost completely isolated from even the smallest enclaves and towns and hamlets, geographically and topographically, Ballard haunts the territory of the mountaineer. When society encroaches, he moves deeper into "hillbilly" territory; Ballard traverses "old woods and deep. At one time in the world there were woods that no one owned and these were like them" (127). Like Arthur Ownby in *The Orchard Keeper* who hikes into the "Harrykin" Wilderness when he is threatened by intrusion on what he views as his space, Lester wanders in the "inaccessible places where misfits escape[d] the law, or their masters, or the army, or simply society's rules" (Sweeney 252). Geography, however, is not the only thing that identifies Lester as a mountaineer; his hillbilly violence marks him too. The community members gather on Ballard's land anticipating the auction of his property in a carnival-like atmosphere that is echoed later in the Mr. Wade's story about the hanging of the last two White Caps (*COG* 165–168). A source of community entertainment already, Ballard waits in the barn beneath the frayed rope that stands as a monument to his father's suicide. Then, as Ballard makes his way to the front of the auction, the crowd silences in anticipation of a conflict. Lester, of course, obliges them. Importantly, though, the county instigates this conflict by seizing and auctioning off his land: as the auctioneer reminds him, "You done been locked up once over this" (7). Ostensibly, Lester has refused to pay his property taxes to the county, but no reason why is given. It is plausible that his father sold the timber rights to the land so that "the trees that shaded him were no longer his property"; for whatever reason, legitimate or otherwise, Ballard becomes an example of the dispossessed mountaineer Caudill describes as "little more than a trespasser upon the soil beneath his feet" (76). With the completion of the auction, he becomes homeless, a vagabond or vagrant, dispossessed and disdained by the society of Sevier County. Ballard loses all the advantages of his traditional white male privilege — land ownership, occupational stability, social interaction, sexual privilege, and cultural as well as monetary currency; he retains only his rifle, an icon of mountaineer individuality. He becomes a mountain-poor-white-trash pariah "at once like us and not like us," emblematic "of a particular definition of mountain life as squalid and degenerate, of the mountaineers as those who lived in squalor and degeneracy, and of Appalachian otherness as a social problem" (Shapiro, *Appalachia on Our Mind* 61).

John Hartigan Jr. maintains that the category of "hillbilly" exists as "a cultural and rhetorical identity, it is a means of inscribing social distance and insisting upon a contempt-laden social divide, particularly (though not exclusively) between whites" (Hartigan 50); it is a way to create rhetorical difference when an apparent racial distinction is unavailable. In his "Name Calling: Objectifying 'Poor Whites' and 'White Trash' in Detroit," Hartigan speaks directly about "white trash" as a rhetorical category and identity, but his deconstruction of that social identity can be readily applied to the "hillbilly" identity as well because the people he examines in Detroit are Appalachian out-migrants. The rhetorical strategy he highlights here is one that disclaims connection between "normative" white society and a "deviant" society — mountain society in this instance (41–56). Mountain whites are problematic because they possess many of the characteristics associated with "normal" white Americans; nevertheless, they become peripheral while remaining central to the discursive strategy that places them on the margins. Henry Shapiro explains it thus:

> Conventional modes of resolving the dilemma posed by the perception of "deviance" from the American norm by a region or a people — ascription of geographic, chronological, or ethnic distance which made such "deviance" seem natural and normal — could not be utilized to explain the "deviance" of white, Anglo-Saxon, Protestant, native-born Americans living in the present and within miles of the older centers of American civilization [*Appalachia on Our Mind* x].

Therefore, a category delineated by behavioral patterns had to be created and applied to the mountaineer. Like Hartigan's article, Shapiro's *Appalachia on Our Mind* does an excellent job of showing both how this category came to be and tracing the cultural ramifications of this naming.

Ballard typifies this rhetorical identity. Made to squat on someone else's land, he lives in the dilapidated Waldrop house (*COG* 13–16); penniless, he is forced to barter with Kirby, unsuccessfully (10–12); unable to attract affections from the opposite sex, he masturbates while watching two other people engaged in sexual intercourse, and then he eventually turns to necrophilia as his sexual outlet (19–20); deprived of employment, he simultaneously becomes a thief and a sexual deviant when he steals the money from a dead man's wallet and a dead girl's purse (89–90); as Walsh asks, "Denied fair and proper legal protection or the consolation of Christian fellowship, where else is there for Lester to go?" (*In the Wake of the Sun* 154). Ballard possesses the distrust of authority demonstrated by mountaineers, especially the mistrust of governmental authorities. The process of Ballard's eviction could have been initiated by a private firm to whom he owed a mortgage; however, had that been the case, it remains unlikely that the county would be responsible for the auction, unless the private firm hired the county to perform the auction, and that seems unlikely. Whether a private firm or the county begins the proceedings against Ballard is immaterial because either way, representatives of a society who demand payments that he seems to believe he does not owe force him off land he claims to have inherited from his father. These representatives' claims to his land mandate his forfeiture; therefore, figures of authority, specifically the authorities of Sevier County — as the auctioneer says, "The high sheriff is standin right over yonder" (*COG* 7) — take Ballard's land and sell it to someone else. Ballard's anger toward the authorities here has historical precedent: the English colonies that would become the United States fought a war with England over taxation; insurgents in western Pennsylvania rebelled against taxes and absentee ownership they perceived as unfair; mountaineers have often resorted to violence when outside corporations and absentee landowners have tried, successfully, to evict them from their mountain habitations, and Ballard, as a denizen of just such a contested area, is no different.

Lester's status as a social anomaly and his geographical isolation cannot protect him from the far-reaching arms of the authorities, as the opening scene of the novel details. Vereen Bell claims Lester "is beyond the pale both socially and psychoanalytically ... but as aberrant as Lester progressively becomes, he is ruled at every turn both by unspeakable appetite and by a warped compulsion to domesticate it" (61). Ballard's need to domesticate and to order things links him inextricably to his community; his society creates him and then uses him to keep potentially subversive members on the periphery. He might be "beyond the pale" psychoanalytically, but his role as *oppositional* to mainstream Sevier County society keeps him within its bounds. As a social pariah, Ballard's otherness helps to define normalcy in

Sevier County, much as the historical and rhetorical mountaineer has done in relation to the rest of America. Where so many Appalachian stereotypes are reproduced in *Child of God*, Ballard is an extreme example. Kirby, the moonshiner, cannot find his stash when Lester approaches him because he was too drunk when he hid it (*COG* 10–12; 114), and the dumpkeeper — whose *nine* daughters parody the muses and fit the images of wanton sexuality associated with hillbillies (including the pregnancy of the twelve-year-old) — sometimes fires "a shotgun just to clear the air" and to ward off would-be impregnators (26–28). The valley and town dwellers congregate about the courthouse steps and gossip about current events. They exchange oral histories of the area like characters on television's *Hee Haw*, comparing the "good ole days" unfavorably with the contemporary degeneration of society. Sheriff Fate Turner, too, is a stereotype: a good ol' boy who polices his constituents firmly but with an even-handed sense of humor — a less folksy Andy Griffith or a less angry Buford Pusser. His interactions with parkers on the turnaround and with Ballard himself demonstrate his practical take on law enforcement (44–45; 56). *Child of God* also comes replete with its own mountaineer vigilante lynch mob — latter-day White Caps whose "mountain justice" never gets carried out thanks to Lester's cunning, not the mob's lack of motivation (154; 177–186). When later in the novel Mr. Wade relates a story about the hanging of two Sevier County White Cap vigilantes, Diane Luce reminds us, "Like the story of Lester Ballard, the White Cap story raises issues of societal and individual standards of morality, the roles of law and social pressure in enforcing community standards, the attitudes of the community towards its most shameful moments in history, and the competition to control the inscription of history that extended into the twentieth century" ("White Caps" 43). This is a society conscious of its collective historical narrative and of its pariahs.

Paradoxically, perhaps, Ballard also possesses traits traditionally associated with American ideals, including "his armed individualism, his perverted consumerism, his clumsy improvisation, and his resilience as the underdog" (Luce, "Cave of Oblivion" 185). Ballard is stubborn and self-sufficient. After he has been evicted from his land, Ballard improves the abandoned Waldrop house enough to live in it (*COG* 13–16). Ballard's prowess with a rifle is legendary within his own community — one narrator says: "He could by god shoot. Hit anything he could see. I seen him shoot a spider out of a web in the top of a big redoak one time" (57). At the county fair, Ballard wins three huge prizes at the shooting booth, prompting the barker to change the rules to get him out of there (63–64). Only a perfectly timed shovelful of dirt keeps his rifle from exacting revenge on John Greer (172–173). The idea of the mountaineer's keen ability with a rifle stems from several places. The memorable defeat of the British forces at King's Mountain in the Revolutionary War by an outnumbered band of backwoodsmen, Cooper's *Leatherstocking* tales, the legends of Daniel Boone and Davy Crockett, and the stories of the Southwestern humorists have all contributed to the notion that the mountaineers can out-shoot any human alive. World War I hero Sergeant Alvin York confirmed this idea and added to the legend: "York was a Tennessee mountain boy who entered the American Expeditionary Forces only with reluctance.... [H]is duty included capturing single-handed a German machine-gun battalion after picking off eighteen men with his rifle and seven more with his pistol.... [H]e captured a total of 132 German soldiers ... [and] received the Congressional Medal of Honor" (Shapiro, *Appalachia on Our Mind* 262). Of course, Gary Cooper's Oscar-winning performance in 1941's *Sergeant York* advanced both York's heroic status and the legend of the mountaineer's prowess with a gun. This image of the mountaineer continues to be reproduced in literature and in pop culture, as Steven Spielberg's *Saving Private Ryan* demonstrates. As the literary progeny of Natty Bumppo, Davy Crockett, and Alvin York, the cross-wearing, scripture-quoting Tennessee sniper played by Barry Pepper accomplishes impossible feats with his rifle, much like the degenerate Lester Ballard.

Ballard also perversely mirrors another Frog Mountain mountaineer— George Washington Harris's Sut Lovingood—who is also a deviant, critical voice on the margins of his society. Both are what Annalee Newitz would term a "lower class white," whose "differences are represented as the difference between civilized folks and primitive ones.... [R]acialized, and demeaned, because they fit into the primitive/civilized binary as primitives" (Newitz 134). Harris, like McCarthy, grew up in Knoxville and likewise wrote about the poor mountaineers he encountered. John Grammer highlights the similarities between the nickname of Cornelius Suttree ("Sut") and Sut Lovingood, but he further notes that the comparison between those two characters ceases there (Grammer 40). Not so with Lester Ballard and Sut Lovingood. They occupy the same space geographically—the "Frog Mountain Range" south of Knoxville (Harris 51; *COG* 19–20)—and rhetorically. Both characters take "the form of a scourge or a moralistic force of retributive justice" (Wenke 206). There are obvious differences between the targets of each and the means of their retribution. Sut's "venom is particularly directed toward certain social types, such as circuit riders, dandies, squires, traveling salesmen, tax collectors, and constables" (Gardiner 181); Ballard's venom is *misdirected* toward the mountaineers around him because he cannot take it out on those who have taken from him—the representatives of the county. This misdirected violence is one of the ways that the authorities of the community use Ballard to maintain their power. Sut's conversations with George serve as running commentaries for not only his own mountain society, but also for the readership of the narrator "George" who can interpret them as he sees fit. Whereas Sut Lovingood takes out his hatred of hypocrisy via practical jokes and his interpretation of those jokes in the stories he tells the hegemonic representative George, Lester punishes wayward members of the Frog Mountain community with lethal violence.

The Frog Mountain enclave, a microcosm of stereotypical *Appalachia* often seen as "a 'deviant subculture' whose problems owe more to physical isolation, depleted gene pools, pathological inbreeding, clan wars, hookworm, moonshining, and welfarism," has all the popular *Appalachian* stereotypes; it needs a figure like Ballard on its periphery to help classify and categorize (Whisnant, *Modernizing the Mountaineer* xix). Stereotypes of the region conveniently have fed ideologies that aid and abet the manipulation of the Appalachian people by making them aberrant. Certainly deviance exists in the Frog Mountain community without Ballard, but his particular deviance allows Ballard's community to "other" him with impunity. Annalee Newitz believes that class stereotypes like those in *Child of God*

> suggest that poor whites are trash who don't deserve the benefits of social welfare, sympathy, or national power. But, at the same time, such stereotypes maintain — in a contained taxonomic sense — images and narratives about poor whites in order to provide something against which "civilized" whites can measure themselves [136].

While Newitz's criticisms directly concern the images of poor whites in general, these ideas and images can directly describe the situations of mountaineers and how their images in a broader cultural sense have helped mark them as "othered" in relation to society at large.

Because of his behavior, Ballard's economic and social disenfranchisement seems warranted. The stories of the men around the courthouse give textual proof that Lester is a standard by which all other community deviance is defined. Ballard resists authority, but he does not escape its control because the citizens of Sevier County use Ballard as a scourge for other social deviants and as a disciplining mechanism for the upstanding members of the community. With Ballard on the loose, the Frog Mountain fornicators must contend with the very real possibility of death when they journey to the outskirts of civilization to commit their sins; the stories of Lester's victims become warnings to potential deviants from the "upstanding" members of the society: "Break our standards and you'll wind up like them kids Lester Ballard carried off."

Ballard the Foucauldian Deviant

Discussing the deviant as a social construct, cultural materialist Jonathan Dollimore uses Michel Foucault's theories in much the same way I have throughout this project. Dollimore observes that "in Foucault's scheme deviants come to occupy a revealing, dangerous double relationship to power, at once culturally marginal yet discursively central" (222). These deviants become the topic and infatuation of their cultures by straddling the edges of human interaction. Dollimore applies this specifically to sexual deviants — particularly homosexuals — in order to show how society defines itself through what it labels as unacceptable. A heterosexual culture remains homophobic and whispers about what is in the "closet" — it defines itself by what it claims it is not. Seven separate narrative instances in *Child of God* show community members telling stories about Lester as though they can glean some moral imperative from his deviance via these stories. Their preoccupation with him proves his discursively central status within the community. Lester polices the social periphery literally, but he is also a monster in the middle of the collective social imagination because his society has internalized him. Vereen Bell believes that for the reader and for the "pocketknife society" loitering around the Sevier County Courthouse, "Lester becomes something like the spirit of the place," that he is "a berserk version of fundamental aspects of ourselves — of our fear of time, our programmed infatuation with death, our loneliness, our threatening appetites, our narcissistic isolation from the world and the reality of other people" (55). Ballard is a member of mountaineer society as seen in a funhouse mirror: he has all the attributes of mountaineer "peculiarity," but he pushes things far beyond the scope and limit of social acceptability.

Foucault, as Kevin Jon Heller distinguishes, "wants to foreground the fact that no use of power is ever inherently either 'power' ... or 'resistance,' just as no subject-position is ever inherently either 'hegemonic' or 'counter-hegemonic.'" Resistances are labeled as resistances only because they are "lesser forms of power, not because they are power-less" (Heller 100; 99). Domination must have its oppositional — resistance. Dialogic and discursive, the opposing ends of the power binary depend on each other for definition. The hegemonic subject-position is given that dominating label because it exercises power more efficiently than the counter-hegemonic subject position. In the case of *Child of God*, the society as represented by the county assumes the dominant subject position because it uses power more efficiently than the resistive Ballard. Ballard's rifle is no match for the series of munitions his society drops on his head, but he is not entirely powerless.

Child of God reveals ways in which the dominant order can use counter-hegemonic subject positions as the "abnormal" position of a power binary to maintain and reinforce its own hegemonic position. In their critique of M.M. Bakhtin's work *Rabalias and His World*, Peter Stallybrass and Allon White quote Terry Eagleton, who suggests that Bakhtin's carnival can be a "*licensed* affair in every sense, a permissible rupture of hegemony, a contained popular blow-off" (13). Foucauldian resistance can be manipulated in a similar way. Social deviance—one form of resistance to domination—can be commandeered by the hegemony in order to legitimate the hegemony's domination over those it considers resistors. This manipulation of the "other" need not be explicitly pursued or acknowledged. The "other" must be allowed; it must not be crushed. A power relationship of this nature means that it is not in the interest of the hegemonic subject position to destroy resistance because "power has to qualify, measure, appraise, and hierarchize rather than display itself in murderous splendor; it does not have to draw the line that separates the enemies of the [community].... [I]t effects distribution *around the norm*" (*HS* 144, emphasis added). Hegemonic domination must be resisted for its power to be exercised, and in the case of *Child of God*, Lester Ballard provides this resistance from the opening scene.

Historically, vagrancy and a lack of property ownership have been characteristics by which normative society defines the mountaineer. The concept of property and its commodification have marked Lester's existence. The auctioneer responds to Ballard's threats by saying, "I didn't take your place off of ye. County done that. I was just hired as auctioneer" (*COG* 7). But whom does the county represent if not the auctioneer and all of the other community members? It might be argued that Ballard's dispossession is indicative of a wider trend in Appalachia where encroaching industrial interests combined with legal confusions about overlapping land deeds to the disadvantage of the mountaineer. Many mountaineers did not understand the value of the timber rights to their land. Timber and coal companies obtained the mineral rights to the land and left the mountaineers with little more to claim than taxes. Furthermore, with the advent of the New Deal, TVA, and the national parks system, the federal government got involved with the Appalachian land grab:

> Federal intervention in Appalachia before 1930 included the designation of national forests from 1911 and the establishment of the Great Smoky Mountains National Park in 1926. Both involved government purchase of land, often from the timber companies after they had felled the trees but also by compulsion from families that had not previously sold out to those companies. The latter purchases generated dislike of federal intervention among local people [Bradshaw 19].

Thus, the county auctioneer's sales pitch references how "they's good timber up here too. Real good timber. It's been cut over fifteen year ago and so maybe it ain't big timber yet," showing evidence of the timber industry's footprints in McCarthy's Appalachia (*COG* 5). This scene was not an anomaly in Appalachia; in fact, it was a fairly common occurrence.

Certainly, it is possible that Ballard's father sold the timber rights to the land and thus the cutting-over, or it is possible that the elder Ballard himself cut the timber, because many "resources — the seemingly endless hardwood forests, for example — have been abused by the people who occupy the land and by outsiders" (Raitz and Ulack 189). Even if this is the case, and the hypothesis is shaky at best, it does nothing to explain *Lester's* neglect of the farm. If he has paid as little attention to the details of the rest of the homestead as he has to the barn where the rope with which his father committed suicide still hangs after several years, then it is no surprise that the opening of the novel depicts the sale of the property. Perhaps Lester's initial affront to his community merely stems from his inefficient use of his land. If, as some scholars have suggested, subsistence or self-sufficient agriculture was an inefficient use of Appalachian properties, then certainly Lester's failure as a landowner makes more sense. The community therefore sanctions Ballard's dispossession via the county auction of his homestead, and thus by extension, his vagrancy. It seems paradoxical that a society would exile a person it wishes to control, but that is what happens in this instance.

The results of this exile are catastrophic, especially for the sexually deviant segment of the population. Lester's vagrancy brings him more into the purview of the community authorities and more into contact with other social deviants. Like all vagrants, Ballard is subject to the rhetorical question "What is your station?" and Foucault concludes, "This question is the simplest expression of the established order in society; such vagabondage is repugnant to it, disturbs it" (*DP* 290). Foucault goes on to say, "One must have a stable, continuous long-term station, thoughts of the future, of a secure future, in order to reassure [society] against all attacks" (*DP* 291). Ballard's vagrancy makes him a challenge to the hegemony and requires that he be observed and controlled and manipulated. This deviance makes him problematic, but it also opens him up to discipline. Authorities ask the question and they know the answer; the question is a tool used to occasion surveillance. The act of questioning requires encounter. When the perpetrator answers the question in the negative, he admits his vagrancy to the authorities and reinforces it to himself. He has no station, no home, and thus, no permanent place within the society. Ballard, of course, has no station and he has no permanent abode. In the middle of the novel, when the sheriff brings him before a judge hoping to incarcerate him for arson, Ballard admits his vagrancy. The judge asks him:

>Is it true that you burned down Mr. Waldrop's house?
>No.
>You were living in it at the time that it burned.
>That's a ... I wasn't done it. I'd left out of there a long time before that.
>It was quiet in the room. After a while the man behind the desk lowered his hands and folded them in his lap. Mr. Ballard, he said. You are either going to have to find some other way to live or some other place in the world to do it in [*COG* 122].

Ballard does. He continually wanders from place to place, from the Waldrop shack to Reubel's junkyard, from the mountain caves to the high mountain roads, from the creeks of Sevier County to the streets of Sevierville. In his wanderings, Ballard encounters sexual deviants at the Frog Mountain turnaround and elsewhere. One such encounter — the one with the "old whore" — makes him a wanted man (41–43). Leaving the courthouse on his way to pick up Ballard for the rape of the old whore, Sheriff Fate Turner tells his driver, "Let's go get the little fucker," revealing that he and Ballard have a history; Turner was present at the auction and this is not Ballard's first arrest and incarceration, after all (49). That Fate Turner knows to look for Ballard at the Waldrop place demonstrates that he or his surrogates throughout the community have kept an eye on Lester since his dispossession. Lester's vagrancy makes him an easy target, a fact made apparent by the sheriff's sarcastic recognition of his station. When he finally reaches the porch of the Waldrop shack, having struggled through the briars and brush, Turner says to Ballard, "Man of leisure like yourself ... you oughtn't mind helpin us workers unscramble a little misunderstandin" (51).

Despite all of his legal run-ins, Ballard never stays in jail. The sheriff has a hard time presenting a watertight case against Ballard in almost every instance because he has only suspicion and circumstantial evidence, but there are other reasons for his release: delinquency and recidivism. Foucault notes, "The conditions to which the free inmates are subjected necessarily condemn them to recidivism: they are under the surveillance of the police; they are assigned to a particular residence, or forbidden others" (*DP* 267). At this point in the novel, the sheriff knows where Ballard resides, though he does not own the property. For the time, Ballard is useful to the community because he remains a suspicious deviant under surveillance, as Sheriff Turner's investigations of Lester's crimes prove. Lester patrols the backwoods of Sevier County, trying to make "things more orderly in the woods and in men's souls" (*COG* 136). His patrols wreak havoc on other deviants, both the transgressors who deviate from sexual norms by fornicating in the back of a car, and representatives of mountaineer trash — as in the case of the idiot boy and Ralph's daughter (118–120). He eliminates some deviants and deters community members from committing transgressive acts.

Lester, nevertheless, remains a man apart from others, alienated within his community. "A cursing, spitting, vengeful, homicidal, necrophilic sociopath ... [who] could serve as stuff for a gratuitously shocking horror story" (Bartlett 3), Lester's threat of violence at the auction of his property licenses Buster's swing of the ax, justifying Newitz's claims that "middle-class whites can use the hatred they inspire in lower-class whites to justify their own violence and to claim that they can't help being violent anyway" (145). Lester's refusal to abide by the wishes of the community and his violent attempt at repelling these wishes give the community reason to attack him. He becomes another felled tree, whittled down and used in the construction of a social observatory. His defiance emboldens the county and allows its citizens to rationalize his dispossession, but not without some consternation. They sell his property to John Greer. One narrator relates, "C B went on with the auction like nothin never had happent but he did say that it caused some folks not to bid that otherwise would of, which might have been what Lester set out at, I don't know" (*COG* 9). Greer may not be from Sevier County, but he more readily meets the criteria for their acceptance. Greer replaces Ballard economically when he buys Ballard's homestead; he is the spearhead of Ballard's dispossession, so it is not a wonder that Lester fixates on him. Ballard's fascination with Greer is a jealous attempt to live a vicariously normal life: "After the snow ceased he went every day. He'd watch from his half mile promontory, see Greer come from the house for wood or go to the barn or to the chicken house" (140). In Ballard's old house, Greer has everything that Ballard does not — food, warm shelter, a livelihood; whereas Ballard could not do the things within the law to prevent his own dispossession — work his land, pay his taxes, communicate in meaningful ways with other members of his society — evidently John Greer apparently can engage the community and its economy. On one occasion Ballard watches him reading "what looked like seed catalogues," in anticipation of ordering for spring planting (109); Greer cuts wood for the stove, his barn is full of hay, and his chickenhouse has chickens in it (136–137); when Ballard finally assaults Greer, the new landowner has "turned out to dig a septic tank at the back of his house" (172). Clearly this man is a "worker," in the words of the sheriff, whereas Ballard is a "man of leisure" (51). George Guillemin is right when he claims: "Far from being invaded by industrialism, Lester's farm is simply taken over by a more ambitious landholder" (*Vision* 40), who has been licensed to run the place by his society via his purchase of the property at public/government auction. As a member of the Frog Mountain community, Ballard is inefficient and unengaged. He neither consumes nor produces effectively, so he gets used in other ways.

Ballard's most telling alienation from the rest of his society directly concerns his sexual ineptitude. The continuance of human communities requires procreative sexual intercourse and Ballard lacks any of the courting skills needed to consumate such a requirement. The dumpkeeper's daughters, it seems, screw anything that offers — one is minimally combative when the dumpkeeper himself assaults her — and yet Lester cannot even aptly negotiate verbal intercourse with one of them, much less anything more (pro)creative (*COG* 28–29). As is the case in so many of his encounters with the opposite sex, he resorts to voyeurism; he watches sex and then punishes it. He yet again proves his ineptitude with the old whore he finds abandoned at the turnaround. He slaps her down, rips off her gown, and takes the trophy with him; he does nothing more (41–43). Their conversation is as combative as their physical interaction, but he does not rape her — he can barely even talk to her. Ballard cannot properly navigate social discourse even before he becomes a lover of the dead. He is not "normal."

Ballard the Foucauldian Delinquent

Categorized and manipulated as a delinquent by the authorities of Sevier County, Lester Ballard illustrates how discipline works within the eastern Tennessee community to ensure the continuation of the hegemonic domination. Foucault's socially constructed delinquent plays an important role in the upholding of social normalcy: "In fabricating delinquency," the hegemony gives "to criminal justice a unitary field of objects, authenticated by the 'sciences,'" it "silently organizes a field of objectivity in which punishment will be able to function openly as treatment and the sentence be inscribed among the discourses of knowledge" (*DP* 256). The discipline of modern penitentiary practices creates a position of alterity in which the prisoner becomes the inverse of the law-abiding citizen; this discipline names, scrutinizes, separates, and characterizes the inmate as the delinquent: "Prisons do not diminish the crime rate," "detention causes recidivism," and thus "the prison cannot fail to produce delinquents. It does so by the very type of existence that it imposes on its inmates" (*DP* 266). Even when released, the ex-inmates are still under strains of observation.

The connections with Lester Ballard become gradually more apparent: he spends time in jail, where he seems tempted to stay; in jail he encounters delinquents whose crimes he will later emulate; when the county forcibly removes him from his home and land and then relegates him to the life of a vagabond, Lester becomes the focus of the sheriff's gaze. When Lester is released from jail the last time before he begins his murder spree, McCarthy specifically names the building he leaves. Ballard walks "out through the front door of the *Sevier County* courthouse" (*COG* 55). As Faulkner details in *Requiem for a Nun*, the courthouse edifice represents the law, the justice, the history, and the public will of a county. It is the symbolic foundation of a town's incorporation; it is the icon of a community's social contract (3–42). When Ballard walks out the front door it is as if the community itself licenses his freedom, and subsequently, all that he brings to that freedom. While the Sevier County jail is more of a holding facility than a penitentiary in the truest sense, his time in jail works on him as prison time works on Foucauldian delinquents: the aim of the penitentiary, according to Foucault, was not "to retrain delinquents or to make them virtuous," but to manipulate them so that they might "serve as a tool for economic or political ends. The problem thereafter was not to teach the prisoners something, but rather to teach them nothing, so as to make sure that they could do nothing when they came out of prison" (*P/K* 42). In jail Lester gets "whitebeans with fatback and boiled greens and baloney sandwiches on light bread," more square meals than he has had in years.

While waiting for the county to decide his fate, Lester encounters a black fugitive cokehead named "nigger John" who has "cut a motherfucker's head off with a pocketknife" and who sings constantly "in the cell opposite" (*COG* 52–53). The verbal exchanges between the two men reveal insights into the gradual transformation of Ballard into a delinquent. Ballard appears much more interested in John than John is in Lester. After Lester asks the crooner his crimes and John responds not by saying he has been accused of murder, but by confessing that he decapitated someone in a most grisly manner, "Ballard waited to be asked his own crime but he wasn't"; nevertheless, bragging tentatively, "after while he said: I was supposed to have raped this old girl. She was nothin but a whore to start with" (53). Interestingly, Lester never admits the fact that he didn't rape her and John never inquires one way or the other. Lester, at this point, has little criminal experience other than petty misdemeanors—"failure to comply with a court order, public disturbance, assault and battery, public drunk" (56). He cannot really identify with the fugitive's plight on a personal level. In response to John's commentary on white women, Lester responds with a cliché: "All the trouble I ever was in, said Ballard, was caused by whiskey or women or both. *He'd often heard men say as much*" (53, emphasis added). John comes back at him with a professional's answer: "All the trouble I ever was in was caused by gettin caught" (53). John is the master of this trade and Lester the apprentice. But Lester learns quickly. Ballard tries to impress the murderer John with his own alleged crimes, and John obviously makes an impression on him. When the judge releases him back into the community, Ballard begins to execute his delinquency.

Delinquency becomes a methodology of discipline "not intended to eliminate offences, but rather to distinguish them, to distribute them, to use them; that it is not so much that they render docile those who are liable to transgress the law, but that they tend to assimilate the transgression of the laws in a general tactics of subjugation" (*DP* 272). A community in which this disciplinary mechanism functions ultimately complies with and licenses the construction of delinquency because in a society where "incarceration is the omnipresent armature, the delinquent is not outside the law; he is, from the very outset, in the law, at the very heart of the law, or at least in the midst of those mechanisms that transfer the individual imperceptibly from discipline to the law, from deviance to offence" (301). As is the case with the delinquents of Foucault's writings, jail does not reform Ballard. He has been in and out of jail. Why does the county release him after each arrest? Again, after the incident with the old whore, Lester spends time in the lockup, but after nine days of confinement and good food, the authorities have no legitimate charges to levy against Ballard, so a judge releases him back into the community: "Ballard stood up and went through the gate and across the room toward a door with daylight in it and across a hall and out through the front door of the Sevier County courthouse. No one called him back" (*COG* 55).

On the way out of town, Lester visits the post office — a federal building — where the FBI posts the faces of its most wanted criminals. Other notorious delinquents stare back at him "with surly eyes. Men of many names. Their tattoos. Legends of dead loves inscribed on perishable flesh" (55). Perhaps Lester's future crimes germinate subliminally. While looking through the pictures, he encounters Sheriff Turner, the man elected by Sevier County as "the ostensible representative of these civil folk" (Bartlett 6), who asks him, "What sort of meanness have you got laid out for next?" (*COG* 56). The conversation that follows demonstrates the sheriff's, and thus the community's, complicity in Lester's delinquency and warrants full recounting:

> I figure you ought to give us a clue. Make it more fair. Let's see: failure to comply with a court order, public disturbance, assault and battery, public drunk, rape. *I guess murder is next on the list ain't it.* Or what things is it you've done that we ain't found out yet?
>
> I ain't done nothin, Ballard said. You just got it in for me.
>
> The sheriff had his arms folded and he was rocking slightly on his heels, studying the sullen *reprobate* before him. Well, he said. I guess you better get your ass on home. These people here in town won't put up with your shit.
>
> I ain't ast nothin from nobody in this chickenshit town.
>
> You better get your ass on home, Ballard.

> Ain't a goddamn thing keepin me here cept you goin on at the mouth.
> The sheriff stepped away from in front of him. Ballard went on by and up the street. About halfway along the block he looked back. The sheriff was still watching him [56, emphasis added].

While Lester sasses the sheriff like a saucy kid, Sheriff Turner, the "ambulatory version of the courthouse image — patient, forceful, and unflappable, heir to the legendary Tom Davis, scourge of the White Caps, a subliminal reminder of what it is that keeps us from becoming Lester," lists the offenses Lester has and has not committed already (Bell 58). Then, in a telling prognostication, the sheriff predicts that Lester might murder someone. When taken alongside his confinement across from a murderer and his examination of the most-wanted poster, it can be argued that Fate Turner himself helps plant the seed of this particular act. Lester's interest in the act of murder grows. The sheriff not only enables Ballard to do his dirty work by releasing him, he gives him the tool of suggestion and even recognizes Ballard as a delinquent ("reprobate").

At the very least, Turner's words draw attention to the indirect process through which discipline helps to produce Lester's delinquency. One could not claim that the sheriff consciously induces Ballard to murder, but one could claim that the jail time and his encounters with legal officials, rather than deterring Ballard and facilitating his rehabilitation, only give him ideas about further crime. Perhaps Foucault's perception of the role of confinement is most telling here: it ensures "the maintenance of delinquency, the encouragement of recidivism, the transformation of the occasional offender into the habitual delinquent" (*DP* 272). Ballard continues to do things that run him afoul of the law. The litany of his offenses progresses by degree until he goes and does exactly what the sheriff has suggested he might.

As a representative of the dangerous "hillbilly," Lester helps control the population through his perversion and sociopathology. The community objectifies Ballard by drawing on his previous social infractions. The auctioneer reveals that Ballard has "done been locked up once" over the conscription and sale of his land (*COG* 7). In the tale about Lester and the Finney boy, according to the teller, Lester hauls off and smashes Finney's face for no reason; the narrator claims that everyone present "just felt real bad"; he says, "I never liked Lester much from that day," even though he concludes Lester "never done nothing to me" (18). Quick to objectify his deviance and delinquency, the community will not accept its complicity in and dependence on the creation of Lester Ballard: "What is not open to community scrutiny ... is the ambiguity of the normal and what is covered over by the collective belief in it and the effort to sustain its placid and reassuring rhythm" (Bell 57). Ultimately, the community around Frog Mountain uses Ballard the delinquent as a disciplinary mechanism to *reinforce* its community values. In all his murderous instances, Lester presents little direct threat to the hegemonic land-owning class that abides by the rules of the community. Law-abiding, monogamous couples have sex in their bedrooms, not in the back seats of cars at the Frog Mountain turnaround. Nevertheless, "since the Frog Mountain turnaround is one of the novel's most significant settings, it is worth noting that the sexual activity it elicits is scarcely limited to Lester Ballard. His role as voyeur depends on others' use of this place" (Lang 107). Evidently, this place is rife with illicit activity, as demonstrated by the detritus surrounding it: "flattened beercans and papers and rotting condoms" (*COG* 20). Were the behavior not transgressive, there would be no reason to hide it and there would fewer reasons for condom use. Ballard opens the dead man's wallet and finds "family pictures within the little yellowed glassine windows" (89). A wife and children, perhaps? The sheriff's deputy later reveals that the girl involved "was supposed to of been goin with that Blalock boy we talked to," and the sheriff responds, "Yeah, well. These young people keep pretty active some of em" (147). The evidence suggests that the girl—who was not found with the Blalock boy when the sheriff questioned him—was promiscuous at best and adulterous at worst. If the words chosen to describe them can be considered an indication of age, the asphyxiated "man" and "girl" most likely are engaged in an illicit *extramarital* affair, and that is most definitely against the values of their society.

With the couplings on Frog Mountain, Lester acts as an extension of authority in two ways: (a) he deters anyone who might be tempted to park and have illicit sex on Frog Mountain by acting as a surrogate sheriff, a sort of "Boogie-man," someone who "could serve as stuff for a gratuitously shocking horror story," a monster sent to punish those who subvert sexual prohibitions (Bartlett 3); and (b) in policing the margins, Ballard also helps keep members of the community from begetting bastards through such illicit sex acts, thereby limiting the possibility that the community will have to provide for those illegitimate children. This is Ballard's version of abstinence-only education.

Diane Luce notes, "Each of Lester's female victims is, in his mind, sexually promiscuous as well as sexually attractive.... [T]hus Lester recaps his White Cap heritage when he judges and kills these 'lewd' yet disturbing young women" ("White Caps" 49). For Luce, the story Mr. Wade tells of the White Cap hangings "is not an extraneous bit of local history" ("White Caps" 43). Her attention to how these groups policed Sevier County between 1892 and 1899—mostly terrorizing "lewd" women—shows how a vigilante group can influence the behavior of a community and how the community can use their potential violence as a deterrent to behavior it considers unsavory. Lester Ballard works in much the same way. Like the young women, the male victims contribute to community deviance by bedding these "loose" women.

Additionally, Lester's execution of Ralph's daughter and the slobbering toddler is no threat to the community at large for this second reason. Ballard surmises that the idiot child is the offspring of the girl and "that old crazy Thomas boy" (*COG* 117). The girl, "all [post-partum] tits and plump young haunch," is obviously not married, so if the child is hers as Ballard believes, then she too is sexually deviant (76). What is more, if one pays attention to the inventory of her yard —"the roof of a car sliced off and propped up on cinder blocks. A light cord [that] ran across the mud and underneath the car roof a bulb [that] burned and a group of depressed looking chickens [that] huddled and clucked"— she also seems to represent a certain hillbilly trashiness associated with mountaineers (76). A few rangy chickens and junk in the yard — garbage and unusable car parts. The mental picture of Appalachian squalor materializes. So the text suggests that Lester polices his own kind: trangressors and hillbillies.

Evidently Ballard is an efficient policeman, or at least an active one. By terrorizing the backseat lovers on Frog Mountain, Ballard performs a necessary function within the society. The sheriff makes a practice of doing the same thing Ballard does — periodically checking on the mountain turnaround's nocturnal visitors. According to one of the pocketknife society talkers — possibly one of Turner's deputies — Turner uses the disciplinary method of embarrassment on the boy whom he pulls out of the car at the turnaround. When the boy steps out of the car with his pants on inside-out, Fate hollers to his rider, "John, come here and see this"; unlike Lester, who later shoots a similar young man, Turner "just told him to go on. Ast him if he could drive like that" (44–45). While Lester, "in his monitoring of the activities on Frog Mountain, explicitly mimics the sheriff when he confronts the young couple on the turnaround directing the flashlight beam into their eyes and demanding to see the boy's license," the sheriff merely makes the deviants go on their way, embarrassed but alive (Luce, "White Caps" 50). They may or may not commit the same acts again. The fear Ballard induces, however, is an even more pressing deterrent than that of the sheriff. Potential death stifles the most potent sexual appetites (except Lester's, of course). As the White Caps did in their preliminary stages, here Ballard's "work" functions as an extension of civic morality.

It might seem a stretch to suggest that community authorities encourage Ballard to murder deviant community members. Yet they do not have to encourage it, they merely have to *allow* it, and there is ample evidence of that allowance. Having jailed him numerous times throughout the novel, the county lets Ballard go every time The sheriff has his suspicions. The sheriff hauls him in at gunpoint, ostensibly for arson in the case of Waldrop's house, but Ballard denies it. Waldrop does not press charges, the sheriff has no case, and Ballard goes free with the judge's warning. When Ballard kills Ralph's daughter and her son, he also burns down the house to destroy evidence. However, he leaves a rifle shell, an explicit connection to him, which he cannot locate in his haste (*COG* 119). Ballard treads thin ice. When Turner and his deputy investigate a car upturned in the ravine below the turnaround — after a missing persons report on the couple who had been in the car and after they have found the asphyxiated man whose lover Ballard burned up — Fate says, "I wisht we'd been here three days ago when they was still some snow on the ground" (147); snow on the sides of the road would have been undisturbed by vehicle traffic and would have revealed the comings and goings of a pedestrian perpetrator. They are trying to figure out where the couple went. Turner says, "They wasn't in the car.... I believe somebody's shoved it off in here" (147). He has investigated this case to the extent that he has discovered the wrecked car has no outstanding lien, excluding the fraud suspected by the deputy as a potential motive. Furthermore, he surmises this disappearance is tied to others. He says when asked where he thinks the driver and passenger have gone, "I reckon they've got to wherever that gal got to that was supposed to of been with that boy we found up here" (146–147). Turner suspects Ballard, clearly. He has done his detective work, but he cannot detain Ballard or charge him with anything. He does not have enough evidence to indict Ballard and he knows it; nevertheless, by not taking Ballard into custody, the sheriff, representative of the county, *allows* Lester to continue his (useful) disciplinary rampaging.

In addition to the policing they do themselves, delinquents like the White Caps and Lester Ballard demand, ensure, and justify the creation of authorities like Tom Davis — a lawman whose existence was solely the result of vigilantism — and Sheriff Fate Turner. Foucault comments on this phenomenon: "Delinquency, with the secret agents that it procures, but also with the generalized policing that it authorizes, constitutes a means of perpetual surveillance of the population: an apparatus that makes it possible to supervise, through the delinquents themselves, the whole social field" (*DP* 281). Were it not for the Lester Ballards of the world, there would be no need for the high sheriffs; they would not be welcomed without the threat of imminent danger: "What makes the presence and control of the police tolerable for the population, if not fear of the criminal?" (*P/K* 47). Sheriff Turner certainly knows that members of the community go to the turnaround — an off-the-beaten-path mountain hideout — to commit deviant acts. He has caught several of them. Given the "pocketknife society's" proximity to his courthouse office, the sheriff might be privy to the conversations of the whittlers there. He is in touch with the society he polices, as his conversations with them during the flood scenes prove (*COG* 160–165). Those people form the disciplinary web through which the panoptic gaze works. Furthermore, Ballard's criminality, his "wrong blood," is essential to the workings of authority in his community because "crime was too useful for them to dream of anything as crazy — or ultimately as dangerous — as a society without crime. No crime means no police" (*P/K* 47). The threat of a figure like Ballard licenses the observation of Turner much as the criminality of the White Caps licensed the advent of Tom Davis. Criminals such as Ballard "can be put to good use if only to keep other criminals under surveillance" (45). Lester watches both Reubel's daughters and Ralph's daughter and her cretin son; he keeps his eye on the Frog Mountain turnaround and the adulterers and fornicators there; he even goes hunting for Kirby's liquor, just like a revenuer might (113).

The disciplinary network grows as the novel progresses. Turner watches Ballard; Ballard watches others; eventually, many members of the community seek Lester and he observes their searches: "Ballard watched them from the saddle of the mountain.... [I]n the night the side of the mountain winked with lamps and torches. Late winter revelers among the trees or some like hunters calling each to each there in the dark" (154). Whereas earlier Lester "stood in the crossroads listening to other men's hounds on the mountain. A figure of wretched arrogance in the lights of the few cars passing," he now becomes the object they hunt (41). Suspicion of Lester's crimes occasions this hunt; his actions cause the community's increased watchfulness. Lester's murderousness assuages their guilt for his dispossession; his sociopathology creates a safety valve for the community's repressed aggressions and violent tendencies. His delinquency proves he deserves social exclusion.

Ballard finally exceeds the bounds of his subject position when he attacks John Greer. His felony is not so much the attack on Greer itself, but the fact that he goes against the will of the community *so directly*. The county, as it represents the community at large, sells the property to Greer and thereby legitimates his place among its citizens as a landowner despite the fact that he is an outsider from Grainger County, not Sevier County. Greer, nonetheless, is the chosen one. He *is not* the typical poor-white mountaineer; to the contrary, he is a handpicked, financially stable landowner, engaged in productive work. Ballard *may not* murder him with impunity. Diane Luce suggests as much: "It is apt that when Lester mediates his assault on Greer, he spies on his bespectacled alter ego as he sits (*in the most recognizably middle-class image of the novel*) in Lester's repossessed farmhouse, engaged in the purchasing of living goods, seeds, from a catalogue (109)" ("Cave of Oblivion" 178, emphasis added). No longer a matter of deviant-on-deviant violence, this attack does not serve as a disciplinary social control. In the subsequent melee with Greer, Ballard's power is illegitimate and unlicensed, and is, therefore, a genuine disturbance to hegemonic domination. Nevertheless, it is not a case of resistance working outside the power relation; it is merely resistance manipulating its position as the potentially violent, deviant Other. It is a case of what Kevin Jon Heller might call a "reversal" of the power dynamic (101). Having conscripted his power and named it as his own, Ballard the deviant is no longer an extension of society's policing power. He is now a problem and must be reeled in.

Ballard the Victim

One of the most bizarre but compelling facets of *Child of God* is that its "protagonist," despite his antagonism to his society and to the whole of human decency, is not outside the bounds of the human condition. Certainly, as Vereen Bell has argued, Lester Ballard is *beyond the pale*, but he is not inhuman and he is not bestial. Making him a pawn, the community conscripts Ballard's resistive power and uses it for the advancement of community goals: "Lester has all of these same wires, but he is wired differently, so he turns out dangerously wrong, an aberration and a norm at the same time, an unconscious being brought forth, as if by sorcery, into the conscious world" (55). I would argue that Lester is wired in the same way as his community, but that his dispossession and ostracism have twisted those wires until their rubberized coating has cracked and the exposed filaments have short-circuited together. Violence does not offend this society. In fact, this Appalachian mountain community has a violent past, as the stories of the White Caps and their executions show; the natural wilderness Lester lives in mirrors this violence: watching two hawks, Ballard "did not know how hawks mated but he knew that all things fought" (*COG* 169). Lester does not fight, he does not hit people with an axe as Buster does to him; he shoots them in the head—his is a superlative violence. And as long as it is released in what the community sees as a constructive outlet, as one that helps control deviance, it can be tolerated.

Lester feels the same emotions as any human. He yearns for socialization and normalcy, especially when so many of his attempts at social interaction with his social peers fail. Ballard is "systematically identified as a scapegoat by a variety of hegemonic cultural institutions" (Walsh, *In the Wake of the Sun* 153); the county, the police, and even the church ostracize him, and yet they allow him to roam the periphery of their community unchecked until he affronts one of their own in John Greer. The result of this ostracism and of Lester's failure at basic socialization is his enduring loneliness. Perhaps this facet alone is what makes Ballard, despite his despicable behavior, almost sympathetic. It undoubtedly makes him pitiable and inextricably human. His actions manifest his yearning. Lester "amasses fragments into a surround[ing] that stands at once as prison and protecting cocoon" (Stewart 42); he fills his room with the stuffed bears and a tiger he won at the carnival and they watch him like family, "their plastic eyes shining in the firelight and their red flannel tongues out" (*COG* 67).

Living without any social skills, as Ballard does, there is little likelihood of female companionship. As perverse as the violation of the first corpse is, he treats her almost tenderly, pouring "into that waxen ear everything he'd ever thought of saying to a woman," as any man might do to his lover (88). Then, once he has taken her home, he walks into town (no small task given the distance and the weather) to buy her gifts with the money her dead lover did not spend on her — a dress, lingerie, lipstick — and comes back home with nearly frostbitten toes. After dressing her up, he poses her, framing her as a picture in the window: "He would arrange her in different positions and go out and peer in the window at her" (103); he desires normalcy. Perhaps he bases whether or not she looks right on what he has observed in "normal" families' windows. After all, he does bear some voyeuristic tendencies. His behavior would be normal were the woman he courted not dead. He misperforms domesticity and courtship, but his desire to emulate them proves that he has interiorized some form of social discipline.

Even as late in the novel as just before he shoots John Greer, Lester watches the progression of a wagon across the valley and sees the world passing normally about him and wishes he could be a part of it: "Squatting there he let his head drop between his knees and he began to cry" (*COG* 170). His structure of life, though perverse, is modeled after that of normalcy. When the house burns down, he rescues his family of stuffed animals first and takes them to a cave. Later he makes for himself a perverse rendition of a family "in the bowels of the mountain ... on ledges or pallets of stone where dead people lay" (*COG* 135). When threatened by the lynch mob and by unrelenting rainfall, Ballard tediously drags his "family" of corpses, one by one, to the sinkhole where they are eventually discovered (158). He makes his own world below a parody of that above. His frame of reference is society, but it rejects him, so he refashions it the only way he can.

The cokehead murderer in the jail cell tells him, "All the trouble I ever was in was caused by getting caught" (53). Ballard takes the advice to heart. He approaches his actions with caution, at least at first. However, as he sinks deeper into his madness, he gets careless; his perversions of normalcy, and his desires to make those perversions emulate normalcy as closely as possible, cause him to throw caution away. His inability to locate the rifle shell ejected from his gun outside Ralph's house possibly results from his desire to romance Ralph's daughter while she is still warm and somewhat lifelike. His carelessness with the boy he shoots in the neck at the Frog Mountain turnaround alerts the community to his delinquency when the boy escapes; subsequently, Ballard's carelessness results in further infiltration of the mountain by authority figures — the search parties that scour the mountain for him.

Ballard's perverse imitations of social norms demonstrate how he has internalized social expectations; his actions reflect how a degree of discipline has influenced him. He tries to be a sheriff, a salesman, a boyfriend. He knows what the norms are and he tries to emulate them in his own way. What is more, Lester, at least to some extent, understands that he is marginalized, that he does not fit into his society's normal expectations. Yet he still possesses a moral and social compass that has been shaped by his interaction with his peers. The fact that he often rejects this moral/social compass does not belie its existence; in fact, throughout the novel ample evidence exists for its confirmation. If Ballard truly cared not what people around him thought, he would never go to a church, much less remove his hat in respect when he entered. He sniffles through the service, but he never challenges the preacher, or the congregation, or the existence of God (31–33). At the carnival fish tank, he cheats, but Ballard is no different from the carnival barker who changes the rules when he realizes Ballard's prowess with a rifle: Ballard cheats a cheater (62–64). When the young hunters invade his shack, Ballard chases them off. He realizes that the young dead girl is frozen in the adjacent room and that the discovery of her would present a problem for him. He stands "in the door where they'd stood and he looked into the room to see could he repeat with his own eyes what they'd seen. Nothing was certain" (94). He knows his actions are deviant and extraordinary and he does not yet want to be caught. When Mr. Fox at the store asks him about the dead boy they found at the turnaround, Ballard either deflects the question or earnestly asks, "What about him?" in an attempt to ascertain what is known about his crime (100). When Ballard tries to sell the watches he has collected from his victims, he has enough sense to travel to a different settlement rather than trying to sell them near Frog Mountain (129–132). Ballard is conscious of his status as a deviant, and he knows that the penalties will be severe if he is found out. He understands his liminal position; he knows that he resists the will of his community and eventually he knows the community will "want [his] life. [Because] he has heard them in the night seeking him with lanterns and cries of execration" (156).

No situation in the novel reveals more about Ballard's own knowledge of his marginal social position than how he interacts with John Greer. Ballard watches Greer and then wanders "about aimlessly in the woods talking to himself. He laid queer plans" (140). Use of the word "queer," of course, draws more attention to Ballard's deviance. At one point in the novel, Ballard runs into Greer and Greer asks him, "You're Ballard ain't ye? Ballard did not raise his head. He was watching the man's shoes there in the wet leaves of the overgrown logging road. He said: No, I ain't him, and went on" (114); he denies his own name.

When Ballard finally works up the courage to confront Greer, his knowledge and acceptance of his outsider singularity are complete. He no longer listens to that "old shed self that came yet from time to time in the name of sanity, a hand to gentle him back from the rim of his disastrous wrath" (158); that self is dead. He watches Greer to calculate his movements, then he appears in the full regalia of a madman, accosting Greer using the object that so closely associates him with the mountaineer — his rifle: "Lester Ballard in frightwig and skirts stepped from behind the pump-house and raised the rifle and cocked the hammer silently" (172). Ballard bizarrely commingles gender by disregarding society's dress codes as he wears the evidence of his murders. No longer does he try to conceal his crimes as "he'd long been wearing the underclothes of his female victims but now he took to appearing in their outerwear as well. A gothic doll in illfit clothes" (140). Greer shoots Lester and then "he picked up what appeared to be a wig and saw that it was fashioned whole from a dried human scalp" (173). This act of scalping his victim links Lester to a litany of "primitives"; both Indians and settlers committed such acts on the American frontier, but such an act in the 1950s represents true barbarism. Ballard becomes a savage. Ballard's attack on Greer is the final straw in his ostracism from his society. His acts of primitivism and gender-bending unearth social taboos that hit too close to home for the community. So as the chosen representative of the community, Greer ends Ballard's reign of terror. The assault on Greer and the subsequent loss of his arm steer Ballard back into the confines of society. They are the genesis for Ballard's reincorporation. Surgeons amputate the remaining flesh, robbing him of his last shred of independence and of the thing that has facilitated his disciplinary capacity — his ability to shoot the rifle. Once disarmed, Ballard enters into the complexities of the modern medical industry. His usefulness has evolved again. Like Arthur

Ownby in *The Orchard Keeper*, he is well on the way to becoming a case study — categorized and compartmentalized as something useful to science. His Sevierville community, on the other hand, tries to use him in a different way.

Ballard the Teacher; Ballard the Legend

Kidnapped from the hospital by a lynch mob who seeks to know where he has hidden the bodies of his victims, Lester manages to escape in the caves. But he is not the same person. Greer's shotgun truncates his power and the caves that once sheltered him have become more like a prison. In the end, "he'd cause to wish and he did wish for some brute midwife to spald him from his rocky keep" (189). And he is midwifed back into the world, reborn from the ground. When he sees himself reflected in the boy at the back of the church bus, his final epiphany comes. The boy, though in the rear of the bus, is in the company of fellow churchgoers; Lester, though on the margin of society, is still in it. He becomes conscious of the fact that he has his place in the community: "Though he tried to shake the image of the face in the glass, it would not go" (191). He makes his way back to the hospital where "the nightduty nurse ... found Ballard leaning against the counter. A weedshaped onearmed human swaddled up in outsized overalls and covered all over with red mud. His eyes were caved and smoking. I'm supposed to be here, he said" (192). Because, as Diane Luce points out, "Civil communities define themselves through a process of exclusion: through opposition to their designated outlaws," they take Ballard back; "paradoxically, then, the community also needs its outlaws, sustains and 'gives suck to the maimed and the crazed'" (156) for just this reason: "to achieve its sense of identity" (Luce, "White Caps" 56). Ballard is a necessary evil and an object of knowledge.

So Ballard is taken from the outlying areas of the country to a more intense and remote level of disciplinary power; he is categorized, classified, and compartmentalized in "the state hospital at Knoxville and there placed in a cage next door but one to a demented gentleman who used to open folks' skulls and eat the brains inside with a spoon" (*COG* 193). Like Ballard who parodies the actions of the sheriff, this "demented gentleman" parodies the work of a surgeon. Both of these "crazies" remain useful within this hospital context. Ballard's incarceration functions for him and his society in the same way that Foucault claims Tuke's work with the insane functioned in his day: "The asylum no longer punished the madman's guilt, it is true; but it did more, it organized that guilt; it organized it for the madman as a consciousness of himself, and as a non-reciprocal relation to the keeper" (*MAC* 247). Ballard has been conscious of his difference all along. He recognizes his guilt, but he is not remorseful. A nurse assumes he cares not whether Greer dies and to her he replies that he does care: he says, "I wish the son of a bitch was dead" (*COG* 176). Ballard acknowledges his guilt, his relation to his fellow man, and his status as a pariah when he tells the nurse at the county hospital, "I'm supposed to be here" (192). His institutionalization takes on a similar meaning for his society: "It organize[s] it for the man of reason as an awareness of the Other, a therapeutic intervention in the madman's existence" (*MAC* 247). In the asylum Lester's position of alterity is solidified and finalized; like the man who ate people's brains, Lester is a crazy ward of the state.

While the community has no simple case against Ballard, his incarceration in the state mental facility serves the community much more than his execution would. Ballard's incarceration "humanizes Ballard rather than allowing him to remain an unsympathetic candidate for slaughter, and it subjects him to the humane violence of civilization rather than to the barbarism outside it" (Ciuba 100). As Foucault points out:

> The ideal point of penality today would be indefinite discipline: an interrogation without end, an investigation that would be extended without limit to a meticulous and ever more analytical observation, a judgment that would at the same time be the constitution of a file that was never closed, the calculated leniency of a penalty that would be interlaced with the ruthless curiosity of an examination, a procedure that would be at the same time the permanent measure of a gap in relation to an inaccessible norm and the asymptotic movement that strives to meet in infinity [*DP* 227].

Therefore, in this situation, the power of the mob is truncated; Ballard escapes and his return to the hospital marks the completion of his panoptical internalization; he has policed himself and commits himself to a perpetual examination.

Lester is never charged with a crime and he is never tried for anything; he is not hanged in the public square like the White Caps Tipton and Wynn. Instead, he becomes a ward of the state, isolated from society as "insane"; however, his use as a case study by the state's medical school hints at the state's complicity in his deviance and thereby in his crimes. He is studied as an extreme example of deviant psychosis and as the bizarre reflection of normalcy. There he dies, evidently of pneumonia, and his body is "shipped to the state medical school at Memphis" (*COG* 194). Guillemin comments on Ballard's social repositioning, noting:

> The novel's ending represents not an exorcism but an epiphanic moment of Lester's coming home.... [H]e is removed from the extreme margin of society that he has occupied, and this is not toward the outside, into death or exile, but

toward the inside.... [T]he strange form this regeneration takes is his institutionalization and the postmortem. Yet this minimal redemption is anything but incidental or ironic. Lester's body is used for scientific procedures that are detailed as barbaric but are *societally sanctioned* [*Vision* 44; emphasis added].

Physically, Ballard becomes a professional educational tool for members of society who wish to advance the human condition, those doctors-in-training who want to extend life, not take it. His eviscerated body reincorporates him into a useful thing, and "at the end of three months when the class was closed Ballard was scraped from the table into a plastic bag and taken with *others of his kind* to a cemetery *outside the city* and there interred" (*COG* 194, emphasis added). He becomes a part of the "pathological anatomy," where cadaver dissection "made it possible for the last stage of pathological time and the first stage of cadaveric time almost to coincide" (*BOC* 141). While the medical residents do not discover the origins of Lester's deviance, his body educates doctors-in-training who will eventually play a disciplinary role in the medical complex of society.

Postmortem, he returns to where he started at the novel's opening — on the margin, "outside the city," a space that has so often been used as a social dumping ground. But that is not the end of Lester Ballard. Ballard becomes the "file that was never closed." Though removed from their midst, his tale becomes the endless interrogation of the community. Were Ballard tried, found guilty, sentenced to death, and the sentence carried out, his effectiveness as legend would be lessened in Sevierville and he could not be the site of knowledge learned by the mental health agents in Knoxville. His would be a closed morality tale, a tale of collective revenge wrought on a lone wolf. As it remains, Ballard becomes an evolving tale of ambivalence as the disciplinary scourge of Frog Mountain in the stories the men around the courthouse tell about him. His community, having dispossessed and ostracized him for so long, is finally forced to deal with him, if only on a rhetorical level; it cannot push the idea of Ballard aside — he remains discursively central. As Vereen Bell so keenly first observed:

> Since it is clear that all of the stories told about Lester are being told at some point after the events of the novel have taken place, it is also clear that Lester has become a part of the mythology of his region and has thereby achieved, ironically, a place in the community that has otherwise eluded him.... [L]ester becomes something like the spirit of the place, a bizarre aberration certainly, but not so totally dissociated from the people of that place that he doesn't seem somehow like their collective nightmare [54].

He is to be talked about, made the superlative, "mythicized when the community needs to tame the terrible story, to domesticate it, to make it 'safe'"

(Cant 90). Certainly, he is not tried because the evidence against him is circumstantial. The bodies are not found until after his death. The attempted murder of Greer is not a capital offense. Besides, Lester is more useful as a madman than as a criminal and his "boogie-man" status remains an occasion for wonder. He simultaneously warns community members that "if you are deviant, Lester Ballard'll get you" and "be nice to your neighbors" so as not to aid in the creation of another Ballard. He is both a warning and a chastisement.

The telling and retelling of his story illustrates the community's lack of comfort with him and with recognizing him as a manifestation of the human condition. Bartlett says that regardless of his crimes against humanity, "Ballard remains a human animal" (14). While his community imagines him as perverse, sexually depraved, antisocial and even demonic, they cannot see him as animalistic: typically animals just do not have sex with dead animals. Necrophilia is a human trait. Whether or not it likes it, Lester's community must rationalize him as human because it cannot escape his human acts — theft, assault, the degradation of corpses, murder. The narrative space created around Ballard

> [n]arrativizes social and moral orders and makes a [narrative] text not just an object of knowledge but the very place where the social code is continually dissolved and reconstructed.... [I]t places the storyteller on the same plane with the story and produces not meanings per se but points of view, voices, and tropes. It implies both the contingency of subject positions and the reversibility of things, the ability to turn time back on itself and to reinscribe events in distinct voices. In such a space, culture itself can be seen as nothing more, and nothing less, than "what people say" [Stewart 38].

While Lester's community may not understand the ambivalence of its narratives, it obviously recognizes storytelling as a space where the meaning of Lester can be reached and contained. The men of the "pocketknife society" whittle down the meaning of Lester's legend in much the same way that the medical students whittle down his body; like the cadaver study, their narratives produce knowledge.

The men around the courthouse talk about the goings-on, about the nature of people, about their collective history, about each other, and about the present. In six of the seven instances of narration presented in the first section of *Child of God*, Lester Ballard serves as a focal point of the storytelling, an exemplary figure against which others are measured. The men try in vain to explain Ballard as: (a) the victim of a massive head wound (*COG* 9); (b) an inherently mean bully (17–18); (c) a child traumatized by a parent's suicide (21); (d) an ignorant, stubborn mountaineer who would kill his cow rather than admit defeat (35); (e) an angry ape backed into a corner who does not abide by rule-governed activity (57); and (f) a descendant of degenerate ancestors hell-bent on extracting from society something that they did not earn (80). The oral histories about Frog Mountain's own Lester Ballard become the "true-crime" stories of Sevier County, a series of "there but for the grace of God [or socialization] go I" fables. Mr. Wade's narrative about the White Caps' hanging serves the same purpose, though it does not directly involve Ballard; nevertheless, Ballard's ancestors are implicated in that vigilante movement (81).

All of these stories demonstrate the attempts of the community to encapsulate Lester and to compartmentalize him as an aberrant, soulless ghoul through its storytelling, but they do not accomplish that goal. Contrary to the desired effects, what the stories show, in their ambivalence, is a genuine nervousness about how to situate Lester in the community and how Sevierville and the surrounding areas might have somehow brought his pathological violence on itself. The man had to keep hitting the ape before it went ballistic. Not once does a narrator suggest, "We forced him into this situation by limiting his economic opportunities when we confiscated his land, and we engendered his hatred through our attitudes and actions toward him." Not once does anyone acknowledge, "Having been formally evicted from his house, Lester is without shelter and is thus exposed in exaggerated manner to the crushing influence of his own facticity, because the related institutions of private property and bourgeois civil law have deprived him of shelter" (Holloway 127). The community must reconstruct Ballard's utility without revealing its own role in his creation or reconstitution through these discursive acts, telling and retelling Ballard's story as its own version of the "truth." In *Child of God*, as in the stories of Dorothy Allison that Jillian Sandell discusses, the "emphasis on storytelling also demonstrates how meanings and histories are always both relational and contestable. There is no single truth, only versions of the 'truth'" (218). Through the varying narrations, the community tries to rationalize its role in the production and destruction of Lester Ballard. Rather than concentrating on his dispossession, created with the reappropriation of Lester's farm, the community tries to inscribe him in their collective consciousness as an inexplicable sociopath.

Bell believes, "Since the narration has been so scrupulously decentralized from the beginning, it seems intended to be as much about the place and the people in it as about Lester himself" (54). The community *needs* him as its collective nightmare. As in most "horror" stories, the objective of the telling is to warn the listener against acts of deviance. Time and time again, the victims of horror genre demons are individuals who engage in deviant acts. The horror tale where the origin and creation of the antagonistic-protagonist is deconstructed remains a recent literary development. Historically, such macabre tales repeat and their victims are most often those of ill repute. Jack the Ripper murdered prostitutes; Jason of *Friday the 13th* and Michael Myers of *Halloween* always kill scantly-clad, fornicating teenagers. When they finally assault the texts' protagonist or the society's selected representative, they meet their match, just like Lester Ballard does. The Frog Mountain community consciously attempts no deconstruction of the "how" of Ballard's creation, but the tales and the acts of telling them reveal continuing attempts at rationalizing Ballard's existence. The community members cannot make him fit easily into the category they have prepared for him. Perhaps this is because "the fact that stories about impoverished whites have been virtually *un*tellable suggests a profound collective anxiety about what such narratives might reveal" (Sandell 213). Carelessly constructed stories might reveal the society's role in them. Therefore, each "pocketknife" narrative is a carefully structured comparative one, with Lester always as the superlative example of deviance.

The narrators, who represent the collective psyche of the community, try to disconnect themselves from Ballard in several ways. According to one narrator, "Ballard never could hold his head right" after Buster smashed his cranium with an axe; Lester "just laid there and was bleedin at the ears" (*COG* 9). Perhaps the head trauma tripped a wire in his brain that made him go berserk. Bartlett claims, "The folk would like to assimilate Ballard by framing him as an example of superlative 'meanness'" (7), as the story told about the Finney boy demonstrates (*COG* 17–18). Another narrator tries to show that Lester "never was right after his daddy killed hisself"; he tries to blame Lester's deviance on the absence of his parents — "mother had run off, I don't know where nor who with" — and the spectacle of seeing his own "old man's eyes ... run out on stems like a crawfish and his tongue blacker'n a chow dog's" (21). The community uses the classic "broken home" scenario. The narrator ends this story by comparing Lester with Gresham, who sang the "chicken shit blues" at his wife's funeral, and who still "wasn't a patch on Lester Ballard for crazy" (*COG* 22). This story takes the responsibility for Lester away from the community's actions and places it on his fickle, disloyal mother and his cowardly dead father.

In the narration about the cow whose neck Lester broke by pulling her off the ground with a tractor, the narrator reveals his opinion of Lester's lack of common sense and on his quick temper, perhaps suggesting that it could be the preface to his delinquency (35). The community even tries to blame Lester's ancestry by tying his grandfather to the infamous White Caps and by saying that his uncle was a criminal hanged in Hattiesburg. Even so, the narrator concludes with this superlative: "I'll say one thing for Lester though. You can trace em back to Adam if you want and goddamn if he didn't outstrip them all," a remark that gets the general agreement of the gathered listeners (81). So, perhaps heredity and genealogy cannot account for Ballard. The ambivalence remains.

Two stories that speak most directly to this ambivalence are not directly related to Lester at all: the story about boxing the carnival gorilla (59–60) and the other about Tom Davis and the White Caps (165–168). These stories bring the ambivalence of the Lester Ballard legend to the surface. One storyteller begins his tale by admiring Lester's prowess with a rifle. This admiration segues into reminiscence about a boxing match with an ape. The ape is a small thing, as the narrator — drunk and trying to impress a girl — remembers, so he gets in the ring with it. After hitting the creature a couple times, the narrator feels pretty good about his boxing skills — that is, until the ape jumps on his head and nearly rips his jaw off (58–60). He forgets that the ape does not play by the rules of the ring; he does not possess an ethical creed against lethal force. He is a mad monkey and he wants to create pain. This story, when interpreted with Lester in mind, posits the sociopath in the position of the ape and reveals two things: (a) never judge an opponent by his size, especially if he does not play by the same rules of engagement; and (b) by assuming his superiority, the narrator backs up the ape just enough and hits him just enough to piss him off. Then the monster emerges. And so it goes with Lester Ballard. He might try to abide by the rules or to parody social norms, but he falls short.

The nervous subtext of this narration is that the man should have known better than to step in the ring in the first place; perhaps the community should have likewise left Lester alone. The narrator's official interpretation, however, leans toward the ape being "wired differently," while a deconstruction of the tale shows that the man should have known better than to push the monkey into a corner. Who was the dumb ape in this situation? The narrator quickly realizes, though, that sometimes discretion is indeed the better part of valor.

The second narrative that indirectly reflects on Ballard and allows an intertextual subversive reading of the community's narratives is the legend about Tom Davis. At first glance, the comparison between Ballard and the two executed White Caps seems fairly simple. Because Lester's grandfather has been identified as a White Cap, and because everyone in the community knows that his uncle was hanged in Hattiesburg, a reader will most likely come to the conclusion that Lester's meanness, like that of his White Cap predecessors, is both unwarranted and worth punishing. This, coupled with the similarities between the auction scene at the novel's opening and the scene of the hanging of the last two White Caps, reveals the collective and unilateral opposition of the community to the perpetrators of such meanness. However, a subversive reading of this story might equate Tom Davis and Lester Ballard — they do, after all, both become legends. Certainly, they might diametrically oppose one another in heroism and infamy, but their stories are both revered as discursive legends that seem to haunt the community landscape, rising to be told and retold, to be reshaped with each retelling. Ballard and Davis both police and punish social deviants; they both clean up the hillbilly riffraff of Sevier County; they both occupy space in Sevier County's discursive tradition.

While Mr. Wade talks, both Sheriff Fate and the deputy identify with Tom Davis and not with the White Caps. Davis represents the law, so this identification seems most logical. But Tom Davis can also be seen as a stronger vigilante who punishes weaker vigilantes. The readers of *Child of God* may also identify most with the community that condemns Lester Ballard as the pathetic, bloodcurdling delinquent. Nevertheless, Mr. Wade's tale complicates the policemen's identification with Davis and the community's condemnation of Ballard. When the deputy asks Mr. Wade if he thinks "people was meaner then than they are now," Mr. Wade replies, "I think people are the same from the day God first made one." Then, as they go up the courthouse steps, Wade segues from the general meanness of the human population to the specific meanness of a community that will not leave alone an old hermit who lived "out on House Mountain" (168). Mr. Wade inverts the focus of his comments from the delinquents of the community to the community members themselves, or the "people who were used to going by his hole in the rocks and throwing in stones on a dare and calling him to come out" (168). He tells this tale at the same chronological moment in the novel that Lester is moving his corpse society to a cave. This inversion highlights the ambivalence of the legends — both Davis's and Ballard's — and demonstrates how attempts to compartmentalize through mythic re-creation inherently fail; it trains the focus of critique on the community rather than just on Ballard or the old hermit.

The problem that Mr. Wade points out is not that a community seeks to reinscribe events in legend, but that it denies the various interpretations of those legends and its own definitive role in those legends. By reifying Lester as a social deviant without recognizing his utility as that deviant, the community remains blind to the necessity of oppositional figures like Ballard. They forget that they at first licensed the actions of the White Caps (Luce, "White Caps" 44). They admit no responsibility for the creation and nurturing of Ballard the man or Ballard the legend. Ballard is inextricably a part of this culture: he is just the perversion of the human condition that allows the recognition of normalcy. In this way, Ballard's status as a resistive delinquent aids and abets hegemonic control. He demonstrates a need for that hegemony's social control in the face of potential anarchy. The community wanted the White Caps to police "lewd women," but when they crossed the line with the Whaley family and others, they, like Ballard, had to be reeled in and reinscribed. That hegemony uses Lester Ballard: alive he is the scourge who disciplines and punishes the other delinquents; institutionalized, he becomes the focus of the state's collection and categorization of knowledge about the extremities of the human mental condition; dead, he trains those who seek to keep people alive, but who also use "illness," "disease," and pathology to classify "others" and to construct "difference." Through his legend Ballard becomes the marginal character who remains discursively central, Sevier County's most nefarious and talked-about favorite son.

Ballard's community constructs him by constraining his economic and social potential. It uses him to control the delinquent populace; when he tries to invert the position approved for him by the hegemony by attacking the civilized Greer, the community cuts him down. They relinquish him to the state, which eventually eviscerates him and finally scrapes him "from the table into a plastic bag" (*COG* 194). The community then repackages him in a form that they think they can control. The result, however, is an even more ambivalent creature — myth.

Four

The Construction and Maintenence of an Icon, or Fantasizing the Mountaineer

In the early nineteenth century, "Appalachia as terra incognita was not seen to differ in this respect from other unexplored or undeveloped areas of the nation" (Shapiro, *Appalachia on Our Mind* xiii). The continent was as yet mostly unexplored by Europeans and pockets of isolation existed everywhere; for colonial and antebellum Americans, "a conception of Appalachia as a distinct region of the nation did not exist in physiographic terms.... [T]he identification of Appalachia as a thing-in-itself was the product of a later consciousness" (xiii). This "product" has since been utilized for the exploitation of a region, the oppression of a people, and the general depopulation of the mountain landscape by entities in positions of authority that possess a variety of ulterior motives and interests. The creation of *Appalachia* was never an accident; the literature about the Appalachian Mountains has not merely described phenomena associated with the region, it has actually created and maintained the entity known as *Appalachia*. According to Ronald Lewis, "Appalachia is a region without a formal history," therefore, *Appalachia* could be "invented in the caricatures and atmospheric landscapes of the escapist fiction [local colorists] penned to entertain the emergent urban middle class. The accuracy of these stories and travelogues, the dominant idioms of this genre, generated little or no critical evaluation of their characterizations of either mountain people or the landscape itself" (21).[6]

Thus, the *mountaineer* has emerged from a whole slew of documentation about a supposedly "other" people existing just beyond the reach of modern culture. Through the cultural creation of the mythical mountaineer, these real mountain people have been categorized, compartmentalized and disciplined; they have been placed "in a field of surveillance [that] also situates them in a network of writing; it engages them in a whole mass of documents that capture and fix them"; though derived from fictional origins, literary and historical examinations of the mountaineer have been "accompanied at the same time by a system of intense registration and of documentary accumulation" (*DP* 189). This process began before white people ever settled the Appalachians. The subjective documentation of surveyors like William Byrd II initiated the encapsulation of poor whites who would later migrate to the mountains and become mountaineers; for instance, Anthony Harkins, in his *Hillbilly: A Cultural History of an American Icon*, locates the genesis of *Appalachian* writing in men like Byrd, Charles Woodmason, D.R. Hundley, Augustus B. Longstreet, George Washington Harris, and others, all of whom had vested economic interests in the development of the mountain region (14–45). Travelers and surveyors continued writing about their Appalachian journeys and continued objectifying the mountain people into the nineteenth century, when Will Wallace Harney published "A Strange Land and Peculiar People" in *Lippincott's Magazine* in 1873 (Shapiro, *Appalachia on Our Mind* 3). By then, George Washington Harris, whose Appalachian tales influenced authors Mark Twain and William Faulkner and even cartoonist Billy DeBeck, had published his stories about the trickster-mountaineer Sut Lovingood in *The Spirit of the Times*, a widely circulated magazine of the 1840s and 1850s (Harkins 18–19). While Harris published his works as fiction, Harney acknowledges no debt to the Southwest humorists—Harris, Augustus Longstreet, Johnson Hooper—or the emerging local-colorists in his depictions of the mountaineers.

Such "documentation" of the mountaineer often moved in conjunction with outside economic interests in mountain development; everyone needed an explanation for the mountaineers' perceived "otherness," and the producers of academic discourse, philanthropic idealism, and popular literature filled this need. So when Berea College (Berea, Kentucky) president William Goddall Frost published "Our Contemporary Ancestors in the Southern Mountains" in 1899, he cemented the connection between fiction and reality and helped to further legitimate the missions of academic and philanthropic institutions like Berea who also had a stake in *Appalachia*.

The Opportunists: Part I

A perfect example of this synthesis is John Fox Jr., who "contributed to a distinct genre of local color fiction that simultaneously created, exploited, and tried to explain images of the mountain South as a place that was vastly out of step, culturally and economically, with progressive trends of industrializing and urbanizing late nineteenth-century America" (Billings and Blee 8). While Fox's novels came to be recognized for their supposed authenticity, his motivation for their creation remains suspect. According to Darlene Wilson, "After his graduation from Harvard in 1883, John himself became an integral absentee player in promoting interest and continued investment in schemes involving the [Big Stone] Gap and its surrounding wealth of bituminous coal and timber" (Wilson 106). She concludes that Fox was an impostor who disliked the mountains he wrote about: "Despite his claims to authenticity, John's experience in the mountains and with mountain people were strictly self-limited — he despised his family's home as 'commonplace' and retreated there only when his pockets were empty, his presence was required for his own bankruptcy or other court proceedings, or when more interesting invitations were not at hand" (106). John Fox Jr. found inspiration not in the true lives of the mountain people, but in the bankable guarantee of the fictions he could extract from the region and sell. The most garish and unseemly fictional "details" about mountain life would simultaneously sell more novels *and* paint a picture of the mountain inhabitants that would lessen their standing in the American consciousness. The mountain degeneracy Fox portrayed in his fiction legitimated the intervention of outside interests while delegitimizing the claims and concerns of the mountain inhabitants. Purposefully or not, "John Fox Jr. perpetrated and then perpetuated the myth of Appalachian otherness to facilitate absentee corporate hegemony by marginalizing indigenous residents economically and politically" (R. Lewis 22). Mountaineers, in the fiction of John Fox Jr., became commodities compartmentalized on the margins of a quickly modernizing America.

So much of the information "gathered" by many of the most well-known local colorists was secondhand. Mary Noailles Murfree "in fact knew very little about Appalachia. Her own observations of the region and its people were limited to girlhood summers spent at Beersheba Springs, a favorite watering place of the Tennessee gentry.... [T]he popularity of Murfree's sketches did not depend on the validity of her private experience so much as on her ability to establish the otherness of Appalachia as a matter of fact rather than of mere unfamiliarity" (Shapiro, *Appalachia on Our Mind* 19–20). Anthony Harkins cites Fox, Rebecca Harding Davis, James Lane Allen, Mary Noailles Murfree, and others as the "local color" writers of the late nineteenth century who continued to embellish the images of the mountaineer, though their fictions had little basis in reality (Harkins 29–33).

Despite the fact that the images the local colorists perpetuated were fictions, a field of writing sprang up around the mountaineer which simultaneously allowed his definition and his objectification in relation to the rest of

American society because "at the heart of local-color writing is comparison, a perception of alternative modes of life, a confrontation between the 'we' readers and the 'them' read about" (*Appalachia on Our Mind* 14–15); what remains problematic about the work of the local colorists, however, is the fact that "what provided the focus for the sketches of the American local colorists was never a contrast between alternative social or cultural systems, but rather a *perception of the peculiarity* of the life in the 'little corners' of America that they described" (14–15, emphasis added). Because of the continued conflation of the mountain reality and the image of *Appalachia*, the real-life mountaineer and the modern American society that seemingly had passed him by were disciplined by a series of fictions whose potency remains today, as the inquiries of Anthony Harkins, J.W. Williamson, Wilma Dykeman, and others prove. Despite the fact that mountain people were then, unlike the stereotypes, neither exclusively subsistence farmers nor completely isolated from the rest of the world, in the minds of the general population they remain "inundated by stereotypical portrayals of shiftless, drunken, promiscuous, and bare-footed people, living in blissful squalor beyond the reach of civilization"; thereby "many Americans outside the southern mountains came to see little or no difference between the 'real' southern mountaineers and their cultural image" (Harkins 4). Efforts to remedy this cultural image have fallen short because they have been grounded in similar stereotypes. Harkins notes:

> In response to such widespread acceptance of these pejorative portrayals, writers, photographers, and artists who were ostensibly sympathetic to the mountain people created a distinct, but parallel construction, the stalwart, forthright, and picturesque mountaineer. But this construct was premised on the same notion of a mythic white population wholly isolated from modern civilization. As a result, images of noble mountaineers intended to delegitimize hillbilly caricatures reinforced these portraits and perpetuated the idea that the southern mountain people were a separate "race" in, but not of white America [4–5].

As an "othered" culture within American society, *Appalachia* and its inhabitants still present a poor, backward, static counterpoint to the rapid industrial advancement of the surrounding areas; the supposed degeneracy and social backwardness of the Appalachian region, based in fictions though they are, make the region's population responsible for its own social and economic disenfranchisement even though much of that disenfranchisement actually results from economic conditions far beyond the inhabitants' control. In conflicts between mountain inhabitants and those in positions of authority — the extractive industries, the benevolent societies, the government — Americans outside the mountains, though they might share economic situations with the mountaineer, have historically sided with those in positions of authority because the fictions associated with hillbillies — bootlegging, feuding, incest, bestiality, laziness, and limited intelligence — have portrayed the mountaineer as unworthy of sympathy and/or advocacy, but nonetheless in need of outside intervention and benevolence.

Cormac McCarthy came to the mountains when his father brought the family to Knoxville, Tennessee, to take a job as a lawyer for the authorities — specifically the Tennessee Valley Authority — in the 1930s. McCarthy's depictions of Knoxville and the surrounding region demonstrate his intimate familiarity with the people and the landscape, but like all interpreters of culture, McCarthy does not escape the influences of regional stereotypes. When *The Orchard Keeper* came out in 1965, President Kennedy's and President Johnson's efforts at regional uplift were ongoing. America was focused on the Appalachian mountains; pictures of squalor filled pages of national magazines and "hillbilly" music inundated the radio airwaves. Harkins says:

> The enormous success of commercially recorded rural white music, today commonly labeled "country music," played a central role in putting the word hillbilly and its image squarely on the national cultural map. Country music's identity was so completely entwined with the "hillbilly" concept that between its commercial origins in the early 1920s and its emergence as a major cultural force in the 1950s it was nearly universally known as "hillbilly music" [71].

McCarthy could not and did not avoid the pervasiveness of these influences, as he proves in *Suttree*, a novel initiated in the 1960s. Suttree and the prostitute Joyce discuss the music on the radio and she asks him, "You like hillbilly?" She claims, "I used to hate it" (*Suttree* 392). McCarthy would have known the music of Hank Williams, Bill Monroe, Flatt and Scruggs, and the Carter Family. Living in Knoxville, he would have had no way to avoid it, and it makes its way into his fiction: when Lester Ballard discovers the asphyxiated couple in the car at the Frog Mountain turnaround in *Child of God*, a hillbilly gospel song plays on the radio (*COG* 86). It seems, too, that McCarthy could have hardly avoided Billy DeBeck's *Snuffy Smith*, or Al Capp's *Li'l Abner*. Again according to Harkins, "At the height of its popularity in the 1940s and 1950s, *Li'l Abner* was carried by nearly 900 newspapers in the United States" (124). These were McCarthy's formative years and the decades prior to the writing of his Appalachian novels. It is reasonable to assume that as a budding writer and observer of culture, McCarthy might have glanced at a newspaper or magazine and that the images put forth in "popular" culture might have affected his musings on mountain characters. It would have also given him notions about the marketability of such images; novels about Appalachian characters were quite topical in the late 1960s and early 1970s, just as they were during John Fox's time. Harkins, in his *Hillbilly: A Cultural History of an American Icon*, has done some of the most extensive research on the hillbilly phenomenon. According to Harkins, Paul Webb's *The Mountain Boys*, created by a man who "did not set foot in the southern mountains until six months after he began" the comic series, ran in *Esquire* off and on from 1934 to 1958 (103–105). Likewise, *Snuffy Smith* and *Li'l Abner* first appeared in 1934. The creators of these cartoons did little original research for their characters, opting instead to fill their pages with stereotypes; they propagated mythic environments that possessed no corresponding realities. McCarthy would have been familiar with these national imaginings of *Appalachia*. To assume otherwise would be naïve.

The Appalachian mountains remained a poor, destitute, liminal space in the American consciousness as late as the 1960s and 1970s, and McCarthy uses that consciousness to his advantage. Duane R. Carr suggests that McCarthy utilizes "some of the most blatant stereotypes of Southern 'rednecks' in contemporary American" literature, and he does, but his work also performs an iconoclastic dismantling of these images (9).[7] Post-structural criticism of history and literature expose the informal history of Appalachia as having an archeology that was motivated by the economic, sociocultural, and political concerns of the people who vested themselves in its creation; postmodern literature presents a "dialectic between past and present [which] serves a purpose antithetical to uses of history that would maintain a sanctified past, turning the tools of this mythic system against the system itself to deconstruct the notion of a bygone golden area" (Guinn 94). Many critics have argued as to whether or not McCarthy is a "postmodern" writer. David Holloway best characterizes McCarthy's relationship to modernism and postmodernism when he says that McCarthy

> clearly shares [Fredric] Jameson's disinclination to pit realist conventions against modernist or postmodernist codes in some rigid binary that would privilege the epistemology of one narrative mode over another.... [M]cCarthy's is a writing that acknowledges the need to accommodate the insights of postmodern thinking but that simultaneously remains attached to the modernist assumption that narrative can and should stand apart from the world, in order to engage and go to work against it [43].

Whether or not McCarthy's work *can* stand outside the world remains a matter of debate.

In his "Atavism and the Exploded Metanarrative," Guinn explores how McCarthy dismantles the myth of the South put forward by authors of the Southern Renascence. He claims that in McCarthy's work "we may observe a clearly delineated struggle between modern and postmodern, old and new, in the evolving landscape of southern literature" (92). In the same way,

Four. The Construction and Maintenance of an Icon

McCarthy's iconoclastic renderings of the iconography of *Appalachia* destabilizes the stereotypes while employing them. On the surface, it appears that he uses recognizable images to expose the "difference" of the mountain people; yet, the way in which he uses his characterizations to indict the cultural creation of those hillbilly images exposes the cultural complicity in their creation and the subsequent social, economic, and political objectification of the mountaineer. McCarthy's characters embody many of the stereotypes associated with mountaineers, but his tales remain complex artifacts wherein he simultaneously engages and deconstructs these stereotypes and images. He foregrounds the process of how stereotypes are manipulated within the scope of his narratives.

Arthur Ownby of *The Orchard Keeper* is the perfect example of this idea. The reader of the novel recognizes "Ownby himself [as] a bastion of a pastoral and communal order that he sees disappearing before his eyes, a character who acts as a conduit for other ways of knowing and understanding the world that are at odds with the rigid modernistic forces" (Walsh, "There's NO Place Like Holme" 32). To the social worker, who presumably has been sent to the mountains to help "uplift" the people there, Ownby presents the quintessential case of the mountaineer: he is Devil Anse Hatfield and Sut Lovingood all rolled up in an aged, antisocial bundle. The young man characterizes Ownby as an "anomic type," not just because of Ownby's hostility, but because he himself possesses a preprogrammed list of stereotypes that posit Ownby — whose motives do not adhere to the prescriptions of the society that incarcerates him — as a vagrant who remains violently resistant to modernity (*OK* 222). Thus, as a representative of "the Welfare Bureau for the county," as one in involved with social services "documentation," the bureaucratic asker-of-questions "would like to have a record of your case for our, our records, you see" (218–219). In the county mental ward, Ownby is "under the gaze of a permanent corpus of knowledge"; the examination of Ownby in this institutional setting helps constitute "a comparative system that made possible the measurement of overall phenomena, the description of groups, the characterization of collective facts, the calculation of the gaps between individuals, their distribution in a given 'population'" (*DP* 190). Foucault is of course describing an individuating function of the examination. Stereotyping — as in the case between the social worker and Ownby and in many instances between authority and the mountaineer — allows those in examining positions to distribute those being examined into characterizations and categories that they may not, in reality, fit into. Mountaineers seldom fit the stereotypes applied to them, but that rarely keeps them from being thusly stereotyped when authority documents their lives. For the social worker attempting to uplift an economically and socially depressed population, Ownby's case gives credence to the theories about the mountaineer. For authorities attempting to discipline a mountain population, literature and documentation about the mountaineer provide the fodder from which descriptions, characterizations, calculations, and distributions are derived. When the social worker hesitates — "for our, our records you see" — it is because his real purpose is not to help Ownby, but merely to make a case of him. Ownby's life story "is no longer a monument for future memory, but a document for possible use" (*DP* 191). The county worker's perceptions of Uncle Ather, and how he subsequently labels him, stem from his prior knowledge of mountaineer circumstance, and his examination of this man will thereafter enter into that body of comparison.

Arthur Ownby initiates a critique of the way his society relates to him as an individual and as a type. The young social worker's flippant characterization of Ownby demonstrates how stereotypes objectify individuals and groups of people, making them shoulder the blame for social and economic conditions far beyond the scope of their control; it also allows those people to become subjects of study, myth, and legend. Extractive industrialists, purveyors of literature, denominational uplifters, and even academics have all benefited from the iconography of *Appalachia*. Some treatments of the mountaineer image remain more complex than others and they provide avenues for subversive readings of those stereotypes. McCarthy's novels are such treatments. Lester Ballard is not the unnamed, brute rapist of Dickey's *Deliverance*; Marion Sylder's understanding of his relationship with Jefferson Gifford is much more complex than Bo and Luke Duke's mindless evasion of Roscoe P. Coltrain; Arthur Ownby might sound like Jed Clampett or Uncle Jesse Duke when he tells John Wesley Rattner, Johnny Romines, and Warn Pulliam a story, but his violent rejection of the government tower more closely resembles the cantankerous, violent attitudes of Snuffy Smith.

McCarthy uses a variety of *Appalachian* stereotypes and simultaneously deconstructs them: the drunken, lazy, degenerate buffoon, the sexually promiscuous mountain woman, the cantankerous old mountain man, the predatory hillbilly vagrant, the innocent mountain lad and lass, the ignorant hillbilly-come-to-town, the anti-establishment, opportunistic bootlegger. Most importantly, he recreates a fantasy-mythic Appalachian space in the environment and setting of *Outer Dark*, one that — much like the historical invention of *Appalachia* itself — reflects the projection of a cultural psychology more than an actual place. Before moving forward with an analysis of McCarthy's manipulation of *Appalachian* iconography, however, I must first examine how and why those fictional images have become so readily associated with the real people of the Appalachian Mountains.

The Engrossers

One of the earliest accounts of travel on the western edge of colonial American settlement helps to form the *ur*-history of *Appalachia* and her mountaineer people. William Byrd II, "an elite Virginia planter who was educated in the finest schools in England," while surveying the borderlands of Virginia and North Carolina in 1728, penned one of the first accounts "of the social category writers and scholars would later label 'southern poor whites'" (Harkins 15). Despite traveling and surveying mainly east of the mountains one hundred years before the removal of the indigenous American tribes, Byrd's characterizations of the people in the Dismal Swamp region of Virginia serve as precursors for many of the images that later appear in descriptions of mountaineers: the "strangely ambivalent perception of the backwoods people he encounters reflects the ambiguity that would thereafter always characterize hillbilly imagery" (15). Byrd's account is oft quoted as the genesis for the mountaineer/hillbilly image:

> Surely there is no place in the World where the Inhabitants live with less Labor than in N Carolina. It approaches nearer to the description of Lubberland than any other.... The Men, for their Parts, just like the Indians, impose all the Work upon the poor Women. They make their Wives rise out of their Beds early in the Morning, at the same time that they lye and Snore, till the Sun has run one third of his course.... Then, after Stretching and Yawning for half an Hour, they light their Pipes, and, under the Protection of a cloud of Smoak, venture out into the open Air; tho,' if it happens to be never so little cold, they quickly return Shivering into the Chimney corner [quoted in Ledford 59].

As Byrd surveyed the land to demarcate the border between North Carolina and Virginia, he endeavored to build curiosity about the mountains in order to encourage westward expansion. His view is that the "geographic terrain is significant only for what can be used or sold from the land.... [W]ith vested interests in the commodification of the region's minerals, plants, and waters, Byrd sees the mountains in a congenial light"; however, "concern over landownership on the frontier and acquisition of mineral rights manifests itself in negative descriptions of settlers, themselves a source of social and class anxiety because of their association with the potentially rich land" (Ledford 58). Similar accounts of poor rural whites can be found in the writings of Charles Woodmason and D.R. Hundley. Woodmason, "a mid-eighteenth-century itinerant Anglican preacher, shared Byrd's contempt for the slothfulness of the southern rural white"; likewise, Hundley doubts the poor rural white's "industry, intelligence, social propriety, and honor, the essential ingredients for political and social equality" (Harkins 16–17). Each man's aristocratic and/or religious background colored his assessment of the rural people. Often, however, these social, political, and economic interests got lost or sublimated in the writing; the remaining opinions became accepted as historical facts. Subsequently, lower-class white people of the westward lands remained unworthy of its richness and unable to develop it efficiently.

Contemporaneously with Byrd's travels, a bait-and-switch technique played itself out in the relationship between the colonists and the Native American peoples of the mountainous region, people who would soon find themselves decimated by European disease, "demon rum," and forced relocation, all three of which made the movement of white settlers into the Appalachian Mountains more fluid. When addressing the indigenous population, white colonial America developed a discursive strategy that would be used later on the mountaineer. The verbal coupling of "noble savage" demonstrates the paradoxical imagery associated with Native Americans. Raitz and Ulack contend "the earliest image of the Indian was that of the noble Red Man, a virtual child of nature whose social and political organization was perceived in light of the European monarchy. The Indian leadership was approved by the tribe's people, and they had individual rights and freedoms and were recognized as the source of the leader's authority" (91). The Cherokee served as a buffer between the British colonies and the French-supported Indians west of the mountains. So the British and Americans formed alliances with these particular "noble red men" who "were probably the most acculturated of the Native American groups; they had adapted a national council patterned after the American legislative and juridical system, and they had developed their own written language" (Dunaway, *First American Frontier* 256). As Dunaway notes, trade with the colonists changed the Native American economy from one that depended heavily on agriculture to one involving more hunting and gathering. Settlers wanted animal skins and medicinal herbs, while the aboriginals wanted commodities the Europeans could provide: guns, liquor, etc. (*First American Frontier* 31–50). This created the illusion that the Native way of life *had always been* one of calculated homelessness or vagrancy. This idea soon motivated the relocation of the Cherokee themselves and the reallocation of Cherokee lands to speculators and white settlers.

When the Cherokee became an impediment to conquering the lands of the mountains and beyond, "settler ideology held that improvident, sexually abandoned 'lazy Indians' were failing to 'husband' or 'subdue' the resources God had provided and thus should forfeit those resources" (Roediger 21). The Native Americans soon became only the savage half of their moniker: the view of the noble Indian "was most inconvenient, and the requirements of whites were better served if the image was changed to the Indian as a ruthless and godless savage" (Raitz and Ulack 91–92). Despite a lifestyle quite similar to that of the European settlers themselves, these Native Americans were systematically demonized, and later murdered or relocated. The "humanitarian" labeling of relocation efforts was a ruse—something to rationalize displacement and genocide. The final solution to the Cherokee problem was, of course, the 1838 Cherokee "Trail of Tears," when "settler greed for territory was culturally guised as a humanitarian effort to relocate indigenous Appalachians to western wilderness areas that were more suitable to their 'barbaric' lifestyle" (Dunaway, *First American Frontier* 256).

Little more than a century later, when the images and stereotypes of the mountaineer came to prominence, the mountaineer, who once took advantage of an iconography's disciplining effects, might have seen it coming. Ironically, the "noble" aspect of the mountaineer developed later in the construction of his image, when he was needed to fight in rich men's wars—the Civil War, World War I, World War II, and even Vietnam. As David Whisnant notes, the treatments of the mountaineers and Native Americans resound similarly:

> The "savagism" of the Indians was functionally analogous to the mountaineers' social and cultural "backwardness"; both derived from a culturally based misinterpretation. Like the Indians, mountaineers were ambivalently characterized as noble ("100% Americans of the best stock") or ignoble (inbred degenerates, feudists, and moonshiners).... [T]he costs to the Indians were ultimately much higher, of course, than were those to the mountaineers [*All That is Native* 257].

Whereas the Cherokee were forcibly marched by the Jackson administration from North Carolina and Tennessee, through Alabama and eventually to Oklahoma, the highlanders moved deeper into the hollows and mountaintops, where they stayed until the authorities wanted the resources under their feet.

William Byrd II and subsequent travel writers had ulterior motives in their descriptions of the inhabitants of North Carolina. Regardless of his "private feelings, [Byrd] clearly saw a need for a negative image of North Carolinians and backwoodsmen during a colonial struggle for land ownership and for control of capitalist resources such as the Roanoke River. Through anecdote, Byrd engaged in a powerful cultural process of representation that had ramifications for generations to come" (Ledford 59). Byrd surveyed for the Eastern elite who speculated in western (mountain) lands. The "backwoodsmen" who might have settled these speculators' lands were often the unlanded whites Byrd described who would eventually be named hillbillies and mountaineers. This squatter segment of the population served as the vanguard for American westward expansion—but only as long as it kept moving. Problems developed when squatters stopped and attempted to settle lands that had already been speculated by men like George Washington, Thomas

Jefferson, John Sevier, and Robert Morris. Like the Native Americans, the unlanded whites simply got in the way of the economic advancement of more powerful men. Unlike the Native American, though, these vagrant settlers were Anglo-Saxon and Christian, so their physical elimination was difficult to rationalize; besides, they had been useful in decimating the Indians and — in cases like the Revolutionary War battle at King's Mountain — essential in ousting the British. They became the buffer between the new United States and the Native American, French, British, and Spanish interests west of the Appalachians, serving in much the same way as the Cherokee previously had before them. Trailblazing frontiersmen like Daniel Boone and later Davy Crockett became quintessentially American and masculine icons, emblematic tintypes of the rugged mountain man penetrating the hinterland for the advancement of white Americans.[8] Yet vanguard squatters of this type also represented the other side of the coin when "folks who determine causes" decided they did. The same systematic paradox used with the Cherokee develops with the mountaineer for the same reasons, as Bruce Ergood suggests:

> To most the mountaineer is not a person but a prototype: in one period he's an ornery, independent, feuding moonshiner. In another he's a proud, honest, God-fearing subsistence farmer. Still another prototype is the ... down-hearted, beaten, welfare recipient rocking on his dilapidated porch "just a setten." No prototype is accurate; most are stereotypes and carry the prejudice of ignorance of the true situation and a broad extension to the many of the attributes of the few [36–37].

The imagery shifts, not with the reality, but with the needs of authority.

The idea of Appalachian subsistence farming, another erroneous supposition used in creating mountaineer iconography, existed *only* in the novels. Misconceptions about the people who inhabited the territory of the Appalachians hinged on the idea of their isolation and independence from the more progressive society of the 1800s, so the myth of their subsistence way of life contributed to the idea of their "otherness" at a cost of ignoring the real economic insufficiencies and legitimate sociopolitical needs. Walter Precourt writes, "The self-sufficient farm economy formed the basis of folklore about the mountains. It was intriguing to outside observers to witness the ability of certain mountain inhabitants to subsist on produce from the farm and forest, and literature on the mountains focused on this type economy" (92). In *The First American Frontier*, Wilma Dunaway maintains that an entire system of exchange — contrary to historical and literary assumptions — pervaded the southern mountains, so that "by the 1830s, several layers of retailers, brokers, speculators, dealers, wholesalers, and forwarding agents had emerged to offer 'ancillary services connected with marketing'" (233). There might have been

Four. The Construction and Maintenance of an Icon

more relative autonomy from a cash exchange economy, but Appalachian agriculturalists did much more than merely subsist. Like the woman who churns butter to sell at Clark's store in *Outer Dark* (*OD* 102–108; 141), Appalachian mountain farmers engaged in trade of all types. Dunaway concludes, "contrary to popular stereotypes, subsistence farming was *not* characteristic of antebellum Southern Appalachia" (*First American Frontier* 125). A debunker of *Appalachian* myths himself, McCarthy rarely describes his characters engaging in agriculture; they more often exchange commodities.

Outer Dark's Rinthy Holme, on the road as she searches for her son, encounters a family who, "on their chairs in such black immobility ... could have been stone figures quarried from the architecture of an older time" (*OD* 77); they are characters quarried from mythic *Appalachia*. They epitomize the stereotypical mountaineer family—hard-working mother, ineffectual father, lazy son, and "an ancient crone who was without a nose" (57). Nevertheless, they engage in commodity exchange; they are not solely farmers. When the family travels to town, the mother carries a quilt, hoping to sell it; she tells Rinthy, "The last one I sold I got three dollars for it, but it was a double wedding ring" (*OD* 66). Not only is she conscious of the commodity value of her handicraft, she also understands the marketability of different styles, the implication being that the "double wedding ring" would bring more money than a patchwork of scraps because of either the craftsmanship involved or the conventional popularity of the design. This family might be carved out of stone, but it is "enmeshed in capitalist activities as semiproletarians" (Dunaway, *First American Frontier* 127). One of the few characters shown with a farm plot, the woman who churns butter to sell at Clark's store, is also a budding capitalist. Her butter has become such a fetishized commodity that destroying it represents her husband's most effective form of inner-marital hostility (*OD* 108).

Dunaway, Billings, Shapiro, and other more recent Appalachian scholars have shown that the real, historical people of the Appalachian region were not the unsophisticated, backwoods dolts that literature has traditionally portrayed. Truthfully, "there is no archival corroboration for the existence of a 'strange and peculiar' Southern Appalachian 'subculture' that 'challenged America's notions of progress'" (*First American Frontier* 257). They were no more homogenous or backward than any other region of the country. So, the question remains: why have they been portrayed as such?

The answer, of course, is that someone stood to profit from such characterizations. Like the "noble" Cherokee, Anglo-Saxon Protestants who inhabited the mountains of Appalachia had to be displaced socially to justify the further engrossment of Appalachian lands by an absentee elite who presumed to understand the land's economic and political potential much better than it was understood by those poor white squatters. Corporations, the extractive industries, and many government entities historically have made these same presumptions. Precourt maintains, "The process of denigrating local populations for purposes of exploitation contributed to the poverty stereotype" (101); the mountaineers' purpose of land use and inhabitation was never wealth maximization, so "the Appalachian way of life did not fit the market model; it was therefore lacking; it was therefore in need of salvation by outside industrial interests" (101). The idea that the mountaineer agricultural way of life did not fit the market model was, like the iconography itself, based on a falsehood. Nevertheless, the icons have persisted just as the very real economic difficulties of the region have proliferated. Within a systematic disenfranchisement that takes advantage of the mountaineer iconography, the difficulties faced by the inhabitants the Appalachian Mountains become their own doing because they are "a 'deviant subculture' whose problems owe more to physical isolation, depleted gene pools, pathological inbreeding, clan wars, hookworm, moonshining, and welfarism than to the nation's unceasing demands on the region for cheap labor, land, raw materials, and energy" (Whisnant, *Modernizing the Mountaineer* xix). The mountaineer's status as an American "other" allows agents and representatives of government or other "authority" entities to exploit and control him. This iconography has been manipulated in an historical reality where the mountaineer has consistently been characterized as "backward" and in the way of "progress." The image of the mountaineer has become yet another tool in his disciplining within modern culture. "Hillbilly" is a compartmentalization that follows the mountaineer wherever he goes, whether to a coal camp, to a cotton mill village, to a northern city, to a city within the Appalachian mountain region, or into a novel.

The Opportunists: Part II

The work of the local colorists highlighted earlier presents only one chapter in the saga of how the mountaineer has been disciplined by the iconic image that represents him to the rest of the world:

> While earlier generations of local colorists and missionaries had publicized and profited from the alleged "strangeness" and "otherness" of southern mountain society, it took [William Goodall] Frost's 1899 essay, "Our Contemporary Ancestors in the Southern Mountains," to place firmly and finally in the national imagination ... the fully developed stereotype of a large, homogeneous, backward, and isolated "other" America he christened "Appalachian" America [Noe 67].

Four. The Construction and Maintenance of an Icon

As the president of Berea College, Frost's job was the collection and dissemination of knowledge. Yet he and other do-gooders built on the images the local colorists propagated and did so to ensure that the train of donations kept chugging along. Like Noe, Shapiro sees Frost as the individual who lent the image of the mountaineer legitimacy. Whereas Fox and Mary Murfree and James Lane Allen and others like them "had been content to see mountain life as quaint and picturesque, and for this reason inherently interesting," they were followed by Frost and "the agents of denominational benevolence [who] necessarily saw Appalachian otherness as an undesirable condition and viewed the 'peculiarities' of mountain life as social problems in need of remedial actions" (*Appalachia on Our Mind* 60). Frost was the "architect" for the view of *Appalachia* as a homogeneous culture: "By describing the mountainous portions of eight southern states as a legitimately discrete region of the nation, Frost did not so much 'discover' Appalachia as invent it" (119, 121). Denominational benevolence organizations like Frost's did not consciously try to disfranchise the mountaineer; they did, however, want to convert the mountaineer to modernity. Therefore, they used the pejorative image of the mountaineer to "support their claim to attention from the churches' boards and societies, and to financial support from their membership, while the very existence of a substantial body of literature describing a strange land and peculiar people in the southern mountains lent credence to their assertions of Appalachian otherness" (*Appalachia on Our Mind* 57). John Fox Jr. and other local colorists "had to insist on the reality of Appalachian otherness lest their work lose its validity and its appeal"; Frost and his denominational contemporaries "had to insist on the reality of the mountaineers' need lest their work lose its purpose" (61). These purveyors of Christian benevolence headed to "the poorest mountain regions they could find to minister good deeds," and then they wrote about their experiences in order to confirm their donors' notions about the mountains so that they might continue to contribute and ensure the continuing mission of Christian benevolence (Williamson 197). The more needy the people of eastern Kentucky appeared, the more essential Frost's Berea College became.

More troubling even than the causal connections between capitalist development and the work of the local colorists, or the way in which the agents of denominational benevolence manipulated the writings of the local colorists for the advancement of their own work, is the complicity of supposedly objective social scientists and reformers in the perpetuation of the mountaineer/hillbilly iconography. Social scientists "inherited a discursive tradition about the region as a place apart, a traditional society in the midst of modern America that was isolated in space and frozen in time, that is, a place 'where time stood still.' That this depiction was false detracted little from its force or longevity" (Billings and Blee 157–158). Ellen Churchill Semple, widely respected and oft quoted among scholars of all things Appalachian, seems to fall into this trap. According to Billings and Blee, in her 1910 essay on the mountain feuds in Kentucky, "The Anglo-Saxons of the Kentucky Mountains," Semple's account of Appalachian feuding "appears, at least in part, to have been lifted without citation from a magazine article by J. Stoddard Johnson published two years earlier in *The Cosmopolitan*" (308). Semple plagiarized her information by paraphrasing Johnson rather than basing her interpretations on research she personally conducted. Additionally,

> [m]uch of what appears to be commentary on Kentucky mountain feuds was really commentary on *writings* about feuds as popular and scholarly authors alike read and borrowed from one another freely.... [S]ince a scholar, Semple, relied on a popularizer, Johnson, who, it turns out, had originally cited an often quoted passage from John Fox, Jr.'s fiction as an authoritative description of the nature of feuds, *it is reasonable to conclude that science, journalism, and fiction writing closely influenced one another* in the creation of the popular imagination about feuding [308–309, emphasis added].

The lines between history, scholarship, literature and profit continue to blur. Ronald Eller gives an answer as to why authors, reformers, social scientists, and outside observers might conflate the fictional imagery and the reality of the mountaineer: "Because metaphor was more interesting than reality, the Appalachian present came to be linked with the American past, and eventually the analogy was accepted as fact" (*Miners* xvi).

    The mountaineer became intimately connected with the white racial past as well. The metaphor may be more intriguing, but the ramifications of such flippancy for real people are immense. For nearly three hundred years, a fictional icon has shaped the economic, political, and social plight of the mountain people. The fiction has served its purpose well. Novels and essays and newspaper reports and films and television shows about delinquent hillbillies have amassed to form the Appalachian equivalent of what Michel Foucault named the *fait divers*, seemingly comprehensive accounts of various "delinquent" activities. According to Foucault, the French society he examines became inundated with daily reports of crime; entire newspapers were devoted to the subject. As with the mountaineer, in France it was "a patient attempt to impose a highly specific grid on the common perception of delinquents: to present them as close by, everywhere present and everywhere to be feared" (*DP* 286). Though perhaps not conscious or purposeful, accounts like William Byrd's and Ellen Churchill Semple's stigmatized the mountaineer as latently criminal and dangerous. Accounts of feuds and Appalachian "backwardness," and pictures of Appalachian degeneracy like those widely published during President Lyndon Johnson's "War on Poverty," desensitized the public, even though they were meant to raise awareness and sympathy. They painted the southern mountains "as a dark zone of chaos and violence in desperate need of 'civilizing' influences from the outside"; they gave "American readers a framework through which to view the profound changes that were taking place" in the mountains (Blee and Billings 134). They brought the mountaineer "problem" into American living rooms. Such "diverse facts" help justify the intrusion of authority into the isolated reaches of the mountains.

The novels and other writings of the local colorists and essays by William Goodall Frost and his denominational contemporaries work in another way too. Detailed in the magazine publications of the day, like Foucault's "crime novel, which began in the broadsheet and in mass-circulation literature," the novels of Fox and Murfree show "an entirely different world, unrelated to [the] familiar, everyday life" of people from metropolitan areas (*DP* 286). The presentation of the mountaineers as "strange and peculiar" makes identification with them difficult. People who share the same socio-economic and political realities, but not the same regional affiliations, cannot relate to their plight. The images in these novels and other writings, like those in the French crime novels Foucault cites, "are there to make the normative middle-class urban spectator feel better about the system of money and power that has him or her in its grasp" (Williamson 20). Furthermore, they

> trivialize complex political and economic issues facing the region to the level of personality traits and cultural quirks. Moonshiners, welfare cheats, coal miners and other Appalachian "types" distance us from the political and economic realities of the region, including our own injustices toward those stereotyped. In the case of Appalachia, such images allow the rest of America to keep the region at arm's length, rather than to confront the systemic problems of a dependent economy, environmental decay, and institutional weakness that challenge mountain communities today [Eller, Foreword x].

These abject stereotypes make it easier to justify the cultural and economic subjugation of an entire region's population.

The Opportunists: Part III

Matthew Guinn demonstrates how McCarthy iconoclastically subverts the literary focus of modernism in general and the Southern Renascence in particular — both of which held that the history presents universal truths for the enlightenment and betterment of humanity. His ideas apply directly to McCarthy's re-creation of *Appalachia's* mythic space in *Outer Dark*. Guinn writes:

Where the modernists used the stability of mythological patterns to inform and order the chaotic present, McCarthy subverts the dialectic. His evocation of the past is antinostalgic; rather than presenting a lost stability, it emphasizes an elemental primitivism that humanity retains, declaring war (in [Vanderbilt new critic Walter] Sullivan's terms) against those venerated "repositories of order and truth" such as cultural mythology and teleological notions of human community [94].

Appalachia is a fictional space generated from the relationship between an Appalachian mountain reality and the collective American psyche; it is a mythic space largely accepted as "truth," at least until recently. McCarthy, in the vanguard of literary mythoclasm, with his "antinostalgic" pen, deconstructs both the mythology of *Appalachia* and the iconography of the mountaineer.

Like so many authors who take Appalachia — both the region and the construct — as their subject, McCarthy uses the associated stereotypes in all of their ambivalence. His novels work in a similar way to Foucault's *fait divers* and crime novels, and they follow the paths cleared by the local colorists and agents of denominational benevolence a century before. The Appalachian characters of his novels often demonstrate sexual deviance, reluctance to engage in legitimate capitalist profit maximization, and other peculiarities of "contemporary ancestors" (though they do not generally engage in subsistence agriculture). They bootleg; they commit violent acts against other mountaineers and outsiders; they go crazy; they talk funny and can barely read; they exhibit an aversion to law enforcement. Rather than merely cashing in on stereotypes, however, McCarthy "takes the language, symbols and images of his culture and inverts their meanings in order to illustrate the destructive consequences of following narratives that are 'false'" (Cant 74); his work foregrounds how *Appalachian* stereotypes are constructed from a collective cultural psyche.

Cormac McCarthy lived in the Appalachian Mountains for much of his life. He moved about "from Knoxville to Asheville to Europe to Waldens Creek outside Pigeon Forge" (Gibson 29), so he is not describing some exotic location he has only heard described by others, as both Mary Noailles Murfree and John Fox Jr. did. McCarthy comes to the Knox and Sevier County courthouse steps toting his own experiences and stories, not hearsay and conjecture. When he crafts Lester Ballard's tale out of the Frog Mountain clay, he "recalls the whelming 60s-era flood that beset Sevierville, leaving merchants to traverse downtown streets in boats"; with Ballard, McCarthy "recalls the early settling of the Waldens Creek area by a real-life Ballard clan" (30). That, of course, is not to say that McCarthy neglects the stereotypes that have historically drawn the mountaineer. To the contrary, he manipulates them with great skill. Ballard, in his vagrancy through the East Tennessee hills and his eventual residence in a cave, perfectly embodies the opposite side of the coin that posits the mountaineer as the vanguard of westward American expansion. He may be a trailblazer, but he is an inverted one; he blazes a trail *under* ground. Lester Ballard is the demonized *Hillbilly*. Nevertheless, McCarthy does not allow the reader to write Lester off as unredeemable or completely *beyond the pale*; he is, after all, the titular "child of God." Lester, who "becomes a hermit and then devolves into a gnome-like creature scampering beneath the ground," is created within his society in much the same way the mountaineer icon itself has been erected monolithically within American culture (Arnold 54). Not privy to the everyday doings of Ballard, his community, as represented by the "pocketknife society" gathered around the Sevier county courthouse, creates the negative images of Ballard (*COG* 48).

The men of the valley town — the county seat of authority, Sevierville — produce a literary icon in Ballard, albeit via oral storytelling, in much the same way as outsiders have constructed the mountaineer. The community representatives struggle to frame Lester, alternately placing the blame for him on themselves (though disguising it in parables) and disavowing him. One narrator who shows admiration for Lester's marksmanship evolves his tale into the story about the boxing ape (*COG* 57–60). In that scene, the narrator tries to read Lester's story as a morality tale for the community: do not mess with a wild animal because he does not play by society's rules. Perhaps the community should not have cornered Lester by repossessing his property. On the other hand, the story about the Finney boy (17–18) demonstrates that Lester was just always mean and took an opportunity to exert his strength over a smaller opponent. In Section I of *Child of God*, a nervousness and guilt bleed through the narrators' words. These narrators want to make sense of Lester and to figure out why he exists amongst them but not *of* them. They blame his immediate ancestors (21–22; 80–81), ascribe to him an inherent violence (17–18; 57–60), and show him as stubborn and unteachable (35–36). Ballard presents other hillbilly attributes, but McCarthy situates these particular characterizations in the mouths of Ballard's own community. Collectively, Ballard's contemporaries' descriptions accomplish the same feat as the literary-historical descriptions of the mountaineer, which "meant the institutionalization of a particular definition of mountain life as squalid and degenerate, of the mountaineers as those who lived in squalor and degeneracy, and of Appalachian otherness as a social problem" (Shapiro, *Appalachia on Our Mind* 61). Even advocates like Harry Caudill and Jack Weller regurgitate some of the stereotypes associated with the mountaineer; when advocates from the mountains themselves or otherwise intimately connected to them buy into the hillbilly image, it goes a long way toward legitimizing that image. This institutionalization is a form of discipline. The men loitering around the courthouse are connected to the authorities, specifically to Sheriff Fate Turner, as some of their conversations indicate. One man, "John," says that he has "rode with [Turner] a lot of times" (*COG* 44) and the sheriff clearly converses with the "pocketknife society" as he passes in and out of the courthouse (48–49; 160–168). The narrators make Ballard "a part of the mythology of his region" (Bell 54). They become spokesmen for a society that "consistently tries to explain Lester's evil acts in such a way as to prove his constitutional difference from them" (Luce, "Cave of Oblivion" 185); they couch him in a collective narration that forms this society's oral equivalent of the *fait divers* and the crime novel where Ballard's "delinquency appears both very close and quite alien, a perpetual threat to everyday life, but extremely distant in its origins and motives" (*DP* 286).

By contextualizing stereotypes in the words of his Sevier County narrators, McCarthy creates a framework of motives and interests for these views. Two things that complicate the use of these stereotypes, however, are the ambivalence of the narrators around the courthouse steps and the extremity to which McCarthy takes Ballard. The pocketknife society never conclusively determines the causes of Ballard's degeneracy; they speculate. McCarthy undercuts the ways the community objectifies Ballard by giving the reader of *Child of God* an objective, matter-of-fact presentation of Ballard and his crimes. He says directly to the reader, "You could say that [Ballard is] sustained by his fellow men, like you" (*COG* 156). The juxtaposition of the superlative degeneracy of Ballard with the fact that he is the titular child of God foregrounds McCarthy's use of stereotype *as stereotype*; it brings the process through which stereotypes are created to the forefront in his fiction; it deconstructs stereotypes through the use and manipulation of them.

To Work or Not to Work

The perception that mountaineers refused to engage the economy in ways that authority might recognize as productive necessitated their discipline. Mountain folk needed be brought into the mainstream economy and into the web of disciplinary relationships of modern culture. The *Appalachian* characters in McCarthy have, in some cases, willfully rejected the institutions of market capitalism; in other situations their positions on the cultural and economic margins make it difficult for them to produce in culturally acceptable ways. Many do not share the modern definition of productivity and efficiency, one that demands work in time-increments rather than a task-completion labor scheme: they, "rather than striving for excellence in corporate relationships, might turn [their] drive for excellence into being a good coon hunter, vegetable gardener, or story teller" (Fisher 18). Marion Sylder, for one, cannot stomach punching the time clock for the pittance he is paid (*OK* 28–31).

Arthur Ownby is the perfect example of a mountaineer who has rejected modern productivity and influence. Ownby's interaction with John Wesley and the other community boys undercuts the jailor's assessment that Ownby is "mean as a snake" (222). Ownby, having once embraced the mechanisms of modernization when he worked on the railroad crew, now actively rejects the intrusion of modernity — with its insistence on enclosure and private property — on what he sees as the natural domain. As far as the reader can tell, Ownby has not held a "real" job since his wife left him for "that goddamned bibledrummer" (156). After that event he allows his homestead to waste away and neglects basic animal husbandry; he sinks into the melancholia of rejection "while the chickens grew thin and the stock screamed for water, while the hogs perished to the last shoat" (155). He rejects the modern world's gradient of occupational validity, choosing instead to take to the woods and gather ginseng for trade. He dismisses the dominant culture's Christianity, subscribing instead to some opaquely defined pantheism. He discards the traditional ideas of productivity: "The orchard went to ruin twenty years before when the fruit had come so thick and no one to pick it that at night the overborne branches cracking sounded in the valley" (52). Ownby himself refused to pick it. He rejects the government installment that represents outside influences, and this rejection of modernity underpins his incarceration. The authorities think him insane because he refuses the essential tenets of the encroaching capitalist society. He operates by seasons, not by a time clock; he is the mountaineer with the (super)natural connection to the wild. The only thing he tends in the orchard is Kenneth Rattner's grave. He needs few commodities; he has no address and he has no job, and for the authorities, such anomie equals sloth — and that too is unacceptable.

Gene Harrogate, Lester Ballard, Culla Holme, and Kenneth Rattner can be seen as other anomic types in McCarthy because none of them will find a residence or *get a job*, though they are industrious in other ways. Harrogate's craftiness takes the inappropriate forms of his many get-rich-quick schemes and his crimes of theft and burglary land him in the state penitentiary. Unable or unwilling to engage in society, Lester Ballard reverts to a barbaric primitivism and becomes a hard-working but perverse version of a hunter/gatherer (Bartlett 4). Culla Holme tries halfheartedly several times to engage in "proper" work and fails every time (*OD* 48–49; 90–94; 207–208). Kenneth

Rattner, a thief and robber, preys on the good will or the bad luck of the people he encounters. Despite his wife's protestations that "he wouldn't take no handout from nobody even if it was the govmint," the elder Rattner works not a single day (*OK* 72–73). He neglects his family, steady work, and the laws of the land, ceasing to be an economic leech only when he encounters a man with stronger financial urges and stronger hands.

Ownby, Harrogate, Ballard, Holme, and Rattner can be characterized by their occupational passivity, but Marion Sylder occupies a place on the social margins *because* of his occupation. As a moonshine runner, Sylder fits an *Appalachian* trope. Appalachian literature and history are full of such characters. Henry Shapiro suggests "conflicts between mountaineers and revenue officers over enforcement of the federal excise tax on whiskey were reported as early as 1867.... [B]y the 1890s, moonshining had become so integral an element in the popular conception of mountain life that discussion of the phenomenon ... became virtually a requirement in descriptive pieces dealing with the region" (*Appalachia on Our Mind* 104). Real mountaineers like NASCAR's Junior Johnson — a blockader-turned-racing champion — and fictional characters like Sylder are making a living *because* their activity is illegal. Moonshiners have gotten so much attention because "the antics of a distiller of corn whiskey in an Appalachian laurel thicket, robbing the federal government of alcoholic beverage revenue, offered much more entertainment than the dry stratagems of a financier coolly juggling accounts and figures to rob thousands of trusting investors of their hard-earned savings" (Dykeman 37). For people writing about *Appalachia*, the illicit manufacture and distribution of distilled spirits evidences the depravity of mountaineers.

Bootlegging, in Sylder's view, is *part of* the legal and economic system, not outside of it. Booze-running is not inherently immoral, as the authorities would suggest; it is just illegal (*OK* 210). Were it not for blockaders, the revenuers would have no reason to treat mountaineers with suspicion, and were it not for the revenuers the blockaders would be nothing more than distributors. Dykeman and other critics demonstrate that the literary and historical focus on conflict between revenuers and moonshiners results from its value as entertainment (37) — that seems mundane enough; but attention to this facet of mountain life without deciphering the economic ramifications inherent therein disproportionately heightens the perception of mountaineer violence and illegality. Under such perceptions the mountaineer operates on the wrong side of the law, and outsiders see only mountaineer subversion. Sylder, however, understands his relationship to authority in a way that can be interpreted as a tacit awareness of Foucauldian power relations where "their existence depends on a multiplicity of points of resistance: these play the role of adversary, target, support, or handle in power relations" (*HS* 95). For Sylder, blockading is a choice; it presents a *better* way to make a living *because* it opposes the mandates of authority (*OK* 213–215). He seems to know that "where there is power, there is resistance, and yet, or rather consequently, this resistance is never in a position of exteriority in relation to power" (*HS* 95). Sylder's problem with Gifford is not that the constable is doing his job, but that he is cheating at it. Gifford cannot catch Sylder, so he must threaten John Wesley with incarceration to gain an upper hand on Sylder. Gifford violates the unspoken parameters of the power relationship, or he has a juvenile understanding of them.

Blood Feuding

The fiction of the local colorists and the writings of the agents of denominational benevolence posited Appalachia as a violent place where people held authority in contempt. The tough-to-reach wilds of the mountains encouraged self-governance but also permitted "mountaineers to engage in feuds, and more specifically the practice of private justice through ambush or 'bushwhacking'" (Shapiro, *Appalachia on Our Mind* 104). Therefore, feuding

> gripped the popular imagination and fastened on the people of southern Appalachia a cultural stereotype of violent irrationality that is still potent today.... [T]his fear, [Henry Shapiro] argues, came not from the reality of Appalachian peculiarity but from but from the needs of middle-class Americans in industrializing America to project their own nostalgia for the past and fears about the future onto a people perceived as different [Waller 348–349].

Waller claims that economic jostling initiated feuds rather than Civil War retribution or family vendettas or some innate mountaineer violence (367). This reality never saw the light of day in traditional depictions because it did not gel with the "sensationalist press coverage" which named the Appalachian region "as 'the land of feuds'" (Billings and Blee 306). In such a context, the mountain people themselves needed to be out of control if the public was to buy the need for civilizing influences, government or industrial intervention, and social reform in the mountains. Furthermore, "as indicators of a disregard for duly constituted authority, feuding and moonshining long had functioned in fiction as overt indicators of the distance which separated Appalachia and America" (*Appalachia on Our Mind* 104). The feud violence Dykeman, Waller, and Shapiro critically uncover in a macro-cultural context, McCarthy reduces to a micro-cultural level, namely in the Rattner-Sylder blood feud and in Arthur Ownby's conflict with the authorities.

Kenneth Rattner deserts his family, but in his wife's mind he has been taken from her and no one in a position of authority will take up her cause of retribution; her desire for private, personal vengeance "might be seen as following naturally from the inadequacy or absence of public agencies to adjudicate disputes between individuals, and/or to provide justice to those who had been wronged" (*Appalachia on Our Mind* 109). In the eyes of the authorities, she and her son are vagrant hillbillies like her husband, as John Wesley himself recognizes: he meets a girl on his way to the creek and his first notion is, "She ain't old enough to own the land to want to run me off of it even if she is big enough" (*OK* 68). They do not pay taxes or otherwise contribute to the economy, so far as the authorities can figure, so why should they bother? The authorities in fact do not care about her situation, as Gifford himself demonstrates when he pokes fun at her, commenting to Mr. Eller, "Wonder if she had a vision about [her husband] bein wanted in three states" (*OK* 235). The inept "law" cannot even find her husband's body, much less avenge his death, so Mildred Rattner makes John Wesley swear to "hunt him out. When you're old enough.... [F]ind the man who took away your daddy.... [Y]ou *swear* it, boy" (*OK* 66–67). That this old crone advocates a vendetta comes as no surprise. According to Blee and Billings, stereotypical "accounts of the feud cast women as steely, ominous characters.... [E]ven in mourning, [Tom] Baker's widow [in the Clay County, Kentucky, White-Garrard feud] looked toward vengeance, swearing her twelve sons to a blood oath to avenge their father's death" (131–132). Even the attitudes of many Appalachian scholars prove how feuding has been misunderstood. Harry Caudill accepts the traditional characterization of feuds, concluding that "the animosities of the feuds shut a prospective bridegroom off from adversary clans," and so contributed to the supposed tendency toward incest (Caudill 84–85).

The irony of the blood feud in the case of *The Orchard Keeper* is twofold: (a) Kenneth Rattner, a no-account highway robber who initiated the conflict with Marion Sylder, was killed in self-defense; and (b) not only does John Wesley never exact vengeance for his father's death, neither he nor his mother ever realizes that the very man who has become one of John Wesley's surrogate fathers actually killed his biological father. In this context, Mildred Rattner's demand of revenge is ridiculous and comical. By soaking the mountain blood feud in irony and impotency, McCarthy exposes the traditional feud as a stereotype. Like Billings and Blee, McCarthy seems to know that "feuds left legacies of understanding, or misunderstanding, of life in the southern mountains," and that erroneously, "this discursive description created an authoritative image of southern mountaineers in the minds of those who lived far outside the Appalachian region" (Billings and Blee 306). McCarthy challenges this "discursive description" by satirizing the traditional blood feud.

Arthur Ownby's battle with the government, on the other hand, is anything but an impotent satire. His personal vendetta with the modernizing culture he sees invading his environment presents a legitimate problem for the authorities — so much so that they come to arrest him three times. The government agents are right to see him as dangerous, but not only because he makes his mark on their tank with homemade shotgun slugs. Ownby's entire existence has been a recurring rejection of modern capitalist culture. He cannot be considered economically productive even by his community's standards, for he harvests nothing from the orchard and he possesses few commodities. As Huffaker says, "He's a right funny old feller, don't have no money at all I don't reckon" (*OK* 197). His true business in the orchard — covering Kenneth Rattner's body with cedar limbs — is a slap in the face of the law. Christopher Walsh claims that Ownby "is unable to comprehend the strength of the forces he is up against, unable to recognize the epochal civil, social, and cultural changes that [are] taking place in Appalachia" (*In the Wake of the Sun* 53), but I see the situation differently. Ownby understands that his "space and mobility are eroded by the increasing influence of state and federal agencies," and he bides his time as long as he can stand it (47). He takes the "twelve circumcised shotgun shells" — a choice of language here that denotes ritual — and becomes a legitimate threat to the authorities by blowing holes in the tank (*OK* 95). His usurpation of modern justice presents "a direct confrontation with the world of more normal American behavior, and in particular with the outsiders' institutions of social control" (*Appalachia on Our Mind* 105). The violence escalates in each episode until a couple of government agents are wounded and Ownby's shack is riddled with bullets and tear gas. Ownby then turns his back on modernity by hiking into the wilderness.

The force opposing the old man simply has more intense power; it "can rely upon 'the law' to further its values and eliminate the key representatives of the opposing tradition" (Brickman 131). The reason Ownby's crime is so offensive to the social order, the reason it must be reined in, lies in the magnitude of the disruption it *could* cause; "the injury that a crime inflicts upon the social body is the disorder that it introduces into it: the scandal that it gives rise to, the example that it gives, the incitement to repeat it if it is not punished" (*DP* 92). Ownby's crime subverts the will and the discipline of authority; it suggests that authority cannot just designate land for its own exclusive use, and that, as Ownby himself thinks, "If I couldn't run em off I could anyway let em know they was one man would let on that he knew what they was up to" (*OK* 229). Ownby makes his "X" on the tank; he signs his name to it. He gives the authorities a big middle finger. They cannot allow that to happen because "one must take into account not the past offense, but the future disorder. Things must be so arranged that the malefactor can have neither any desire to repeat his offense, nor any possibility of having imitators" (*DP* 93). John Wesley's desire to give the hawk bounty back toward novel's end validates the authorities' need to quell Ownby's personal insurrection. The old man does have imitators. But his is a doomed resistance, for the web of discipline is vast and sticky. It extends throughout the social and economic sphere so that like Sylder — whose beef with the authorities is more economic than philosophical — Ownby finds himself caught as he engages in commodity exchange. The authorities institutionalize him at novel's end as part of "these 'ignoble' archives, where the modern play of coercion over bodies, gesture and behaviour has its beginnings" (191). In the crazy house, agents of society's authorities document and categorize him as "light in the head" (*OK* 227).

In a stereotypical feud narrative, Ownby would be fighting with a neighbor over who owned the orchard or who had timber rights on what land; in fact, at one point in his life, he did engage in just such a traditional feud over his wife and it left him with lead shot in his leg (230–231). The incident over the tower, however, is not mountaineer-on-mountaineer violence; it is a specific act of defiance. Ownby is not running from the authorities at that point, he is shooting (at) them. Like Gifford, who in the eyes of Sylder breaks the rules of engagement, Ownby violates the parameters of authority and resistance by attacking the tank and then the men who come to arrest him. This is no petty blood feud, but rather open hostility to the will of the authorities. While the social worker who questions Ownby and the intern who examines him in the state hospital both assume he is merely a disgruntled old delinquent — the intern asks him "What were you doing [to get shot], robbing a henhouse?" (230)— the text makes it blatantly clear that Ownby, even at his advanced age, remains a lucid character with legitimate claims against the authorities' intrusion.

The feud Ownby has with the government uncovers another side of the blood feud stereotype. The characterization of the old orchard keeper allows the reader to sympathize with the old man: he is real and three-dimensional, whereas the agents of authority remain nameless automatons in "clean gray chinos" (196). Ownby is a teacher who upholds the community's code of conduct while the agents of authority betray their neighbors for the paycheck they receive at the end of the month. In this instance and throughout much of McCarthy's work, the people doing the labeling are stereotypical bureaucrats who lack sympathy for their fellow man and the mountaineers are flesh and blood individuals who understand the plight of their economic and social community. Sylder, Ownby and Mildred Rattner seem to legitimate the image of Appalachia as a violent place and mountaineers as violent people hellbent on resisting authority, but McCarthy's text deconstructs the tomes that posit Appalachia as a region more intensely violent and less disciplined than other American regions because he delivers ironic reconceptualizations of so many mountaineer stereotypes, including those of the blockader and the blood feud.

"Unnatural" Sexual Nature

As with the blockader and the blood feud, McCarthy reconceptualizes some of the sexual imagery associated with the Appalachian iconography. Iconographically, hillbillies have a notorious predilection for bestiality. John Boorman, in his film adaptation of James Dickey's *Deliverance*, cemented this image to hillbilly violence when he had the backcountry rapist tell Bobby Trippe to "squeal like a pig." This aspect of the rape scene is exclusive to the movie adaptation, as it appears nowhere in Dickey's novel. Clearly Boorman wanted to make this mountain man more than just a rapist/sodomite, and the bestial associations solidified the deviance. This adaptation shows one method of taking stereotype to the extreme. Swine were the choice livestock for the mountain folk, so it comes as no surprise, given the proximity, that they would become the favored object of deviance. Harkins's analysis of the film's affect on the perception of the mountaineer is especially keen (205–214). Obviously it worked. There are now T-shirts that read "Paddle faster, I hear banjo music." So when Culla Holme encounters the hog drive in *Outer Dark*, the reader anticipates the linkage.[9] McCarthy fulfills expectations when the drover claims his brother "says he goin to get him some poontang when we get sold but I told him he'd be long done partialed to she-hogs" (216).

An infinitely more creative take on this particular Appalachian stereotype, and one that comments subversively on the stereotype itself, occurs in *Suttree* when Gene Harrogate makes love to an entire watermelon patch (*Suttree* 31–35). McCarthy squeezes the scene for every bit of humor, especially once the prisoners at the workhouse find out about the "moonlight melonmounter":

> Yeah, sang out Callahan, we get out we goin to open a combination fruitstand and whorehouse.
> Harrogate smiled nervously.
> Callahan was sketching for them a portrait of his brothel. Melons in black negligees.
> Watch out the niggers don't hear of it.
> The niggers is liable to lynch ye.
> Other fruits discussed. A canteloupe turned queer. Do you buy them a drink [*Suttree* 49].

This scene, when juxtaposed with the one so obvious and expected in *Outer Dark*, disarms the stereotype while using it. With Harrogate, an undersized Jethro Clampett in oversized shoes, McCarthy hilariously explodes the image of hillbilly bestiality, taking it to an extreme that is so absurd as to be barely believable. Suttree, one of McCarthy's few educated bourgeois characters, recognizes Harrogate as this stereotype: "this adenoidal leptosome that crouched above his bed like a wizened bird.... [S]ly, ratfaced, a convicted pervert of a botanical bent. Who would do worse when in the world again. Bet on it" (54). Sut knows perfectly well that Harrogate represents the degenerate mountaineer to everyone he comes in contact with, and he tries to warn Gene when he comments, "You look wrong. You will always look wrong" (60). Being the naïve rube that he is, Gene does not take the hint. Nevertheless, even Suttree is surprised by the truth of Harrogate's nighttime exploits. Gene tells Suttree (himself an interlocutor as G.W. Harris's "George" was for Sut Lovingood), "My lawyer told em a watermelon wasnt no beast. He was a smart son of a bitch." Suttree's response sums up his amazement at Gene's hillbillyness: "Oh boy, said Suttree" (49). The absurdity of Harrogate's deviance confounds a character who has the social background and life experience to recognize him as stereotype incarnate.

Suttree also knows that because Gene is so readily identified as a hillbilly, his lot is cast as a delinquent. Gene will always have some crazy scheme to keep himself from doing "real" work, he will always look wrong, and the authorities will always catch him at whatever illegality he conjures up. That is why Suttree advises him to get out of town when the telephone police come after him. Gene is afraid he will take the wrong bus, but Suttree tells him, "There's not any wrong bus. Not for you" (436). Sut anticipates Harrogate's robbery and his incarceration. Gene Harrogate foregrounds how stereotypes can categorize and compartmentalize.

"Nowheres" or the Space of Appalachia

One mythic metanarrative for *Appalachia* is incest — a culture isolated and turned inward on itself so much that everything remains within the family. According to the *Appalachian* iconography, if a mountaineer cannot locate livestock as a sexual outlet, he turns to his cousin or his sister. This degeneracy — an act of uncontrolled sexual impulses — this violation of an anthropological taboo, allows the outside world to blame the mountaineer's problems on the mountaineer himself. McCarthy's work examines the specter of Appalachian incest in *Outer Dark*, a literary site where all things hillbilly can be projected and recognized. Culla Holme, the central figure of this novel, cannot hold a steady job, trespasses when he has to, and steals when he can. And that is not the worst of it. *Outer Dark* seems to confirm both notions of mountaineer hyper-violence and images of *Appalachia* as the iconography of discord and degeneracy. As John Grammer hypothesizes, "The whole social atmosphere of *Outer Dark* is one of near-total estrangement: we are shown a community, presumably once unified and solid, now shattered to atoms" (37). The physical environs of the novel *seem* built from no known template. The feel is primarily Appalachian, antiquated, and agrarian. Yet the presence of swamps and alligators indicates a more southerly clime. The aggregate effect creates a sensational otherworldliness, awash with both possibility and limit, a dreamscape unreality filled with tangible references. In *Outer Dark* "the realism of [*The Orchard Keeper*] is resolutely abandoned and the adoption of mythic form is overt" (Cant 74). But this is a familiar territory for those whose work centers on *Appalachia*.

In this novel McCarthy does what so many other writers have done before him: he re-creates *Appalachia* as space of legend and as a projection of a collective psyche. Unlike the standard iconography, however, McCarthy's re-creation is a mythoclastic one; he "dismantles our metanarratives, deconstructs our preconceptions, and throws us into epistemological uncertainty at every turn" (Metress 154). He undermines the classic images of *Appalachia* as truisms and shows them to be projections of his readership as much as the novel's physical environment and social "landscape" are projections of his main characters' psyche. *Outer Dark* deconstructs *Appalachia* as nothing other than a mythic space that answers the fantastic and phantasmal needs of its readers. *Appalachia* and *Outer Dark* are literarily "nowheres."

The unreality of *Outer Dark*'s landscape has precedence: the environs are reminiscent of Al Capp's "Dogpatch," a setting that was a "part of the mythic South, a land where mountains border on bayous, where caves and caverns stretch for miles, and where two day's walk beginning in the Appalachian hills brings one to the southwestern desert" (Harkins 127). Harkins further states: "Although Capp initially situated Dogpatch in Kentucky, he later relocated the community to the Ozarks, a move never explained in the strip or commented on in the press. To an even greater extent than [Billy] DeBeck [creator of *Snuffy Smith*], Capp thus conflated the vast array of southern landscapes" (127). Al Capp, of course, was not the first to convolute the mythic geographical space of the mountains. Billy DeBeck, the creator of the *Snuffy Smith* comic strip, "was instrumental in freely blending Ozark and Appalachian settings into a single mythological geographic location. Although the strip was initially set in the North Carolina mountains, characters in an early episode refer to ordering store-bought clothes from the nearby big city of 'Little Rock'—in reality, 600 plus miles to the west" (123). DeBeck re-creates *Appalachia* in pop culture. According to Harkins, DeBeck

> read dozens of nineteenth- and twentieth-century novels and nonfiction books about the hill folk and his debt to earlier fabrications of southern Appalachia and the mountaineer is obvious. He was strongly influenced by the works of Mary Murfree and George Washington Harris, and his copy of *Sut Lovingood* is liberally annotated and includes his preliminary sketches of Snuffy Smith [114].

Like so many others, DeBeck, whose comic strip reinforces the iconography of the hillbilly, bases his comic-book fiction on a long-running fiction.

Cormac McCarthy grew up in the mountain South. Of him childhood friend Jerry Anderson said, "We spent an awful lot of time running around Brown's Mountain.... [W]hen I read his descriptions of it today, I'm always amazed at his eye for detail. He didn't just see a dirt road; he saw the lizard paths that crossed it and the lichens that grew on the nearby rocks" (quoted in Gibson 26). A writer with such an eye for detail would not randomly or accidentally throw an alligator into an Appalachian creek; he would know that the cold winter climate of even the most southern Appalachian mountains would preclude the inhabitation of such a large cold-blooded reptile. Christopher Metress suggests a "murkiness surrounds the time and place of the novel, and no number of rereadings will dispel it; we simply have to accept that these events occur in a setting that cannot be fixed with certainty" (151). Metress, Walsh, and many other critics have suggested that this "murkiness" exists because the point of the geography in *Outer Dark* is not to place the setting in a legitimate climate or region, but rather, to situate it in the realm of a fantastic mythology, in an allegorical space that conflates Appalachian and Southern geography and blends features often "separated in some cases by thousands of miles, into a single mythic space," thus foregrounding the process of the construction of *Appalachia* itself (Harkins 127). Academics, purveyors of benevolence, and industrialists have always wanted to explain why mountaineers do not fit into modern American culture and they have constructed this *Appalachian* metanarrative to accomplish this goal. The purveyors of pop culture have merely cashed in on already existing tropes.

Like Fox Jr., Frost, Semple, DeBeck, Capp, and others before him, McCarthy works in the imaginary realm of *Appalachia*; but unlike these writers, who wanted to fit the mountain people into categories that made them either the epitome of American transcendence or of American degeneracy, unlike these purveyors of culture who consciously or unconsciously sought to explain and discipline a heterogeneous culture *vis-à-vis* such a mythic creation, in *Outer Dark* more than in any of his other novels, McCarthy highlights this imaginary dimension itself by creating a phantasmal regionality that can only be satisfactorily explained as a projection of some character's unconscious — alternately Culla's and Rinthy's. McCarthy thus exposes the meta-geography of *Appalachia*. Under McCarthy's mythoclastic scrutiny, *Appalachia* looks less like a real place and more like what it has always been — fantasy space. The novel's setting appears nightmarish because the entire realm of experience — the geography and even the three marauders who make up the "Grim Triune" — is a psychological projection colored by Culla Holme's guilt. Ample textual evidence suggests that both the confused landscape of the novel and the Grim Triune exist only as manifestations of Culla's psyche, "figments of his dreams, projections of his inner dark, forecasting or representing his own dark impulses and deeds" (Luce, *Reading the World* 63).

In re-creating *Appalachia*, McCarthy does reproduce certain mountain realities as well as mountain stereotypes. One of the major tangible references tying the environment of *Outer Dark* to Appalachian reality can be found in the swine drive Culla stumbles upon wherein the drovers are heading "crost the mountain to Charlestown [Charleston?]" (*OD* 214). Wilma Dunaway notes that "by 1860, western North Carolina and East Tennessee were exporting more than 764,000 hogs, at least half of them overland via the French Broad Trail," so this aspect of *Outer Dark* remains rooted in an Appalachian reality (*First American Frontier* 218–219). However, even within this scene — a situation based on an historical reality — McCarthy calls to attention the conjoined relationship of *Appalachian* myth and Appalachian mountain reality. The drover mentions the mulefoot "mountain hog from north of here" (*OD* 214). According to The American Livestock Breeds Conservancy, "the Mulefoot is an American hog breed that is named for its most distinctive feature, the solid, non-cloven hoof which looks like the hoof of a mule," yet it is not a breed indigenous to the Appalachian mountains (*The American Livestock Breeds Conservancy*); rather, it probably "descended from the Spanish hogs brought to the Americas beginning in the 1500s" and by 1900 was "common along the Mississippi River Valley, where farmers ranged their hogs on the islands in the river" (*The American Livestock Breeds Conservancy*). The breed's prevalence in this region, along with other geographical indicators, leads Wesley Morgan to conclude that *Outer Dark* takes place somewhere in the Mississippi River Valley — Missouri, Arkansas, or northern Louisiana ("Mulefoot Hogs"). Regardless of whether Morgan is accurate, McCarthy's reference illustrates the same fluidity of *Appalachian* geography present in the work of Al Capp or Billy DeBeck. Oklahoma State University's web page *Breeds of Livestock* claims that "F.D. Coburn, in his classic 1916 book *Swine in America*, notes that the Mulefoot hog was found in Arkansas, Missouri, Iowa, Indiana, across the southwest and in some parts of Mexico." (In southern

Missouri and northern Arkansas, Mulefoots were sometimes called "Ozark pigs.") Evidently neither F.D. Coburn nor Oklahoma State nor the American Livestock Breeds Conservancy has been able to locate evidence that the "rarest of American swine breeds" ever foraged in Appalachian forests (*Breeds of Livestock*). Yet, like writers before him, by referencing the mulefoot hog, McCarthy convolutes geographical space, making *Outer Dark* yet another "part of the mythic South, a land where mountains border on bayous" and geographies coalesce in fantasy (Harkins 127).

This question of ontology within McCarthy's mythic *Appalachian* setting draws attention to the setting's fantastic quality. About the mulefoot hog, the drover asks Culla, "Well is he a hog or ain't he?" (215). One might ask the same question about *Outer Dark*'s setting: Well, is it Appalachian or ain't it? Culla answers, "I'd say he was a hog if he didn't have nary feet a-tall," but the drover does not permit this flippant response. The drover concludes: "If he was to have feet you'd look for em to be hog's feet. Like if ye had a hog didn't have no head you'd know it for a hog anyways. But if ye seen one walkin around with a mule's head on him ye might be puzzled" (115). *Outer Dark* walks around with a mule's head on it.

In the 1960s, the image of Appalachia in the national media remained confused because *it* was wearing a mule's head — the pictures and writings confirmed national ideas about Appalachian people because those very perceptions colored the selection of images produced from the mountains. The degradation and depravity of the mountains were the product of national fears and anxieties projected onto mountain spaces and populations. With an unpopular war raging and urban upheaval simmering, the Kennedy and Johnson administrations needed the Appalachian region to need the government as much as the benevolent organizations needed the mountaineer for their own survival fifty years earlier, if as nothing more than a diversion. The truth of the Appalachian reality yet again was less important than the myth of *Appalachia*.

Outer Dark exposes the puzzling iconography of *Appalachia* by forcing the reader to see the landscape of the novel as Culla and Rinthy perceive it. Diane Luce succinctly connects this facet of *Outer Dark* to the readers' need to project: "Our experience of the world is always a projection of our inner grace or darkness, and the world of 'reality' is largely subjective. The differing experiences of Culla and Rinthy as they travel the 'same' surreal world are central to this" (*Reading the World* 63). Just as the mulefoot hog is pure invention, the Appalachian *reality* of the novel remains bracketed within and distorted by consciousnesses under psychological pressures — pure myth, pure *Appalachia*. Tales within the text like the mulefooted hog story expose the connections between Appalachian mountain reality and *Appalachia* as fantasy. *Outer Dark* dramatizes this insight.

The brother and sister characters of the novel travel through the same geographical area, almost immediately behind or in front of one another: their "alternating scenes, which emphasize their isolation from one another and from any sense of community, occur with striking discontinuity" (63). When Rinthy inquires about Culla with the store clerk, he replies, "Why he just left here. Quiet feller? Come in here this afternoon" (56). Culla works for Squire Salter, for whose murder "two itinerant millhands" hang (95); Rinthy sees these "two men hanged in a tree like gross chimes" (100). Rinthy steals turnips from the man whose wife churns butter to sell in Clark's store (100) — "Bud," as Clark calls him — who later accuses Culla of carrying cholera (138). Incidentally, the millhands happen to be hanged in Bud's field, and that, not his wife's butter, is what brings him into an encounter with Holme at Clark's store. The horse that nearly kills Culla on the ferry (166) crosses over a bridge under which Rinthy sleeps (97). And at the end of the novel, Rinthy sleeps in the same glade where Culla bears witness to the murder of their son (236–238).

Nevertheless and in incredibly queer ways, the settings through which the siblings move do not resemble one another at all. With Culla's movement, with his running, "social conventions are constantly broken, relations teeter on the brink of violence, and each encounter is a confrontation marked by phobia and paranoia" (Guillemin, *Vision* 66). As "dried blood sifted in a fine dust from the lines of his palm," Culla carries his newborn son out onto a woodland path and to a bridge, "the swollen waters coming in a bloodcolored spume from about the wooden stanchions and fanning in the pool below with a constant and vicious hissing" (*COG* 15). It is as though a nightmarish fairytale forest conspires against him: "With full dark he was confused in a swampy forest, floundering through sucking quagmires and half running" (16–17). He stumbles back to where he has abandoned his son (18). Perhaps his confusion in the woods mirrors his vacillation about abandoning his child and its mother. Perhaps that is why "before he slept he saw again the birth-stunned face, the swamp trees in the dark bower above the pale and naked flesh and the black blood seeping from the navel" (27).

Rinthy, on the other hand, experiences none of the environmental maliciousness Culla endures. She passes through "sunshine that washed fitfully with the spring wind over the glade, turning her face up to the sky and bestowing upon it a smile all bland and burdenless as a child's" (53); she goes "happily, flushed, shuffling through the woods and plucking the shy wildflowers that sat upon the sunpatched earth" (32). While even the road to town requires

Culla to wade through "mud slathered to his knees" (37), little sister follows the footprints of the German storekeeper, easily "walking out his tracks to the crossroads" (54).

How could the siblings encounter the same environments and persons to such dramatically opposite effects? The answer is that each character projects his or her individual psychic states onto the surroundings. McCarthy is highlighting within his text the same processes at work behind the fantasy construction of this fictional domain—*Appalachia* itself.

Culla and Rinthy both violate the taboo of incest, but their reactions to the originary sin differ dramatically. Rinthy feels no guilt for the act. "I wasn't ashamed," she tells the doctor (156); she tells the tinker "I'd care for [the baby].... [T]hey wouldn't nobody like me" (193) despite the fact that "it's no right child" (194). She is perfectly conscious of the child's origins and she does not care, unlike Culla, whose guilt spurs him to first attempt infanticide. Her conscience remains unmarred and perhaps that is why she sleeps "through the first wan auguries of dawn, gently washed with river fog while martins came and went among the arches," and why "butterflies attended her and birds dusting in the road did not fly up when she passed" (97–98). As Edwin Arnold notes, "She is at peace with nature, and it with her" because she is at peace with herself (48).

Conversely, Culla tries to disguise their sin at every turn. To keep the tinker away, he warns him, "Sickness here, he called. Got sickness" (*OD* 6). Both Edwin Arnold ("Naming" 47) and Ann Fisher-Wirth ("Abjection" 129) have noted that Culla refuses to fetch a midwife, telling Rinthy, "I caint. She'd tell," to which his sister responds, "Who is they to tell?" "Anybody," Culla concludes (*OD* 10). He obviously wants to hide his guilt from the outside world, while Rinthy seems not in the least concerned about the potential condemnation of their transgression. Fisher-Wirth claims that "so extreme is Culla's despair that it as if he has suffered not a change of heart but a change of ontological status between the incestuous coupling and his son's birth.... [Y]et, repudiating that incest, he plunges himself further into the 'outer dark,' beyond the circle of the family" (129–130). This happens when ontology is a product of psychology. The repudiation of the incest takes the form of infanticide.

While Rinthy would accept her motherly duties regardless of their origin, Culla rejects all the responsibilities of a father and partner when he leaves both the child and his sister to die. The environment through which he moves manifests his guilt for this abandonment—an act as unacceptable as incest, an act tantamount to murder. Culla travels, shrouded in his guilt, through "a sunless wood where the road curved dark and cool, overlaid with immense ferns, trees hung with gray moss like a hag's hair, and in this green and weeping fastness birdcalls he had not heard before" (117), or in the dark where "the road before him went winding chalky and vaporous through the black woods. Swamp peepers hushed constantly before him and commenced behind as if he moved in a void claustral to sound" (131). He is "always met with suspicion" (Arnold 49); he is not at peace with himself and therefore not contented in the world.

Rinthy experiences no such despair, so she finds herself "cradled in a grail of jade and windy light," while Culla ends up in "a spectral waste out of which reared only the naked trees in attitudes of agony" (*OD* 242). Given that they travel the same roads in the same small geographical area, the vast differences in the landscapes through which they journey can be explained only by concluding that the differences are the direct results of the projections of their separate psychological states.

Enter the Grim Triune. "Bearing spades and brush hooks through a barnyard, frightening the stock, ... they are that community's nightmare, the seed of destruction which lurks" within the realm of the mountaineer iconography (Grammer 35–36). They are Culla's nightmare. Presented on the first page of the novel, they literalize many of the mountain stereotypes: "ragged, filthy, threatful," they wear the shabby stolen clothes of the dead (*OD* 182); the unnamed one, a manifested evolutionary reject, drools and whimpers like a grown version of the simian idiot baby in *Child of God* or an adult version of Culla's nameless child; the leader, scowling "redly out of a great black beard" (*OD* 170) could double for "Devil" Anse Hatfield, the "mountain patriarch with a flowing dark beard" (Harkins 37). These three, who darkly resemble sinister versions of Paul Webb's *The Mountain Boys*, are the nightmare figures Culla conjures up to embody his own horror at his transgression (105). Another interpretation of Culla's psychology might posit the three marauders as Culla's id, ego, and superego, and that could be a valid assessment — but that is not the current project. Christopher Walsh maintains, "We can find a potential historical antecedent for [the Triune] in the murderous Harpe brothers, an evil group who roamed parts of Appalachia in the late 1700s" (*In the Wake of the Sun* 118). More than any literary mountaineer characters, however, the dark triune resemble Al Capp's Romeo Scraggs and his sons Lem and Luke, the terrors of "Dogpatch" and foils to Capp's Li'l Abner: "Always the symbol of unmitigated violence and social chaos ... in a 1938 sequence, their path across the countryside best resembles that of a deadly tornado, and their hideous grinning faces fill civilized society with dread anytime they appear." It makes sense that "the Scraggs became increasingly savage by the late 1930s and the years of World War II" because they represent projections of the

Depression-era and World War II-era American psyche (133–134). Likewise psychological projections in their fictional realm, the triune of *Outer Dark* are an intensified scourge of the land, the Scraggs on crystal meth, capable of unspeakable deeds — murder, infanticide, cannibalism. They manifest the mountaineer at his scariest and most demonically inhuman. Yet "the novel makes it increasingly clear that these evil raiders are not so different from Culla Holme," that they manifest some sinister, blacker wraith of his already darkened self (Spencer 86).

I will go one step further than Spencer: no Grim Triune really exists. These three scourges are nothing more than Culla's psychological projections; he commits all the crimes attributed to them and his conversations with them are interior monologues that manifest the deep confusion of his soul. Spencer suggests, "McCarthy calls into question the humanity of the band of murderers in *Outer Dark* even further through the typography of this novel.... [T]he italics make them seem unreal or surreal, and nightmarish" (85). Throughout the novel, the actions of the Triune, minus their interactions with Culla himself, are described in the italicized sections (*OD* 3; 35; 51; 95; 129; 229). The one exception is when they encounter the Squire in his wagon (*OD* 50). Each incident in italics precedes or follows Culla's interactions with the same character(s).

In *The Orchard Keeper*, McCarthy often uses italics to register the inner thoughts of his characters, and it is plausible that the italics work in a similar fashion in *Outer Dark*. Kenneth Rattner, John Wesley Rattner, Marion Sylder, and Arthur Ownby all remember past events and think to themselves, and those rememberings are related in the text via italics: Kenneth Rattner (*OK* 23–27); Ownby (52–54, 155–156, 184, 224, 227–229, 230–231); John Wesley (68–72, 77–85, 133–136); Sylder (161–164, 168, 214–215). The triune could be chronicled thusly because "they are too far out of the bounds of normal humanity to be described in the usual typeface" (Spencer 85), or they could be figments of Culla's imagination textually registered in similar ways to the thoughts and rememberings of characters in McCarthy's first novel.

Proximity, too, would suggests Culla's intimate familiarity (beyond his personal encounters) with the three road agents. They seem to haunt his every move. Spencer claims that the "commotion of hens from the barn" trumpets the triune's arrival when Culla goes to work for Squire Salter (86), but it seems fairly clear that the Squire himself blames Holme for the theft of both his boots and his brush hook (*OD* 41–49). The Squire is then murdered with a brush hook that "missed his neck and took him in the small of the back" (51). Interesting coincidence. Culla just happens to show up after graves have been robbed (87–88) and again after the millhands have been hanged (140–

141). The man who "wouldn't turn Satan away for a drink" (127) should have turned Culla away; he finds himself disemboweled shortly after their interaction (129). Clark, too, hangs from a tree soon after meeting Holme (146). Everyone who comes into contact with Holme, even the tinker, dies at the hands of the triune, except Rinthy and Holme himself. Spencer asks the pertinent question: "Why don't these three cold-blooded killers murder Culla?" (Spencer 86). Bell believes that "the spectral magi treat Culla as an apprentice member of their group" (Bell 41), while Arnold answers the question by suggesting that "Culla's destiny has not yet worked itself out" (50). Bell gets closer to the answer when he claims "Culla is often suspected of the atrocities [the triune members] commit" (41); Luce gets closest when she writes, "Culla's direct encounters with the triune may be read as his inward experience ... the triune may be seen as outward projections of Culla's unconscious" (*Reading the World* 96). Culla would have to commit suicide to be murdered by the "spectral magi."

Culla's first direct encounter with the triune comes after the destruction of the ferry and the disappearance of the ferryman. He washes up on the side of the river, makes toward their camp, and warms by their fire. The bearded one compliments Culla on his boots. Such a "jimdandy pair of boots" certainly draw attention to Culla (*OD* 173). Culla claims that the boots were "bought for somebody else. He died," and so they were given to him. How does he know the Squire has died? Regardless, those boots present a liability for Culla. They might be part of the reason everyone seems to chase him; the boots are not "all right," so he has to get rid of them, rationalizing by imagining that they were taken from him by fantasy figures (178–179). The leader of the triune, whose own shoes "were cracked and weatherblackened and one was cleft from tongue to toe like a hoof," forces a boot swap, so that Culla ends up walking in the shoes of the drooling idiot (176); the shoes he receives "were mismatched, cracked, shapeless, burntlooking and crudely mended everywhere with bits of wire and string" (180). Spencer reminds critics that Satan "has cloven hooves" (84). The crude and shapeless footwear he "receives" might have once belonged to a millhand, or one of his other victims. It might be argued that the triune are demons of Holme's imagination as the hillbilly is the imaginary demonic persona of the mountaineer or of a wider society that projects its gremlins onto *Appalachia*.

The conversations Culla has with the leader of the trio bear out his pervasive guilt (Arnold 50). The leader assumes an accusatory tone in their initial direct encounter. He rationalizes Culla's lack of a horse by suggesting "maybe you was afraid to take it. That makes sense." The bearded one implies that Culla has killed the ferryman, asking "Did that ferry man not have nary better shirt than that?"(*OD* 176). In fact, the whole episode on the ferry remains suspect. Readers (as well as various characters in the novel) recognize Culla as a liar, so perhaps his rendition of these events is questionable. While Culla's version of the ferry scene has the overflowing river causing the cable to snap (157–166), the leader of the three claims that his mute companion is "the one set the skiff adrift this morning" with the purpose of bringing Culla to them: "Even if it just drifted off he still done it. I knowed they's a reason. We waited all day and half the night. I kept up a good fire" (178). Holme tells the man he is hunting Rinthy because he thinks "she run off with this tinker," but that is purely false (177); even had Rinthy run off with the tinker, there is no way Culla could have known it since he was gone before she was. The leader digs deeper, asking,

> How come ye to run your sister off?
> I never.
> How come her to run off?
> I don't know. She just run off.
> You don't know much, do ye? [178].

Culla does not know much, and his dialogue with the leader of the triune reveals how the events are confused in his mind.

The second interaction between Culla and the Grim Triune uncovers Culla's interior struggles even more blatantly. The three "wore the same clothes, sat in the same attitudes, endowed with a dream's redundancy" (231). The tone of this encounter, perhaps because of the presence of the physical manifestation of Culla's transgression, becomes more bitter, more accusatory, and more brutally close to revealing truth. In their first encounter, Culla never even lets on that he or his sister have a child, and yet in the second meeting the leader of the three intuitively tells Culla, "I figure you got this thing here in her belly your own self and then laid it off on that tinker," to which Holme responds, "I never laid nothing off on no tinker" (233). He never denies committing incest; as Luce notes, "He denies the wrong half of the charge, in effect obliquely admitting to the incest that he has tried all along to repress psychologically and literally (*Reading the World* 97). How does the leader figure it out? Luck? Maybe. Perhaps the leader possesses some supernatural clairvoyance. The more plausible explanation, however, is that Culla makes up the triune in his own mind to rationalize his deeds: "McCarthy's tripartite personification of evil emphasizes that part of Culla's nature which could be termed 'sinfulness'" (Spencer 91); the "triune are a manifestation of Culla's psyche" (Luce, *Reading the World* 97).

At the novel's beginning, Holme lacks the gumption to destroy his progeny, so he passively leaves the child to die amongst the cottonwood trees:

"When Culla decides to leave his baby to die and then lies about it to Rinthy, he is guilty of the same abuse of authority, malevolence, deception, violence, and destruction that are embodied in McCarthy's parodic trinity, which is thus presented as the incarnation of man's own inner darkness" (91). More aptly, the trinity is an incarnation of Culla's *inner* darkness. As the novel progresses, if he becomes the familiar of murder, then by the novel's end he can finish what he started. He comes full circle and destroys what he created; he negates one taboo act with another.

With a landscape difficult to name and place, and characters that appear more parody than real, McCarthy shows exactly how *Appalachia* was created as a manifestation of cultural anxiety and need. The reader sees the environment and the inhabitants of *Outer Dark* alternately through the rose-colored glasses of Rinthy Holme and the darkly tinted lenses of her brother; each jilted vision constructs how each character perceives the events of the world he or she encounters. What McCarthy does in microcosm with *Outer Dark*, sensationalists, industrialists, government authorities, denominationalist do-gooders, and academic scholars have done with *Appalachia* in macrocosm. *Appalachia* describes no known reality, but rather reflects the mythological/psychological projections of its creators.

This is why the iconography of *Appalachia* and the mountaineer has worked to discipline both the mountaineer and the corresponding society for over a century. The mountaineer, because of this invented image and despite its illegitimacy, becomes immediately categorized and fitted into the vessel of stereotype. He becomes either *Hillbilly* or the "noble" mountaineer. The outside culture recognizes these stereotypes and wants to be anything but them. If an individual in American society does not sleep with animals or his kinfolks, does not feud with his neighbor or the authorities, engages his fellow citizens in commerce, and works hard by modern standards, then he receives all the benefits of citizenship and will not be ostracized as the mountaineer has been. The mountaineer, thereby, becomes a scapegoat with whom no one wants to identify despite potentially similar economic situations. Furthermore, such stereotyping legitimizes the infiltration of the mountain world and society by the authorities and their minions just as rejecting a whiskey excise once did.

The ending of *Outer Dark* provides a metaphor that sheds light on the entrapment of the mountaineer. Walking down a dirt road, Culla Holme comes to where the road ends in a swamp. He tries to place "his foot in the mire before him and it rose in a vulvate welt claggy and sucking"; all around him is wasteland — "there were only the charred shapes of trees in a dead land where nothing moved save windy rifts of ash that rose dolorous and died again down the blackened corridors"—a premonition of the *Appalachia* McCarthy returns to in *The Road*. As Culla turns back from the road's dead end, the blind man he has previously passed smiles "upon him his blind smile" (242). Is it a smile of ignorance or knowing? McCarthy gives no clue. Perhaps he is suggesting that the mountaineer will always move blindly in a world of unfair stereotypes if he does nothing to combat them and allows them to continually define him: "Someone should tell a blind man before setting him out that way" (242).

McCarthy uses the blind man motif throughout his work. In *Outer Dark*, the man called Harmon comments to Culla on the subject of eyes and blindness, "Some folks has two and cain't see" (232); the blind man himself tells Culla, "Them old eyes can only show ye what's done there anyways. If a blind man needed eyes he'd have eyes" (241). What's "done there" is not always reality. When a reader looks at *Outer Dark*, he sees through Culla's or Rinthy's eyes; when he assesses *Appalachia* with his two good eyes, he sees what is already there, the invention. The history of the Appalachian region, those paradigms by which it is defined and on which it is constructed, stands in the swampy foundation of myth. Readers do not readily see into the substructure of the Appalachian region's creation, but it remains there nonetheless. McCarthy exposes that substructure. He foregrounds the process, revealing that what the reader of Appalachian representations gleans from literature and history is a projection of psychological and ideological need mapped onto the region and mistaken for it. Like so many recent Appalachian scholars and critics, McCarthy performs an archeology of the history of the Appalachian mountain region and her people via his fiction.

Coda

Atavising the Mountaineer
The Road

> Turning and turning in the widening gyre
> The falcon cannot hear the falconer;
> Things fall apart; the centre cannot hold;
> Mere anarchy is loosed upon the world,
> The blood-dimmed tide is loosed, and everywhere
> The ceremony of innocence is drowned;
> The best lack all conviction, while the worst
> Are full of passionate intensity.
> Surely some revelation is at hand ...
> — W.B. Yeats, "The Second Coming"

Around the time of *Suttree's* publication, Cormac McCarthy left East Tennessee and the Appalachian Mountains, lighting out for the territory of western Texas, southern New Mexico, and northern Mexico. Self-exiled there for thirty years, he has made his literary reputation via postmodern, mythoclastic representations of the American Southwest. In his Pulitzer Prize–winning *The Road*, McCarthy returns to the geographical region of his youth and to the mythical land of his early novels; but that environment remains only as ruins, "uncoupled from its shoring. Unsupported in the ashen air. Sustained by a breath, trembling and brief" (*TR* 10). Mike Clark and Jim Branscombe predicted McCarthy's post-apocalyptic re-visioning of the Appalachian landscape when they concluded in the nineteen seventies that

> there are only three things that could prevent the annihilation of Appalachia, no matter who owns it. *The first thing would be a nuclear war that makes it a moot point by ending everything.* The second is if the Lord intervenes. And the third would be some kind of dramatic, unbelievable awakening of the people and a changing of life styles that would reverse — break us away from — massive overconsumption [quoted in Egerton 241, emphasis added].

In *The Road*, a holocaust and the subsequent reversion of humanity to barbarism finalizes the demise of the Appalachian region, murders God, and reduces the world entire to the ruins of mythic *Appalachia*. "Ruder forms survive," they walk upright on two legs, and they call themselves men (*Suttree* 5).

The annihilation of the modern world that pre-dates the action of *The Road* is a result of the same anthropocentric worldview that rips up the natural world and replaces it with the government installation in *The Orchard Keeper*. In that novel, the mountaintop becomes a vacant, lifeless, fenced-off space where "the great dome stood complacent, huge, seeming older that the very dirt, the rocks, as if it had spawned them of itself and stood surveying the work" (*OK* 93). A metal and mineral world replaces an organic one so convincingly that it seems to have been originary itself. Even if the storage facility is not connected with the nuclear laboratory at Oak Ridge, as Natalie Grant suggests (78), it demonstrates a mindset that privileges the "advancement" of civilization over the conservation of nature. The destruction of the space surrounding the storage tank and the government-erected fence that guards it both designate this mountain spot for the government's (read: authority's) exclusive use. Such an "exclusive" mindset has directed land use in the Appalachian Mountains for nearly two hundred years. Land owners in the Appalachian region — whether absentee entities, industrial corporations, or even mountaineers themselves — have maintained that they alone have the right to decide how the land is used. The effort, time, and money spent in clearcutting timber and strip-mining coal have been relatively low compared to the yield of resource, but both environmentally unfriendly processes have annihilated ecosystems and have left the mountains desolate and bereft of life. The inhabitants, pushed off the land and out of the region by "modernizing" techniques, have abandoned "traditional" lifestyles for lives that lock into modern occupational, social, political, and monetary systems.

For at least two centuries the timber, mineral, energy, and human resources harvested from the Appalachian region have powered the modernization of the United States, a modernization seen as "progress." Accordingly, it is no accident that the United States has developed into an international superpower in that span of time, a superpower that needed and subsequently developed nuclear technology to maintain its status on the world stage.

Jean-François Lyotard would debate this idea of "progress." He maintains, "Technoscientific development has become a means of deepening the malaise rather than allaying it. It is no longer possible to call development progress. It seems to proceed of its own accord, with a force, an autonomous motoricity that is independent of us.... [H]uman entities — whether social or individual — always seem destabilized by the results and implications of development" (49). Arthur Ownby might agree. The government facility, described in *The Orchard Keeper* as a "barren spot, bright in the moonwash, mercurial and luminescent as the sea, the pits from which the trees had been wrenched dark on the naked bulb of the mountain as moon craters," is a microcosm of the wider destruction of the actual Appalachian Mountains (*OK* 93), which in turn is a minor representation of *The Road*'s holocaust, whether it be accidental or the result of man's unquenchable quest for dominion over other men.

As Walter Benjamin suggests, "There is no document of civilization which is not at the same time a document of barbarism" (quoted in Docherty 11). The creation of the atom bomb stemmed directly from the desire to end the bloodshed of World War II and from the desire to conquer what the Allies saw as Axis barbarism. The United States' possession and use of nuclear technology was hailed as a triumph for civilization. The bomb saved thousands of Allied soldiers but destroyed thousands of civilians at Hiroshima and Nagasaki. Though not as dramatic or as easy to pinpoint as the dropping of the atom bomb, hundreds of thousands of mountaineers have been displaced by "progress" in the Appalachians. Civilization's overall advancement required the resources of the Appalachian Mountains, but it was barbaric to displace their inhabitants. Civilization required the defeat of the Japanese via the bomb, but it was barbaric to drop it. According to Docherty, "The civilized face of modernity is attended constantly by a barbarism which is its other side" (12).

In *The Road*, barbarism survives civilization.

The pitted, desolate, "lunar" mountain landscape of *The Orchard Keeper* becomes the global landscape of *The Road*. A barren wasteland. The central character of the novel, "the man," lies awake as "the ashes of the late world carried on the bleak and temporal winds to and fro in the void. Carried forth and scattered and carried forth again" (*TR* 9–10). It is the end of the world as humanity has known it, and the darkness to come slowly dims "like the onset of some cold glaucoma" (3). All of humanity is going blind. The destruction of *almost all* living things brings on the unanticipated death of sociocultural constructs: "Maps, calendars, currency, and alphabets are all obsolete here, therefore destabilizing our claims to order or accurately representing the world" (Walsh, *In the Wake of the Sun* 257); time, names, history, regions, literature, taboos, class, and even God become as extinct as the dinosaurs.

What remain are the inorganic constructions of humanity — the buildings, the vehicles, the roads — and human beings themselves, at least for a while. In this panorama of ruin, McCarthy's most recent novel certainly resembles his previous work. As Rick Wallach writes in an analysis that pre-dates the publication of *The Road*, "McCarthy's works are littered with the detritus of numerous failed potentials: trashed and abandoned bodies, vehicles, mansions.... [T]he narratives anticipate the exhaustion and failure of culture at every turn" (xii-xiii). "Progress" brings culture's ultimate failure to fruition. While there is no exact textual evidence to prove unequivocally that the event that precedes the world's destruction in *The Road* is a nuclear holocaust set off by human means (it could be an explosion created by the impact of a meteorite, for instance), the pervasive tone of the text makes one think that human beings have done this thing to themselves. There is no evidence of a crater, as one would find in a cataclysmic impact scenario, and the attention paid to other evidences of human modifications of the world — gas stations, dams, bridges, etc. — lead me to believe that environmental destruction present in this novel is a direct or indirect result of human activity and its insatiable need to "advance."

In the novel, the material artifacts of progress — buildings and vehicles — provide the lingering humanity with temporary shelter from the natural elements and from each other. The man and his son come "upon a roadside gas station" where they drain old motor oil bottles and collect "oil for their little slutlamp to light the long gray dusks, the long gray dawns" (*TR* 5–7). In this post-apocalyptic world roads become central fixtures and fixations. The techniques of discipline outlast most of their objects. Roads remain spatial denominators, yet there is little left to denominate. The space surrounding the roads remains too, of course, but with little meaning to fill or articulate it. These traditional lines of transit literally become the *centers* of everything. Ambivalent spaces of encounter in much of McCarthy's work, concrete and asphalt thoroughfares in this novel both threaten and give hope. Roads provide sustenance, grim though it may be. They evidence the last vestiges of human society, reordered as a barbaric survival of the fittest. They are life and death. They are all that is left.

The Road marks McCarthy's return of a sort to the American South and to the Appalachians; the apocalypse has changed everything, though — the vegetation, the people — and it has blurred or demolished the cultural lines of demarcation that worked to posit the Appalachian region as distinct and "other." Living things are dead and all of the people look and act like stereotypical literary hillbillies, the ones who at any moment might kill you and then rape your wife or daughter or son. *The Road* is peopled with men who resemble Lester Ballard or the triune of *Outer Dark*. The world has become "largely populated by men who would eat your children in front of your eyes," just as the unnamed imbecile of *Outer Dark* does (*TR* 152).

Intertextually, "the man's" journey in this novel is also a regional homecoming, a reversal of the hillbilly diaspora that took so many "Tennessee wetbacks" to northern and midwestern industrial towns in the middle decades of the twentieth century (*Suttree* 398). The father and son characters slowly traverse the southern Appalachian landscape, the region of the man's youth turned into a "cauterized terrain," an "ashen scabland," with "the pieced farmland still visible, everything dead to the root along the barren bottomlands" (*TR* 12; 13; 18). They encounter the ruins of industrial towns, tourist attractions, concrete dams, and cotton-mill villages. They traverse high mountain passes, deep river gorges, and vast scorched valley lands. They escape the elements in barns, fallout shelters, and the shells of old southern homesteads. All of these sites dimly trace southern Appalachian culture. The man and his son, like so many other characters in McCarthy's oeuvre, cannot stop moving once they take to the road. They trek, they plod, they run, they stumble, and yet they carry within themselves the last vestiges of human decency and discipline. They carry *the fire*.

Return to the Mountains and to Appalachia

There can be no discerning exactly where the journey begins for the man and his son, but it is reasonable to assume that the boy was born somewhere near larger cities in the northern or midwestern area of the United States, since the man and his wife "sat at the window and ate in their robes by candlelight a midnight supper and watched distant cities burn" and the child is born only days after the incident (50). When the three family members — the man and his wife and their child — set out for more a southerly clime, the child is walking on his own and talking in coherent complete sentences, so several years have passed since the event initiated the end of all things. By the occasion of the story's recounting, the woman has committed suicide (49), and the man and his son have made it to "the foothills of the eastern mountains," once known as the Appalachians (23). The proper name, which carried a cultural context, has been exchanged for an abstract geographical bio-regionalism that draws focus to the empty and abstract space of this novel where "McCarthy once again manages to destabilize his readership, to force us to question the validity and permanence of the systems through which we know the world and our place in it" (Walsh, *In the Wake of the Sun* 267).

In their travels on the road, the father and son encounter the remains of a forest that the man remembers as "a rich southern wood that once held mayapple and pipsissewa. Ginseng. The raw dead limbs of the rhododendron twisted and knotted and black" (34). Arthur Ownby, Marion Sylder, Lester Ballard and other McCarthy characters once traversed similar woods. Over the mountains, the two encounter an Appalachian socio-economic regionalism in "the dark stacks of a mill" and a once-grand Southern estate where "chattel slaves had once trod those boards bearing food and drink on silver trays" (66, 89–90). The vegetation and housing, even the "aluminum [manufactured] houses," mark the setting as the southern Appalachian region (12).

Were the topography, skeletal vegetation, and housing not enough to convince the reader of *The Road*'s Appalachian setting, McCarthy includes Appalachian-specific signifiers throughout the early pages of the text. As K. Wesley Berry says about *The Orchard Keeper*, "Nowhere in the fiction are mentioned the Tennessee Valley Authority, coal companies, pulpwood plants, or other prominent industries," but the evidence of their presence manifests itself (Berry 50). The man and boy "sat on a bench and looked out over the valley where the land rolled away into the gritty fog. A lake down there." The boy asks,

> What is that, Papa?
> It's a dam.
> What's it for?
> It made the lake. Before they built the dam that was just a river down there. The dam used the water that ran through it to turn big fans called turbines that would generate electricity.
> To make lights?
> Yes. To make lights [*TR* 16–17].

In fact, "Five of the main dams built by the Tennessee Valley Authority on the Tennessee River and sixteen dams constructed on tributaries are within [the Appalachian region]" (Morris 140). The government never undertook such an extensive hydroelectric power project anywhere else in the United States. Power lines extended from the dams all across the Appalachian South, creating a connective power grid similar to the strands of a spider's web. Even with the people gone, the dams and lakes will remain "there for hundreds of years. Thousands, even" (*TR* 17). Besides the dams and lakes, the most telling sign (a literal sign, in this instance) of the Appalachian regionality of *The Road* is the cultural phenomenon of the painted barn roof. The southeastern United States, and especially the Appalachian mountain region, even in 2012, has hundreds of barns "with an advertisement in faded ten-foot letters across the roofslope. See Rock City" (18). All signs point to the Appalachians.

McCarthy reflects the historical hillbilly diaspora at the end of both *The Orchard Keeper* and *Suttree* when John Wesley Rattner and Cornelius Suttree leave the Appalachian region. As John C. Belcher notes, "Between 1940 and 1960 nearly 2,000,000 more people moved out of the Southern Highlands than moved in" (45). Suttree and Rattner were not alone. McCarthy reverses the diaspora after the apocalyptic incident in *The Road*. People escape the cities to rural areas so that "within a year there were fires on the ridges and deranged chanting," perversely reflecting the region's charismatic religious practices (28). The mountains become the refuge isolated from the "looted and exhausted cities" (152).

Like others, the man returns to, or at least through, the mountains that he once called home. At one point on their southbound escape, the man remembers "in that long ago somewhere very near this place he'd watched a falcon fall down the long blue wall of the mountain and break with the keel of its breastbone the midmost from a flight of cranes" (17). After he and the boy swim in the pooled river, he recalls that "he'd stood at such a river once and watched the flash of trout deep in a pool" (35). The text is full of such reminiscence of his Appalachian mountain childhood. He and the child visit his boyhood home "some few miles south of the city at a bend in the road and half lost in the dead brambles" (21). Of course, like the rest of the world, all of these rememberings are traced in the same gray charcoal pencil. While the exact route of the protagonists is as elusive as an ashen snowflake, I am forced to venture a guess. The two travelers come to the outskirts of a city where the man finds a Coca-Cola and gives it to his son. Region, state, and nation have all been extinguished by this catastrophe, but the great Southern corporate cola brand survives! Then, "by the dusk of the following day they were at the city. The long concrete sweeps of the interstate exchanges like the ruins of a vast funhouse against the distant murk" (*TR* 20). Later, "they crossed the high concrete bridge over the river. A dock below. Small pleasure boats half sunken in the gray water. Tall stacks downriver dim in the soot" (21). They continue south and east, to the man's childhood home and beyond, until they reach "the foothills of the eastern mountains" (23). They then head into the mountains toward the eastern watershed and through "the ruins of a resort town" where they take "the road south" (25). In these passages, I surmise that McCarthy is revisiting the stomping grounds of his own youth in eastern Tennessee, much as Wes Morgan does in his "The Route and Roots of the Road" (Morgan 39–47). The man and his son travel through Knoxville, across the Henley Street Bridge, south through Gatlinburg, and then up through the Newfound Gap, over the watershed and down into the mill country beyond. They make for the coastal areas of Charleston, South Carolina, or Savannah, Georgia, or some other "boarded ruins of a seaside resort" (228).

More important than McCarthy's return to the Appalachian region is his return to *Appalachia*, that mythical-literary-historical realm of the American cultural imagination. As has always been the case, mythical *Appalachia* remains rooted in the geographical reality of the Appalachian Mountains, but often the characteristics of the inhabitants and the details of their ways of life must be viewed through the sepia-tinted lens of *Appalachian* iconography. McCarthy reminds the reader of this relationship early in *The Road* when the man remembers "the perfect day of his childhood. This day to shape the days upon" (11–12). He and his uncle on a local Appalachian lake in the dying days of autumn, harvesting not trees themselves, but the dead stumps of trees felled by a hurricane, whose trunks "had long been sawed for firewood and carried away" (11). Even in the man's dream, the reality of Appalachian degradation intrudes and commingles with an idealized memory.

Humanity, as portrayed in *The Road*, physically resembles the stereotypical mountaineer. The protagonist himself is bearded and gaunt and filthy, clothed in whatever he can find. He is forced to kill a man who wears a "beard that had been cut square across the bottom with shears" and who "dressed in a pair of filthy blue coveralls and a black billcap with the logo of some vanished enterprise embroidered across the front of it" (53–54). Like many instances elsewhere in his work, McCarthy here plays with the notions of Appalachian stereotypes. The reader can perfectly envision the man because he has seen this character before as Devil Anse Hatfield, Al Capp's Romeo Scraggs, a bearded Cooter from the *Dukes of Hazzard*, or the leader of *Outer Dark*'s menacing triune. When earlier in the novel the man thinks to himself, "No more balefires on the distant ridges. He thought the bloodcults must have all consumed one another," one is reminded of Appalachian blood feuds (14). Such feuding, Altina Waller claims, "gripped the popular imagination and fastened on the people of southern Appalachia a cultural stereotype of violent irrationality that is still potent today" (Waller 348). It matters not that the images of Appalachian feuds "came not from the reality of Appalachian peculiarity but from the needs of middle-class Americans in industrializing America to project their own nostalgia for the past and fears about the future onto a people perceived as different" (349). McCarthy foregrounds these images when he labels some survivors of the holocaust "bloodcults." Unfortunately for the man and his son, these bloodcults are not dead. Rather, like the novel's two protagonists, they have taken to the road. He and the boy encounter such a cult

> marching with a swaying gait like wind-up toys. Bearded, their breath smoking through their masks.... [T]he phalanx following carried spears or lances tassled with ribbons, the long blades hammered out of trucksprings in some crude forge upcountry.... [B]ehind them came wagons drawn by slaves in harness and piled with goods of war and after that the women, perhaps a dozen in number, some

of them pregnant, and lastly a supplementary consort of catamites illclothed against the cold and fitted in dogcollars and yoked each to each [*TR* 77–78].

In this explicitly archaic depiction, this "army in tennis shoes," who dress "in clothing of every description, all wearing red scarves at their necks," resemble mountaineers (77).

While in the novel these characters are not labeled or constructed literally as mountaineers, the socially constructed images remain part of the reader's experience. The post-apocalyptic world of *The Road* exposes these images as social constructions. In past and contemporaneous accounts, historians and writers and politicians objectify the attitudes and the appearances and the general culture of the Appalachian mountain people. They become "our contemporary ancestors." For instance, whenever one wishes to refer to the epitome of degradation, one only need recall Dickey's *Deliverance* or McCarthy's *Child of God*. The death of everything in *The Road* makes everything the outer dark of *Appalachia* — the mysterious, dark, strange, and violent fantastic or phantasmal landscape. Referents fade like the fleeting light. Everyone in this novel is a mountaineer. Everyone is a hillbilly. McCarty performs a ubiquitous extension of *Appalachia*.

The Death of the Natural World

In this novel, McCarthy presents a radically demystified imagery of overconsumption, the end result of a culture that has not taken Clark and Branscome's warning to heart. The consumption habits of people have changed in fact, but not for the better, as Clark and Branscome hoped they might. If anything, consumption has accelerated, and the general destruction of the world has left the consumers with nothing to devour but themselves. Fires cremate the landscape. Ashes permeate the air. The characters encounter "cars in the streets caked with ash, everything covered with ash and dust. Fossil tracks in the dried sludge. A corpse in a doorway dried to leather" (10). Footprints in the ashes mark their passing. The end result of the progress of modernity in this novel is a barren natural landscape dotted with gas stations that stand as token reminders of an out-of-control consumerism where the desire to industrialize and modernize superseded any consideration of the potential damage caused by such quick "advancement."

The Appalachian region (and *Appalachia*) is a site possessing an historic intimacy with such blatant consumerism, as the work of so many Appalachian historians and critics have demonstrated. So it stands to reason that McCarthy picks the region as the setting for a novel that deconstructs the American culture of overconsumption. As much or more than his previous work, *The Road* highlights and critiques what David Holloway sees as manifestations of American "late-capitalism," where:

> Imperial ambition, anarchic competition and recurrent crises of accumulation, lead to increasingly entrenched disparities between competing classes on a global basis and the fragmenting of the ruling class into competing "capitals" and devolved class strata.... [W]e see the decaying of those ideological discourses whose function it is to legitimate the contradictions driving capitalist socialization — the performance of those tasks appropriate to one's class, but a simultaneous belief in the classlessness of the capitalist world; a belief in the self as an instrumental agent, alongside deference to institutional authority and patriarchal norms; the notional segregation of public and private, alongside a continual ratcheting up in the administration and commodification of leisure and labor; the work-ethic, but also the "narcissism" of consumer culture; a commitment to the universality of Western progress and democracy, but also to the legitimacy of the abominations practiced in their name; the absurdity that "human nature" is given full reign under capitalist system whose structure itself makes imperative the subjugation of humans and nature like [42].

Humans have harnessed the power of nature via discipline, industrialization, and modernization, but their greed and overconsumption unleash a nightmare scenario where the fire of human invention directly and indirectly causes the end of human society. Human beings resort to cannibalism because there is literally nothing else to consume, unless it has been processed and placed within a metal cylinder.

By the time of *The Road*'s chronicle, virtually all the world is dead. The once green and fertile vegetation of the southern Appalachian highlands has "gone to rows of black and twisted brambles" (18), and once prolific stands of oak and maple and hickory and pine and birch have followed the chestnut to extinction. Lightning and human campfires have turned them to "charred and limbless trunks of trees stretching away on every side" (7). The migratory birds of the air have "circled the earth as senselessly as insects trooping the rim of a bowl" (45), and crows exist "just in books" (133). The man enters a barn where "there was yet the lingering odor of cows," but only the odor lingers (101). They too are extinct. In *Suttree* the river is "a symbol: of life, since it gives Suttree the fish which sustain him, and of death — in the opening scene the bloated body of a suicide is grappled from its depths" (Grammer 42). Even the rivers in *The Road* are completely dead. When the boy inquires about the possibility of fish inhabiting the lake they view, the man replies, "No. There's nothing in the lake" (*TR* 17).

What the initial nuclear blast(s) did not destroy has been carried away by the resulting inclement weather or human consumption. Human beings themselves have fared only slightly better than other living things. Many, like the man and his son, take to the roads in search of a better place, only to end up as the "pilgrims [who] sank down and fell over and died" (153). Some become members of protected communes, some members of the bloodcults. Some become "the mummied dead ... shriveled and drawn like latterday bog-folk, their faces of coiled sheeting, the yellow palings of their teeth" (20). Others are victimized by their fellow men, "field-dressed and hauled away" like hunted hinds (76). Cannibalism, like the fires that devour the landscape, becomes the final evidence of an unchecked consumerism. People become a plague on the earth. They become what they have always been, just a rawer form — locusts preying on a world that is unable to rejuvenate.

The Death of Social Constructions

Human constructs quickly follow living things to extinction in the world of *The Road*. All the things that order and make sense of human existence vanish into the coming darkness. Time stops at the touchstone moment of "1:17. A long shear of light and then a series of low concussions.... [A] dull rose glow in the window glass" (45). From that moment on, the clock becomes irrelevant. Hunger alone delineates time and the world becomes less and less articulated. Fewer and fewer distinctions make a difference. Day and night are barely discernible as "the nights [are] now only slightly less black. By day the banished sun circles the earth like a grieving mother with a lamp" (28). Human calendars — Roman, Aztec or otherwise — cease to have meaning. The man "hadnt kept a calendar for years" (4). What would be the point? As the man "Ely" says, "People were always getting ready for tomorrow. I didnt believe in that. Tomorrow wasn't getting ready for them. It didnt even know they were there" (142). Anthropocentrism deconstructed. Time never cared for man and here the tables turn. No way to tell a person's age. The boy? The man struck by lightning? (42–43). "Ely" says he is ninety, but the protagonist doubts it (140–141). All things time-related are suspect in this world. There are "no lists of things to be done. The day providential to itself. The hour. There is no later. This is later" (46). Everything is *now*. In the world of *The Road*, time has ceased to be a factor. People live in the continual present and human denominations of time are without moorings, like everything else.

Likewise, names mean little in this post-apocalyptic realm. On the one hand, there are "advertisements [naming] goods that no longer existed" (108). On the other, the places, the roads, the landscapes through which the man and the boy move have no given names. There are no road numbers, and McCarthy gives neither the cities nor the states specific monikers. Names mean nothing. Even people remain nameless. The boy is "the boy" or "the child" and the man is "the man" or "papa," but they are never properly named. The old man they meet calls himself "Ely" but that name too is suspect. The man asks,

Is Ely really your name?
No.
You dont want to say your name.
I dont want to say it.
Why?
I couldnt trust you with it [144].

The old man's words highlight the fact that names are social constructions that present ways human beings order the world and structure things. Like time itself, those structures are irrelevant in this world that is losing "colors. The names of birds. Things to eat. Finally the names of things one believed to be true. More fragile than he would have thought. How much was gone already? The sacred idiom shorn of its referents and so of its reality" (75). "Ely" is wrong. There is no way to reference him, not even via a name. A society must exist for social constructs like names to matter.

History too is false and literature becomes a lie when "blackened books lay in pools of water. Shelves tipped over. Some rage at the lies arranged in their thousands row on row.... [The man would] not have thought the value of the smallest thing predicated on a world to come. It surprised him" (158). Literature, history, culture and language are all predicated on the stability of the world. The social constructs that establish the parameters of people's relationships with one another are as dead as the birds of the air. They have become a lie. The man's marriage, undoubtedly licensed by a now defunct state, is ultimately destroyed by the coming terror. His wife tells him, "Sooner or later they will catch us and they will kill us. They will rape me. They'll rape him. They are going to rape us and kill us and eat us and you wont face it" (48). The taboos against suicide, murder, and cannibalism are all devoid of meaning. The Grim Triune's world of taboo is the only world that exists. The man's wife kills herself (49), murder is "everywhere upon the land" (152), and cannibalism has become the easiest method of obtaining food (60; 76; 93–96; 167). The very idea of friends is laughable, as the man suggests when he tells the boy that all of his friends have died (50), and even the concept of ancestors no longer holds weight. The religious illustrations that structured his predecessors' existence are no longer tenable. The man thinks, "Do you think that your fathers are watching? That they weigh you in their ledgerbook? Against what? There is no book and your fathers are dead in the ground" (165). All the denominators of society are extinct, even class: "The frailty of everything revealed at last. Old and troubling issues resolved into nothingness and night. The last instance of a thing takes the class with it" (24). Everyone is finally the same. The advancements of modernity have become useless or close to it: the train (150–151), the diesel truck (52). The pistol remains useful to the man only as long as the two bullets remain. McCarthy smelts modernity and technology down into one thing: power by way of violence.

The man and his son move south through the Appalachians to the Carolina or Georgia piedmont and on to the Atlantic Ocean, but those regions and that ocean are never given specific referents either. They are "the eastern mountains" or "the valley below" or "the coast" or "the ocean." Political regional orderings are gone. They "used to be called the states," but those distinctions are now unimportant (36). Borders are no more. The man "had pored over maps as a child, keeping one finger on the town where he lived. Just as he would look up his family in the phone directory. Themselves among others, everything in its place. Justified in the world," but in *The Road* there is no justification and there is no overarching social order (153–154).

The only map that matters is the grid of "good" and "bad."

A society of a sort does exist, but only in the relationship between the man and child, and recreating a world of referents remains a difficult task, as the man quickly discovers. He and the boy play cards with a deck they find, but the man has trouble remembering the rules and the boy has never known them. The man "made up new games and gave them made up names. Abnormal Fescue or Catbarf. Sometimes the child would ask him questions about the world that for him was not even a memory. There is no past. What would you like? But he stopped making things up because those things were not true either" (45–46).

That Which Remains in the Ruins

Truly, only the physical, material results of history and culture remain in *The Road*—roads, dams, buildings, and ruins. Like the thoroughfares of the ancient Romans, the roads will remain quite a while because "there's nothing to uproot them" (37). They are relatively indestructible. They serve some of the same functions they served before the nuclear incident, though the methods of carrying out those functions have changed. After the nuclear incident "the roads were peopled with refugees shrouded up in their clothing. Wearing masks and goggles, sitting in their rags by the side of the road like ruined aviators. Their barrows heaped with shoddy. Towing wagons or carts" (24). They are the only remaining migratory animals. They still move on the roads, albeit more slowly. But the road is no longer merely a vehicle for movement and/or escape. It has become *the world*. All human-to-human encounters chronicled in this novel occur on or near a road. The man and boy rely on the same ambivalent spaces that brought modernization into the mountains and provided the mountaineer with the opportunity to participate in the modern economy. Along roads they find food and shelter, yet these paths present them with the specter of death on multiple occasions. The two travel south on the roads because roads still present the most unobscured routes, the most clearly marked paths, and the greatest likelihood of survival, despite the dangers. Both the "good guys" and the "bad guys" continue to survive because roads help them procure sustenance, grim though it may be.

However, to suggest that roads occupy the disciplinary function in this novel they once possessed would be an overstatement. Vagrants can no longer be separated from inhabitants, as was the case in *Outer Dark* or *Child of God* or *Suttree*, because in this space everyone is a vagrant. The industrialization of Appalachia is finally, wholly complete: everything is smelted together in the consuming fires. There are no longer any addresses to claim as one's own. All humans become road agents and marauders to some extent (14). All become versions of Kenneth Rattner or Culla Holme or Lester Ballard. As it concerns the Appalachian region, the roads originally built to facilitate the industrialization of the mountains (and the subsequent removal of their inhabitants) have outlasted everything else in *The Road*. The roads make hunting food more efficient, as the people who capture their victims on the road and store them in the cellar of the antebellum mansion prove (97), but roads only separate, categorize, or compartmentalize individuals as "good" or "bad." They are the remaining sites where people demonstrate their (in)humanity. Only this rudimentary moral and ethical articulation survives, and only in certain characters who have interiorized it. There is no "higher" moral or social authority to determine what is "good" or "bad," only the interior self.

The Remaining Discipline in The Road

Importantly for this study, where the concepts and concerns that structure society are gone, there seems to be little need for Foucauldian discipline. What remains to be made more efficient? Foucault criticizes a modern, industrial, capitalist society that no longer exists in *The Road*. In such a world, Foucault's deconstruction of what David Holloway would label a "late-modernist" society (borrowing from Terry Eagleton, Fredric Jameson and others) seems ridiculous. Holloway states:

> Deconstruction concludes that the Western *logos*, far from carrying any determinate insight into the workings of the world, connotes instead an arbitrary system

of values that orders the world hierarchically, empowering certain peoples, histories, or practices in a privileged central position while relegating others to a deprivileged, relatively disempowered, or otherwise marginal status. Deconstruction, in other words, identifies metaphysical structures of binary thinking as a mechanism for the production and disguising of power relations [15].

In *The Road*, good and evil are deciphered along lines of consumption practices: "good men" eat out of cans and "bad men" eat other people. What applies in the recently primitive world of *The Road* for most of humanity is only who can more quickly bludgeon another human to death and field-dress him before he himself is attacked. The "arbitrary system of values" Holloway speaks of dies with the rest of culture, and so the insights provided by Foucault's analysis of power relations can only apply to the distinction of good and evil and how the man, who has internalized these concepts, tries to instill them in his child. This is what he means when he tells the child that they are "carrying the fire" (*TR* 70). This is the perfect image for discipline: ambivalent — a fire provides light and heat, but simultaneously consumes — the ethics internalized by the man structure his and the boy's existence in a dangerous, absurd, and existential way.

In *The Road* everything is "shrinking down about a raw core of parsible entities. The names of things slowly following those things into oblivion" (75). For most of humanity, the oblivion has swallowed every mechanism that traditionally has ordered human society. The basic rules are as dead as the vegetation on the side of the road. Yet filial responsibility, paternal responsibility, and prohibitions against murder and cannibalism have survived in the father and son. They have internalized some modicum of discipline. And thus, the conflict of *The Road* becomes one of primal instinct versus discipline. On one side, surviving at all costs. And on the other, retaining the vestiges of a culture that mandate certain attitudes and actions and prohibit others, even if the cost is the sacrifice of one's own life. In such a savage world, morality and ethics are impediments to survival. So it is for the man and his son. They will not eat certain things. They run instead of fighting. The man instills a moral code in the boy, as the boy demonstrates when he gives thanks to the people who left the food in the fallout shelter (123).

It seems paradoxical, given how the critique of discipline and authority and the mountaineer has unfolded in this project, to suggest that McCarthy might be rescuing and rehabilitating discipline in this novel, but I do believe that is part of what happens in *The Road*. Discipline mandates some internal compass, some vestige of a civilized self. For some survivors, the death of all these things — society, taboo, God — becomes a license for anarchy and chaos. It becomes a license to murder at will and to consume the flesh of one's fellow man, to construct "a frieze of human heads, all faced alike, dried and caved with their taut grins and shrunken eyes" (76), or to place "a charred human infant headless and gutted and blackening on the spit" (167). With everything dead, the alternative to chaos for the man and his son is a conscious, strained, and disciplined effort to "cobble together some passable ghost" of what once was. As one must do with a fire, they must "coax it along with words of love. Offer it each phantom crumb and shield it from harm" (49). They have to structure a reality from within and only the man has a frame of reference — a fading memory of the society that once was — to "construct ceremonies out of the air and breathe upon them" (63). This he does. He instills this frame, this series of parameters of human behavior, in the boy. For him and the boy, rules that say "thou shalt not kill" exist even when "blackened books lie in pools of water" (158). The prohibition against eating human flesh still remains for the man and his son:

> We wouldn't ever eat anybody would we?
> No. Of course not.
> Even if we were starving?
> We're starving now.
> You said we werent.
> I said we werent dying. I didn't say we werent starving.
> But we wouldnt.
> No. We wouldnt.
> No matter what.
> No. No matter what.
> Because we're the good guys.
> Yes [108–109].

The man cobbles together a morality, a culture, and a god for the boy. The man himself eventually takes on the traditional role of God for the boy: the boy comes to the realization that "the best thing was to talk to his father and he did talk to him and he didnt forget" (241). He *prays* to his father. Though the father himself remains "a being from a planet that no longer existed. The tales of which were suspect," and though "he could not construct for the child's pleasure the world he'd lost without constructing the loss as well," he does construct it (129–130). Being the "good guys" and "carrying the fire" means upholding the discipline of the gone society despite its death. It means sustaining the increasingly ghostly human spirit: "This is what the good guys do. They keep trying. They dont give up" (116). They live within certain parameters. They do not kill themselves. They do not kill others unless it is absolutely necessary. They do not eat one another in any circumstance. They show compassion when they can. They order life even in its bleakness.

Turning Around from the Spectral Wastelands

The Road was published twenty-seven years and five novels after McCarthy's previous foray into Appalachian literature, *Suttree*. It is not out of the question that he might have adjusted or augmented his worldview, and to some extent, his work might reflect that adjustment. Of *Suttree*, Douglas Canfield suggests, "McCarthy untiringly presents us with a new, albeit sometime comic, dawning to balance against the abject evening redness of the west," and this novel's end is no different from *Suttree* or *The Orchard Keeper* or *Outer Dark* or *Child of God* in that respect (Canfield 694). Like Suttree, the man struggles not against the natural world or even against the elements. Such a struggle would be futile. The man knows that "every day is a lie," but that he is "dying. That is not a lie" (200). His entire struggle in this novel is not against the world or against death. Suttree battles the futility of life and the man fights against his own despair and an indiscipline that would allow him to descend into murder and cannibalism. Suttree divests "himself of the little cloaked godlet and his other amulets ... and [takes] for a talisman the simple human heart within him" (Suttree 468). The man has been divested of the world entire, yet in his fight he carries the "fire"— the vestiges of human society, its history and myth and prohibition and ascension. He does it for the child. His project is not to master the world. His project is to discipline himself and to instill that discipline in his son. The novel's transitional moment comes just after the two survivors consign a thief to death on the beachfront road and the man is at the height of his despair:

> The man looked back up the road.
> He was just hungry, Papa. He's going to die.
> He's going to die anyway.
> He's so scared, Papa.
> The man squatted and looked at him. I'm scared, he said. Do you understand? I'm scared.
> The boy didn't answer. He just sat there with his head bowed, sobbing.
> You're not the one who has to worry about everything.
> The boy said something but he couldnt understand him. What? He said.
> He looked up, his wet and grimy face. Yes I am, he said. I am the one [218].

With the boy's statement, the man realizes his success in training the boy. He can die at peace.

In actuality, as in McCarthy's other Appalachian novels, discipline and the power relationships between people take on ambivalent characteristics in *The Road*. Certainly, it can be argued that the modernity discipline has enabled subsequently hastens the destruction of the natural world in *The Road*. However, discipline also apparently saves the man and his son from barbarism. In the Appalachian region itself, historically, industrialization and modernization and the discipline that has made them more efficient have provided some mountaineers with more economically and socially stable lives. The quality of life has improved, and yet the natural environment has been eviscerated. If McCarthy, as Canfield suggests, examines "the deepest conundrums of human existence," then this paradox of discipline and modernization and internalization is one such conundrum.

I do read McCarthy's latest novel as a revision of his Appalachian works. Many scenes in *The Road* echo scenes from the previous novels. The vegetation, though blackened by flame, corresponds to that of Appalachia, and the people themselves resemble spectral mountaineers of *Appalachia*. And perhaps it is a turn from his other *Appalachian* novels. Perhaps McCarthy has become a conservative, humanistic moralist in his latest work. Perhaps there is some underlying theoretical premise for dedicating *The Road* to his son, John Francis McCarthy. If that is the case, and one can certainly argue that point, the transformation has been hardly a rapid about-face. To assume such a speedy turnaround would be to neglect nearly thirty years, five novels, and two plays. *Blood Meridian, All the Pretty Horses, The Crossing, Cities of the Plains, The Stonemason, No Country for Old Men*, and *The Sunset Limited* all show the strains of power and resistance. They all juggle discipline and the threat of human barbarism. The huntsman always waits "in the gray wood ... and in the brooming corn and in the castellated press of cities" within McCarthy's oeuvre (*Suttree* 471). And there are always characters who resist a resort to barbarism or who evidence some interiorized discipline. John Wesley Rattner tries to return the bounty for the hawk (*OK* 233) and adopts characteristics of his mentor Sylder (*OK* 245–246). Lester Ballard returns to the fold of society (*COG* 192). Something in "the kid" of *Blood Meridian* causes him not to fully engage in the barbarism of his companions. John Grady Cole, Billy Parham, and Tom Ed Bell all have internalized some ordering structure that disciplines their existences, something that makes them the "good guys," though they are overbalanced, perhaps, by the "bad guys" of their respective novels. McCarthy's Western novels, like the Appalachian works, reveal things about the humanity that raise more questions than they answer, than can be answered. That is what makes them worth reading more than once.

But those novels are a study for another time and another project.

Discipline and how it has historically worked in the relationships between authority and the mountaineer — through the building of roads and the infiltration of the mountains by modernizing industry, through the voluntary relocation of mountain folk to "modern" spaces like cotton mill towns and other regional cities, through an iconography that makes deviants and delinquents out of the people who have chosen to remain in the hills—seems to have aided in the disfranchisement of the Appalachian people, but it has also given them employment, electricity, mobility, and so many other advantages of modern life. The formal history of Appalachia, scant though it is, so often has privileged the latter benefits and downplayed the former detriments. Not so McCarthy. His is a fairly even hand. As any competent archeologist would, McCarthy excavates everything he can find, he turns it and shapes it, and then he fires the story of the present and the future from the shards of the past.

Notes

1. This same methodology was employed by the federal government at the end of the Civil War in order to disenfranchise the Southern states. Paul Salstrom maintains, "The most important effect of the 1865 law terminating state-bank banknotes was the financial advantage that it conferred on the region that held the most financial reserves as of then. This was not a 'natural' advantage. Indeed, the Northeast had itself acquired its substantial financial assets largely by issuing banknotes against other forms of assets — slaves, land, timber, fish, rum, etc. In effect, the 1865 law denied to other regions the right to follow the Northeast's path to acquiring large financial reserves" (125). Salstrom further argues that this development was a major factor in how the Appalachian Region became dependent on Northeastern investment; but it goes back farther than the Civil War.

2. In the frontier regions of Virginia, North Carolina, and Georgia, as in western Pennsylvania, the excise tax was largely ignored. Hamilton chose western Pennsylvania as the site of enforcement because of its close proximity to the seat of the central government, Philadelphia, and perhaps because of Washington's substantial personal holdings in the area.

3. Several critics have touched on Ownby's resistance to authority and the conflict his value system engenders with the coming modernization. Vereen Bell's section on *The Orchard Keeper* in *The Achievement of Cormac McCarthy* was one of the first. See also Natalie Grant's "The Landscape of the Soul: Man and the Natural World in *The Orchard Keeper*," David Paul Ragan's "Values and Structure in *The Orchard Keeper*," John M. Grammer's "A Thing Against Which Time Will Not Prevail: Pastoral and History in Cormac McCarthy's South," and George Guillemin's *The Pastoral Vision of Cormac McCarthy*.

4. See Dunaway, *The First American Frontier*, and Billings and Blee.

5. The version in *The Gardener's Son* differs only in small detail. Martha relates: "Me and mama went back up to Pickens about a year fore she died. I was just a young girl. Went up on the train. We'd had this horse and his name was Captain and I used to ride him just everywheres and he'd foller me around like a dog and I remember whenever we got ready to leave from up there why they sent me over to Mamaw's because the feller was fixing to come and get him. They had done sold him, you see. But me and mama went up there. We went up there and we was in Greenville that Saturday afternoon and I looked and there in the street was old Captain. He was harnessed up in an express wagon standin there in front of a store and whenever I seen him I just run across the street and throwed my arms around his neck and kissed him and I reckon everbody through I was crazy standin there in the middle of the street and me about growed, huggin and kissin an old horse and just bawlin to beat the band" [*GS* 93].

6. In this section of the project I will distinguish the geographical region of Appalachia from the rhetorical construct of *Appalachia* by italicizing the latter.

7. While Carr tries to belittle McCarthy's work as pure stereotype, his "careful re-evaluation" of McCarthy's work, it turns out, is not so careful. His connection of McCarthy's work and DeBeck's *Snuffy Smith* rings true, but his convolution of the stereotypes of rednecks and hillbillies — he suggests that "the source of some of [McCarthy's redneck] humor seems to spring from the [hillbilly] comic strip 'Snuffy Smith'" — remains an objectionable mistake. Worse yet, he cannot substantiate his claim that McCarthy must have been familiar with the "'scientific'

studies.... *On Aggression, The Territorial Imperative, Human Aggression,* and *The Naked Ape*" (10). I find it most difficult to take Carr seriously, however, when he so blatantly misconstrues the events in McCarthy's novels. He claims that Culla buries his son alive (16) which he does not (*OD* 16–18); he maintains that the leader of the Triune in *Outer Dark* slits the belly of Culla's son (Carr 12), which he does not (*OD* 236); he even misquotes McCarthy, calling Gene Harrogate "the moonlight melonmaster" (Carr 19), when, in fact, McCarthy terms Harrogate "the moonlight melonmounter" (*Suttree* 48). These mistakes make it impossible to buy Carr's supposition that "Arthur Ormsby" is "another sentimental character whose actions and thoughts are frequently cliché-ridden" (Carr 15). Arthur *Ormsby*? Carr and I must have read different versions of *The Orchard Keeper.*

    8. Williamson in his *Hillbillyland: What Movies Did to the Mountains and What the Mountains Did to the Movies* and Harkins in *Hillbilly: A Cultural History of an American Icon* both discuss the image of Davy Crockett as the emblem of sacrifice for a good cause. They further demonstrate that, like the mountaineer, Davy Crockett, the Alamo hero, is a cultural construct of fiction. The real Crockett, lampooned by the publishers (and readers) of *Davy Crockett's Almanack* as what Harkins labels "the original media-fabricated hillbilly," was a bit of a rube, but, during his stints in the Tennessee Legislature and the United States Congress he never appeared in public in a coonskin cap and buckskin clothes as his iconic portrayal would maintain (Harkins 23; Williamson 78–86). Nevertheless, he becomes the first iconic American hillbilly hero.

    9. Harkins is not the only scholar to link mountaineers and hogs, and the historical record confirms McCarthy's use of the hog drive scene. See also Billings and Blee's *The Road to Poverty: The Making of Wealth and Hardship in Appalachia* (44), McWhinney's *Cracker Culture: Celtic Ways in the Old South* (53) and Salstrom's *Appalachia's Path to Dependency: Rethinking a Region's Economic History* (7–8).

References

The American Livestock Breeds Conservancy. "Mulefoot Hog." *ALBC*, 1993. Web. 19 Mar. 2013.

Andrews, Mildred Gwin. *The Men and the Mills: A History of the Southern Textile Industry*. Macon, GA: Mercer University Press, 1987.

Appalachian Land Ownership Study. "Inadequate Taxes, Services Linked to Outside Land Ownership: Appalachian Land Dominated by Few Outside Owners." *Mountain Life and Work* 57.4 (April 1981): 13–20.

Appalachian Regional Commission. "Appalachia Today: Issues and Problems. Material Prepared for Public Meetings to be Held During the Preparation of the Regional Plan." GPO, 1977.

———. *The Appalachian Experiment: 1965–1970*. Ed. Judith K. Ballangee. Washington: GPO,1971.

Arnold, Edwin T. "Naming, Knowing and Nothingness: McCarthy's Moral Parables." In *Perspectives on Cormac McCarthy*. Ed. Edwin T. Arnold and Dianne C. Luce. Jackson: University Press of Mississippi, 1999. 45–69.

Bartlett, Andrew. "From Voyeurism to Archaeology: Cormac McCarthy's *Child of God*." *Southern Literary Journal* 24 (Fall 1991): 3–15.

Batteau, Allen, "Appalachia and the Concept of Culture: A Theory of Shared Misunderstandings." In *Appalachia: Social Context Past and Present*, second edition. Ed. Bruce Ergood and Bruce R. Kuhre. Dubuque: Kendall/Hunt, 1976. 109–125.

———. "Rituals of Dependence in Appalachian Kentucky. In *Appalachia and America: Autonomy and Regional Dependence*. Ed. Allen Batteau. Lexington: UniversityPress of Kentucky, 1983. 142–167.

———. ed. *Appalachia and America: Autonomy and Regional Dependence*. Lexington: The University Press of Kentucky, 1983.

Behr, Edward. *Prohibition: Thirteen Years That Changed America*. New York: Arcade, 1996.

Belcher, John C. "Population Growth and Characteristics." In *The Southern Appalachian Region: A Survey*. Ed Thomas R. Ford. Lexington, KY: University of Kentucky Press, 1962. 37–53.

Bell, Vereen M. *The Achievement of Cormac McCarthy*. Baton Rouge: Louisiana State University Press, 1988.

Berry, K. Wesley. "The Lay of the Land in Cormac McCarthy's Appalachia." In *Cormac McCarthy: New Directions*. Ed. James D. Lilley. Albuquerque: University of New Mexico Press, 2002. 47–74.

Biggers, Jeff. *The United States of Appalachia: How Southern Mountaineers Brought Independence, Culture, and Enlightenment to America*. New York: Shoemaker and Hoard, 2006.

Billings, Dwight B. Introduction. *Confronting Appalachian Stereotypes: Back Talk from an American Region*. Ed. Dwight B. Billings, Gurney Norman, and Katherine Ledford. Lexington: University Press of Kentucky, 1999. 3–20.

———, and Kathleen Blee. *The Road to Poverty: The Making of Wealth and Hardship in *Appalachia*. Cambridge: Cambridge University Press, 2000.

Blee, Kathleen M., and Dwight B. Billings. "Where 'Bloodshed Is a Pastime': Mountain Feuds and Appalachian Stereotyping." *Confronting Appalachian Stereotypes: Back Talk from an American Region*. Ed. Dwight B. Billings, Gurney Norman, and Katherine Ledford. Lexington: University Press of Kentucky, 1999. 119–149.

Bolton, Charles C. *Poor Whites of the Antebellum South: Tenants and Laborers in Central North Carolina and Northeast Mississippi*. Durham: Duke University Press, 1994.

Boyd, Steven R., ed. "Alexander Hamilton to George Washington, Report on the Western Country, August 5, 1794." In *The Whiskey Rebellion: Past and Present Perspectives*. Ed. Steven R. Boyd. Westport, CT: Greenwood, 1985. 31–47.

Bradshaw, Michael. *The Appalachian Regional Commission: Twenty-five Years of Government Policy*. Lexington: University Press of Kentucky, 1992.

Breeds of Livestock. "Mulefoot Hog." Oklahoma State University. 19 June 1996. Web. 19 March 2013.

Brickman, Barbara Jane. "Imposition and Resistance in Cormac McCarthy's *The Orchard Keeper*." In *Myth, Legend, Dust: Critical Responses to Cormac McCarthy*. Ed. Rick Wallach. Manchester: Manchester University Press, 2000. 55–67.

Brown, James S., and George A. Hillary, Jr. "The Great Migration, 1940–1960." In *The Southern Appalachian Region: A Survey*. Ed Thomas R. Ford. Lexington: University of Kentucky Press, 1962. 54–78.

Butterworth, D. S. "Pearls as Swine: Recentering the Marginal in Cormac McCarthy's *Suttree*." In *Sacred Violence: Volume One — Cormac McCarthy's Appalachian Works*, second edition. Ed.Wade Hall and Rick Wallach. El Paso: Texas Western Press, 2002. 131–138.

Byerly, Victoria. *Hard Times Cotton Mill Girls: Personal Histories of Womanhood and Poverty in the South*. Ithaca: ILR Press, 1986.

Canfield, J. Douglas. "The Dawning of the Age of Aquarius: Abjection, Identity, and the Carnivalesque in Cormac McCarthy's *Suttree*." *Contemporary Literature* 44.4 (Winter 2003): 664–96.

Cant, John. *Cormac McCarthy and the Myth of American Exceptionalism*. New York: Routledge, 2009.

Carr, Duane R. "The Dispossessed White as Naked Ape and Stereotyped Hillbilly in the Southern Novels of Cormac McCarthy." *Midwest Quarterly* 40.1 (Autumn 1998): 9–20.

Caudill, Harry M. *Night Comes to the Cumberlands: A Biography of a Depressed Area*. Boston: Little, Brown, 1962.

Cawelti, John G. "Cormac McCarthy: Restless Seekers." In *Southern Writers at Century's End*. Ed. Jeffrey J. Folks and James A. Perkins. Lexington: University Press of Kentucky, 1997. 164–76.

Ciuba, Gary M. "McCarthy's Enfant Terrible: Mimetic Desire and Sacred Violence in *Child of God*." In *Sacred Violence: Volume One — Cormac McCarthy's Appalachian Works*, second edition. Ed.Wade Hall and Rick Wallach. El Paso: Texas Western Press, 2002. 93–102.

Cobb, James C. *Industrialization and Southern Society 1877–1984*. Lexington: University Press of Kentucky, 1984.

The Constitution of the United States, In *The New York Public Library Desk Reference: Second Edition*. New York: Prentice Hall General Reference, 1993. 799–807.

The Declaration of Independence, In *The New York Public Library Desk Reference: Second Edition*. New York: Prentice Hall General Reference, 1993. 795–797.

Ditsky, John. "Further Into Darkness: The Novels of Cormac McCarthy." *Hollins Critic* 18 (Apr. 1981): 1–11.

Docherty, Thomas. "Postmodernism: An Introduction." In *Postmodernism: A Reader*. Ed. Thomas Docherty. New York: Columbia University Press, 1993. 1–31.

Dollimore, Jonathan. *Sexual Dissidence: Augustine to Wilde, Freud to Foucault*. Oxford: Clarendon Press, 1991.

Dunaway, Wilma A. *The First American Frontier: Transition to Capitalism in Southern Appalachia, 1700–1860*. Chapel Hill: University of North Carolina Press, 1996.

_____. "Speculators and Settler Capitalists:

Unthinking the Mythology about Appalachian Landholding, 1790–1860." In *Appalachia in the Making*. Ed. Mary Beth Pudup, Dwight B. Billings, and Altina L. Walker. Chapel Hill: University of North Carolina Press, 1995. 50–75.

Dyer, Richard. *White*. New York: Routledge, 1997.

Dykeman, Wilma. "Appalachia in Context." In *An Appalachian Symposium: Essays Written in Honor of Cratis D. Williams*. Ed. J. W. Williamson. Boone, NC: Appalachian State University Press, 1977. 28–42.

Egerton, John. "Appalachia: The View from the Hills." In *Appalachia: Social Context Past and Present*, second edition. Ed. Bruce Ergood and Bruce R. Kuhre. Dubuque: Kendall/Hunt, 1976. 238–242.

Eller, Ronald D. "Appalachian Oral History." In *An Appalachian Symposium: Essays Written in Honor of Cratis D. Williams*. Ed. J. W. Williamson. Boone, NC: Appalachian State University Press, 1977. 2–13.

_____. Foreword. *Confronting Appalachian Stereotypes: Back Talk from an American Region*. Ed. Dwight B. Billings, Gurney Norman, and Katherine Ledford. Lexington: University Press of Kentucky, 1999. ix-xi.

_____. *Miners, Millhands, and Mountaineers: Industrialization of the Appalachian South, 1880–1930*. Knoxville: University of Tennessee Press, 1982.

Ergood, Bruce. "Toward a Definition of Appalachia." In *Appalachia: Social Context Past and Present*, second edition. Ed. Bruce Ergood and Bruce R. Kuhre. Dubuque: Kendall/Hunt, 1976. 31–41.

Evenson, Brian. "McCarthy's Wanderers: Nomadology, Violence, and Open Country." In *Sacred Violence: Volume One — Cormac McCarthy's Appalachian Works*, second edition. Ed. Wade Hall and Rick Wallach. El Paso: Texas Western Press, 2002. 51–60.

Faulkner, William. *Requiem for a Nun*. 1950. New York: Vintage, 1975.

Fisher, Stephen L. "Folk Culture or Folk Tale: Prevailing Assumptions About the Appalachian Personality." In *An Appalachian Symposium: Essays Written in Honor of Cratis D. Williams*. Ed. J. W. Williamson. Boone, NC: Appalachian State University Press, 1977. 14–25.

Fisher-Wirth, Ann. "Abjection and 'the Feminine' in *Outer Dark*." In *Cormac McCarthy: New Directions*. Ed. James D. Lilley. Albuquerque: University of New Mexico Press, 2002. 125–140.

Ford, Thomas R. "The Passing of Provincialism." In *The Southern Appalachian Region: A Survey*. Ed Thomas R. Ford. Lexington: University of Kentucky Press, 1962. 9–34.

Foucault, Michel. *Birth of the Clinic: An Archeology of Medical Perception*. 1973. Trans. A.M. Sheridan Smith. New York: Vintage, 1994.

_____. *Discipline and Punish: The Birth of the Prison*. 1975. Trans. Alan Sheridan. New York: Vintage, 1995.

_____. *The History of Sexuality — An Introduction: Volume One*. 1978. Trans. Robert Hurley. New York: Vintage, 1990.

_____. *Madness and Civilization: A History of Insanity in the Age of Reason*. 1965. Trans. Richard Howard. New York: Vintage, 1988.

_____. *Power/Knowledge: Selected Interviews and Other Writings, 1972-1977*. Ed. Colin Gordon. New York: Pantheon Books, 1980.

Fowler, Gary L. "Up Here and Down Home: Appalachians in Cities." In *Appalachia: Social Context Past and Present*, second edition. Ed. Bruce Ergood and Bruce R. Kuhre. Athens, Ohio: Kendall/Hunt Publishing Company, 1976. 90–95.

Fox-Genovese, Elizabeth, and Eugene D. Genovese. *The Mind of the Master Class: History and Faith in the Southern Slaveholders' Worldview*. Cambridge: Cambridge University Press, 2005.

Gardiner, Elaine. "Sut Lovingood: Backwoods Existentialist." *Southern Studies* 22.3 (Summer 1983): 177–189.

Gaventa, John. *Power and Powerlessness: Quiescence and Rebellion in an Appalachian Valley*. Urbana: University of Illinois Press, 1980.

Gibson, Mike. "Knoxville Gave Cormac McCarthy the Raw Material of His Art. And He Gave It Back." In *Sacred Violence: Volume One — McCarthy's Appalachian*

Works, second edition. Ed. Wade Hall and Rick Wallach. El Paso: Texas Western Press, 2002. 23-34.

Gordon, Colin. Afterword. *Power/ Knowledge: Selected Interviews and Other Writings, 1972- 1977*. By Michel Foucault. Ed. Colin Gordon. New York: Pantheon, 1980. 229-259.

Grammer, John M. "A Thing Against Which Time Will Not Prevail: Pastoral and History in Cormac McCarthy's South." In *Perspectives on Cormac McCarthy*. Ed. Edwin T. Arnold and Diane Luce. Jackson: University Press of Mississippi, 1999. 29-44.

Grant, Natalie. "The Landscape of the Soul: Man and the Natural World in *The Orchard Keeper*." *Sacred Violence: Volume One — Cormac McCarthy's Appalachian Works*, second edition. Ed. Wade Hall and Rick Wallach. El Paso: Texas Western Press, 2002. 75-82.

Gray, Richard. "Recorded and Unrecorded Histories: Recent Southern Writing and Social Change." *The Southern State of Mind*. Ed. Jan Nordby Gretlund. Columbia: University of South Carolina Press, 1999. 67-79.

Guillemin, George. *The Pastoral Vision of Cormac McCarthy*. College Station: Texas A&M University Press, 2004.

Guinn, Matthew. "Atavism and the Exploded Metanarrative: Cormac McCarthy's Journey to Mythoclasm." *After Southern Modernism: Fiction of the Contemporary South*. Jackson: University Press of Mississippi, 2000. 91-109.

Hamilton, Alexander. *The Papers of Alexander Hamilton, vol. 8: February-July 1791*. Ed. Harold C. Syrett, et al. New York: Columbia University Press, 1967.

_____. *The Papers of Alexander Hamilton, vol. 17 August 1794-December 1794*. Ed. Harold C. Syrett, et al. New York: Columbia University Press, 1967.

Harkins, Anthony. *Hillbilly: A Cultural History of an American Icon*. Oxford: Oxford University Press, 2004.

Harris, George Washington. *Sut Lovingood's Yarns*. Ed. M. Thomas Inge. Schenectady, NY: New College and University Press, 1966.

Hartigen, John, Jr. "Name Calling: Objectifying 'Poor Whites' and 'White Trash' in Detroit." In *White Trash: Race and Class in America*. Ed. Matt Wray and Annalee Newitz. New York: Routledge, 1997. 41-56.

Heller, Kevin Jon. "Power, Subjectification, and Resistance in Foucault." *Substance* 79 (1996): 78-110.

Herring, Harriet L. *Passing of the Mill Village: Revolution in a Southern Institution*. Chapel Hill: University of North Carolina Press, 1949.

_____. *Welfare Work in Mill Villages: The Story of Extra-Mill Activities in North Carolina*. Chapel Hill: University of North Carolina Press, 1929.

Hogeland, William. *The Whiskey Rebellion: George Washington, Alexander Hamilton, and the Frontier Rebels Who Challenged America's Newfound Sovereignty*. New York: Scribner, 2006.

Holloway, David. *The Late Modernism of Cormac McCarthy*. Westport, CT: Greenwood, 2002.

Kohn, Richard H. "Judge Alexander Addison on the Origin and History of the Whiskey Rebellion." In *The Whiskey Rebellion: Past and Present Perspectives*. Ed. Steven R. Boyd. Westport, CT: Greenwood, 1985. 49-60.

Lang, John. "Lester Ballard: McCarthy's Challenge to the Reader's Compassion." In *Sacred Violence: Volume One — Cormac McCarthy's Appalachian Works*, second edition. Ed. Wade Hall and Rick Wallach. El Paso: Texas Western Press, 2002. 103-111.

Ledford, Katherine. "A Landscape and a People Set Apart: Narratives of Exploration and Travel in Early Appalachia." *Confronting Appalachian Stereotypes: Back Talk from an American Region*. Ed. Dwight B. Billings, Gurney Norman, and Katherine Ledford. Lexington: University Press of Kentucky, 1999. 47-66.

Lemert, Ben F. *The Cotton Textile Industry of the Southern Appalachian Piedmont*. Chapel Hill: University of North Carolina Press, 1933.

Lewis, Helen. "Fatalism or the Coal Industry?" In *Appalachia: Social Context Past and Present*, second edition. Ed. Bruce Ergood and Bruce R. Kuhre. Dubuque: Kendall/Hunt, 1976. 180–189.

Lewis, Ronald L. "Beyond Isolation and Homogeneity: Diversity and the History of Appalachia." *Confronting Appalachian Stereotypes: Back Talk from an American Region*. Ed. Dwight B. Billings, Gurney Norman, and Katherine Ledford. Lexington: University Press of Kentucky, 1999. 21–43.

Longley, John Lewis, Jr. "Suttree and the Metaphysics of Death." *Southern Literary Journal* 17.2 (Spring 1985): 79–90.

Luce, Dianne C. "'The Cave of Oblivion': Platonic Mythology in *Child of God*." In *Cormac McCarthy: New Directions*. Ed. James D. Lilley. Albuquerque: University of New Mexico Press, 2002. 171–198.

_____. "Cormac McCarthy's First Screenplay: 'The Gardener's Son.'" In *Perspectives on Cormac McCarthy*. Ed. Edwin T. Arnold and Dianne C. Luce. Jackson: University Press of Mississippi, 1999. 71–96.

_____. *Reading the World: Cormac McCarthy's Tennessee Period*. Columbia: University of South Carolina Press, 2009.

_____. "White Caps, Moral Judgment, and Law in *Child of God* or The 'Wrong Blood' in Community History." In *Cormac McCarthy: Uncharted Territories*. Ed. Christine Collier. Champagne-Ardenne: Universite de Reims, 2003. 43–59.

Lyotard, Jean-François. "Note on the Meaning of 'Post-.'" In *Postmodernism: A Reader*. Ed. Thomas Docherty. New York: Columbia University Press, 1993. 47–50.

Malizia, Emil. "Economic Imperialism: An Interpretation of Appalachian Underdevelopment." In *Appalachia: Social Context Past and Present*, second edition. Ed. Bruce Ergood and Bruce R. Kuhre. Dubuque: Kendall/Hunt, 1976. 189–194.

Marius, Richard. "*Suttree* as a Window into the Soul of Cormac McCarthy." In *Sacred Violence: Volume One—Cormac McCarthy's Appalachian Works*, second edition. Ed. Wade Hall and Rick Wallach. El Paso: Texas Western Press, 2002. 113–130.

McCarthy, Cormac. *Child of God*. 1973. New York: Vintage, 1993.

_____. *The Gardener's Son*. Hopewell, NJ: The Ecco Press, 1996.

_____. *The Orchard Keeper*. 1965. New York: Vintage, 1993.

_____. *Outer Dark*. 1968. New York: Vintage, 1993.

_____. *The Road*. New York: Alfred A. Knopf, 2006.

_____. *Suttree*. 1979. New York: Vintage, 1992.

McCoy, Clyde B., and James S. Brown. "Appalachian Migration to Midwestern Cities." In *The Invisible Minority: Urban Appalachians*. Ed. William W. Philliber and Clyde B. McCoy. Lexington: University Press of Kentucky, 1981. 35–78.

_____, and Virginia McCoy Watlins. "Stereotypes of Appalachian Migrants." In *Appalachia: Social Context Past and Present*, second edition. Ed. Bruce Ergood and Bruce R. Kuhre. Dubuque: Kendall/Hunt, 1976. 100–105.

McDonald, Michael J., and William Bruce Wheeler. *Knoxville, Tennessee: Continuity and Change in an Appalachian City*. Knoxville: University of Tennessee Press, 1983.

McKenna, Frank, and David Anderson. "United States." In *International Handbook of Transportation Policy*. Ed. Tsuneo Akaha. New York: Greenwood, 1990. 269–300.

McWhiney, Grady. *Cracker Culture: Celtic Ways in the Old South*. Tuscaloosa: University of Alabama Press, 1988.

Menzer, Joe. *The Wildest Ride: A History of NASCAR (or How a Bunch of Good Ol' Boys Built a Billion-Dollar Industry out of Wrecking Cars)*. New York: Touchstone, 2001.

Metress, Christopher. "Via Negativa: The Way of Unknowing in Cormac McCarthy's *Outer Dark*." *Southern Review* 37.1 (Winter 2001): 147–54.

Miller, Wilbur R. *Revenuers and Moonshiners: Enforcing Federal Liquor Law in the Mountain South, 1865–1900*. Chapel Hill: University of North Carolina Press, 1991.

Mitchell, Broadus. *The Industrial Revolution in the South*. 1930. New York: AMS Press, 1969.

_____. *The Rise of Cotton Mills in the South*. 1921. Baltimore: Johns Hopkins University Press, 1966.

Morgan, Arthur. *The Making of the TVA*. Buffalo: Prometheus, 1974.

Morgan, Wesley G. "Mulefoot Hogs." Message to Gabe Rikard. 20 March 2013. Email.

Morgan, Wesley G. "The Route and Roots of *The Road*." *The Cormac McCarthy Journal* 6 (Autumn 2008): 37–47.

Morris, John W. "The Potential of Tourism." In *The Southern Appalachian Region: A Survey*. Ed Thomas R. Ford. Lexington: University of Kentucky Press, 1962. 136–148.

Munn, Robert F. "The Latest Rediscovery of Appalachia." In *Appalachia: Social Context Past and Present*, second edition. Ed. Bruce Ergood and Bruce R. Kuhre. Dubuque: Kendall/Hunt, 1976. 8–10.

Newitz, Annalee. "White Savagery and Humiliation, or a New Racial Consciousness in the Media." In *White Trash: Race and Class in America*. Ed. Matt Wray and Annalee Newitz. New York: Routledge, 1997. 131–154.

Newman, Monroe. *The Political Economy of Appalachia: A Case Study in Regional Integration*. Lexington, MA: D.C. Heath, 1972.

Noe, Kenneth W. "'Deadened Color and Colder Horror': Rebecca Harding Davis and the Myth of Unionist Appalachia." *Confronting Appalachian Stereotypes: Back Talk from an American Region*. Ed. Dwight B. Billings, Gurney Norman, and Katherine Ledford. Lexington: University Press of Kentucky, 1999. 67–84.

Precourt, Walter. "The Image of Appalachian Poverty." In *Appalachia and America: Autonomy and Regional Dependence*. Ed. Allen Batteau. Lexington: University Press of Kentucky, 1983. 86–110.

Ragan, David Paul. "Values and Structure in *The Orchard Keeper*." In *Perspectives on Cormac McCarthy*. Ed. Edwin T. Arnold and Dianne C. Luce. Jackson: University Press of Mississippi, 1999. 17–28.

Raitz, Karl B., and Richard Ulack, with Thomas R. Leinbach. *Appalachia, a Regional Geography: Land, People and Development*. Boulder, CO: Westview Press, 1984.

Reck, Una Mae Lange, and George G. Reck. "Living is More Important than Schooling: Schools and Self Concept in Appalachia." In *Appalachia: Social Context Past and Present*, second edition. Ed. Bruce Ergood and Bruce R. Kuhre. Dubuque: Kendall/Hunt, 1976. 284–289.

Reed, John Shelton. *Southern Folk, Plain and Fancy: Native White Social Types*. Athens: University of Georgia Press, 1986.

Roediger, David R. *The Wages of Whiteness, Revised Edition: Race and the Making of the American Working Class*. New York: Verso, 1991.

Rovetch, Warren, and John J. Gaskie. *Program Budgeting for Planners: A Case Study of Appalachia with Projections through 1985*. New York: Praeger, 1974.

Salstrom, Paul. *Appalachia's Path to Dependency: Rethinking a Region's Economic History 1730–1940*. Lexington: University Press of Kentucky, 1994.

Sandell, Jillian. "Telling Stories of 'Queer White Trash': Race, Class, and Sexuality in the Work of Dorothy Allison." In *White Trash: Race and Class in America*. Ed. Matt Wray and Annalee Newitz. New York: Routledge, 1997. 211–230

Shackelford, Laurel, and Bill Weinberg. *Our Appalachia*. New York: Hill & Wang, 1977.

Shapiro, Henry D. "Appalachia and the Idea of America: The Problem of the Persisting Frontier." In *An Appalachian Symposium: Essays Written in Honor of Cratis D. Williams*. Ed. J. W. Williamson. Boone, NC: Appalachian State University Press, 1977. 43–55.

———. *Appalachia on Our Mind: The Southern Mountains and Mountaineers in the American Consciousness, 1870–1920*. Chapel Hill: University of North Carolina Press, 1978.

Shelton, Frank W. "*Suttree* and Suicide." *Southern Quarterly* 29 (Fall 1990): 71–83.

Simpson, William Hays. *Life in Mill Communities*. Clinton, SC: P. C. Press, 1941.

Slaughter, Thomas P. "The Friends of Liberty, the Friends of Order, and the Whiskey Rebellion: A Historiographical Essay." In *The Whiskey Rebellion: Past and Present Perspectives*. Ed. Steven R. Boyd. Westport, CT: Greenwood, 1985. 9–30.

———. *The Whiskey Rebellion: Frontier Epilogue to the American Revolution*. New York: Oxford University Press, 1986.

Slotkin, Richard. *Gunfighter Nation: The Myth of the Frontier in Twentieth-Century*

America. Norman: University of Oklahoma Press, 1992.

Spencer, William C. "Cormac McCarthy's Unholy Trinity: Biblical Parody in *Outer Dark*." In *Sacred Violence: Volume One—Cormac McCarthy's Appalachian Works*, second edition. Ed. Wade Hall and Rick Wallach. El Paso: Texas Western Press, 2002. 83–91.

Stallybrass, Peter, and Allon White. *The Politics and Poetics of Transgression*. Ithaca: Cornell University Press, 1986.

Stewart, Kathleen. *A Space on the Side of the Road: Cultural Poetics in an "Other" America*. Princeton, NJ: Princeton University Press, 1996.

Sweeney, Gael. "The King of White Trash Culture: Elvis Presley and the Aesthetics of Excess." In *White Trash: Race and Class in America*. Ed. Matt Wray and Annalee Newitz. New York: Routledge, 1997. 249–266.

Traber, Daniel S. "'Ruder Forms Survive,' or Slumming for Subjectivity: Self-Marginalization in *Suttree*." *Southern Quarterly* 37.2 (Winter 1999): 33–46.

Tullos, Allen. *Habits of Industry: White Culture and the Transformation of the Carolina Piedmont*. Chapel Hill: University of North Carolina Press, 1989.

Wallach, Rick. "Foreword." *The Late Modernism of Cormac McCarthy*. By David Holloway. Westport, CT: Greenwood, 2002. xi-xiv.

Waller, Altina L. "Feuding in Appalachia: Evolution of a Cultural Stereotype." In *Appalachia in the Making*. Ed. Mary Beth Pudup, Dwight B. Billings, and Altina L. Walker. Chapel Hill: University of North Carolina Press, 1995. 347–376.

Walls, David S., and Dwight B. Billings. "The Sociology of Southern Appalachia." In *Appalachia: Social Context Past and Present*, second edition. Ed. Bruce Ergood and Bruce R. Kuhre. Dubuque: Kendall/Hunt, 1976. 41–51.

Walsh, Christopher J. *In the Wake of the Sun: Navigating the Southern Works of Cormac McCarthy*. Knoxville: Newfound Press, 2009.

_____. "There's NO Place Like Holme: The Quest to Find a Place for McCarthy's Southern Fiction." In *Cormac McCarthy: Uncharted Territories*. Ed. Christine Collier. Champagne-Ardenne: Universite de Reims, 2003. 31–42.

Weller, Jack E. *Yesterday's People: Life in Contemporary Appalachia*. Lexington: University of Kentucky Press, 1965.

Wenke, John. "*Sut Lovingood's Yarns* and the Politics of Performance." *Studies in American Fiction* 15.2 (Autumn 1987): 199–210.

West, Don. "Romantic Appalachia." In *Appalachia: Social Context Past and Present*, second edition. Ed. Bruce Ergood and Bruce R. Kuhre. Dubuque: Kendall/Hunt, 1976. 10–13.

Whisnant, David E. *All That Is Native and Fine: The Politics of Culture in An American Region*. Chapel Hill: University of North Carolina Press, 1983.

_____. *Modernizing the Mountaineer: People, Power, and Planning in Appalachia*, Revised Edition. Knoxville: University of Tennessee Press, 1994.

Williams, Cratis D. "Who Are the Southern Mountaineers?" In *Appalachia: Social Context Past and Present*, second edition. Ed. Bruce Ergood and Bruce R. Kuhre. Dubuque: Kendall/Hunt, 1976. 54–58.

Williams, John Alexander. *Appalachia: A History*. Chapel Hill: University of North Carolina Press, 2002.

Williamson, J. W. *Hillbillyland: What Movies Did to the Mountains and What the Mountains Did to the Movies*. Chapel Hill: University of North Carolina, 1995.

Wilson, Darlene. "A Judicious Combination of Incident and Psychology: John Fox Jr. and the Southern Mountaineer Motif." *Confronting Appalachian Stereotypes: Back Talk from an American Region*. Ed. Dwight B. Billings, Gurney Norman, and Katherine Ledford. Lexington: University Press of Kentucky, 1999. 98–118.

Yeats, William Butler. *Selected Poems and Four Plays*. Ed. M. L. Rosenthal. New York: Scribner, 1996.

Young, Thomas D., Jr. "The Imprisonment of Sensibility: *Suttree*." In *Perspectives on Cormac McCarthy*. Ed. Edwin T. Arnold and Dianne C. Luce. Jackson: University Press of Mississippi, 1999. 97–122.

Index

Adams, John 12
Addison, Alexander 13
All the Pretty Horses 224
Allen, James Lane 33, 169, 181
Allison, Dorthy 162
alterity 10, 24, 33, 37
American Daily Advertiser 15
American Livestock Breeds Conservancy 197–198
American Revolution 7–8, 10–12
American Southwest 207
Anders, Sabine 5
Anderson, David 43–44, 51
Anderson, Terry 196
Andrews, Mildred Gwin 97, 102
anthropocentrism 69, 208
Appalachia 24–25, 28, 32, 38–40, 42, 140, 167, 170, 172–175, 179, 183–184, 188, 194, 198, 200
Appalachian diaspora 90; *see also* hillbilly diaspora
Appalachian Experiment 48, 50, 113
Appalachian Highway Development 57
Appalachian Land Ownership Study 50
Appalachian Oral History 31
Appalachian Regional Commission 57–58, 91, 131–132
Arnold, Edwin T. 185, 200–201, 203
Articles of Confederation 7
Asheville, NC 53, 113, 184
Atomic Energy Commission 113
Aunt Alice 129–130

Bacon's Rebellion 93
Bakhtin, Mikail 142
Ballard, Lester 3–4, 35, 37–38, 55–56, 63–67, 73, 75, 81, 83, 132, 166, 171, 184–187, 211, 220, 224
Bartlett, Andrew 145, 148, 150, 161, 163, 187
Batteau, Allen 23, 52
Beersheba Springs, TN 169
Behr, Edward 73
Belcher, John C. 113, 212

Bell, Ed Tom 224
Bell, Vereen 5, 34, 72, 75, 137, 141, 149, 162, 203, 227
Belloc, Hilaire 43
benevolent organizations 198; *see also* benevolent societies; denominational benevolence; denominational philanthropists; denominational uplift; social uplift
benevolent societies 170; *see also* benevolent organizations; denominational benevolence; denominational philanthropists; denominational uplift; social uplift
Benjamin, Walter 209
Benthum, Jeremy 27, 109
Berea College 168, 181
Berry, K. Wesley 42, 68, 74, 81, 84, 132, 212
beyond the pale 34, 133, 137, 154
bibledrummer 68, 187
Biggers, Jeff 90
Billings, Dwight B. 24, 30, 88–89, 99, 169, 1779, 182–183, 188–190, 227
Black Belt 114
Blee, Kathleen 24, 88–89, 99, 169, 182–183, 188–190, 227
Blind Richard 125
blindness 206
blockaders 73; *see also* bootlegger; whiskey runner
blood feud 189–190, 192, 214
Blood Meridian 224
bloodcult 214, 217
Bolton, Charles 93–94, 107
Boone, Daniel 139, 178
Boorman, John 193
bootlegging 21, 35, 41, 47, 74–77, 79–81, 118, 122, 171, 174, 184; *see also* blockader; whiskey runner
Braddock's Field 16
Bradshaw, Micheal 132–143, 142
Branscombe, Jim 19, 207, 215
Brickman, Barbara Jane 70, 77, 191
Brookside Village 114
Brown, James S. 52, 113

Index

Brown's Mountain 1, 196
Brushy Mountain Penitentiary 76, 81, 128–129; *see also* Petros penitentiary
Bumppo, Natty 139
Buncombe Turnpike 53–54
Buttersworth, D.S. 119
Byerly, Beverly 99–100
Byrd, William II 11–18, 168, 175–177, 182

Caldwell, Erskine 135
Callahan, Billy Ray (Red) 120, 122–123, 193
Campbell, John C. 91
Canfield, J. Douglas 119–120, 223–224
cannibalism 216–217, 221–222
Cant, John 5, 31, 38, 106–107, 132, 161, 184, 195
Capp, Al 171, 195–197, 201, 214
Captain the horse 129–130, 227
carnival gorilla 164
Carolina Piedmont 94–95; *see also* Piedmont
Carr, Dwane R. 172, 227–228
carrying the fire 211, 221, 223
Carter Family 171
Caudill, Harry 27, 47, 54, 73, 76, 81, 91, 112, 116, 132–133, 136, 185, 190
Cawelti, James G. 115
Charleston, SC 94–95, 213
Cherokee [Indians] 176–179; *see also* Indians; Native American; noble savage; red man
Cities of the Plain 224
city rat 126; *see also* Harrogate, Gene
Ciuba, Gary 159
Civil War 86, 88, 95, 100, 113–114, 177, 189, 227
Clampett, Jed 174
Clampett, Jethro 194
Clark, Mike 19, 207, 215
Clark's store 179
Clay County, KY 190
Clinton Highway 122
Cobb, James C. 98, 101
Coburn, F.D. 197–198
Coca-Cola 213
cognitive dissonance 33
Cole, John Grady 224
Coltrain, Roscoe P. 174
Columbia, SC 129–130
Constitution, United States 7–9, 11–12, 16
contemporary ancestors 30, 48, 180, 215
Cooper, Gary 139
Cooper, James Fenimore 139
The Cosmopolitan 182
cotton mill village 35–36, 46, 81, 88, 95–96, 98, 100, 118, 180, 211; *see also* mill village; textile mill village
counter-hegemony 119, 134, 141–142; *see also* hegemony
Crockett, David (Davy) 139, 228
The Crossing 224
Cumberland Gap 53

Davis, Rebecca Harding 169
Davis, Tom 164–165

DeBeck, Billy 171, 195–197, 227
Declaration of Independence, United States 7, 16
deconstruction 24, 39, 56, 106, 163, 172, 186, 195
delinquency 14–16, 27, 29, 35–37, 41, 75, 78, 80, 92, 117–120, 122, 124, 128, 133–134, 136, 146–147, 149–150, 152–153, 163; *see also* reprobate
Deliverance 174, 193, 215
denominational benevolence 32–33, 181, 189; *see also* benevolent organizations; benevolent societies; denominational philanthropists; denominational uplift; social uplift
denominational philanthropists 34; *see also* benevolent organizations; benevolent societies; denominational benevolence; denominational uplift; social uplift
denominational uplift 174; *see also* benevolent organizations; benevolent societies; denominational benevolence; denominational philanthropists; social uplift
Detroit, MI 72
deviance 31–32, 47, 63, 79–80, 140–141, 143–144, 149, 153–154, 156–157, 161–162, 180, 220
Devil Anse Hatfield 173, 201, 214
Dickey, James 174, 193, 215
Discipline and Punish 8, 15, 17, 23, 26, 36–37, 45, 49, 62, 73, 88, 97–99, 108–109, 116–118, 120–123, 125, 128, 143–144, 146, 148, 159, 168, 173–174, 182, 186, 191–192
disenfranchisement 15, 30, 82, 118, 132–133, 140, 170, 180, 225, 227
Dismal swamp 175
dispossession 143, 145
Docherty, Leo 209
Dogpatch 30, 195, 201
Dollimore, Jonathan 141
Dollywood 131
Duke, Bo 174
Duke, Luke 174
Duke, Uncle Jesse 174
Dukes of Hazzard 214
dumpkeeper 137–138, 146; *see also* Kirby, Ruebel
Dunn, Durwood 74
Dyer, Richard 94
Dykeman, Wilma 52, 170, 188

Eagleton, Terry 220
East Tennessee 185, 207
Egerton, John 19, 207
Eisenhower, Dwight D.
Eller, Ronald 29, 31, 34, 53–54, 132–133, 182–183
Ely (*The Road*) 217–218
ephiphany 66, 158
Ergood, Bruce 178
Esquire 172
excise tax 188, 227; *see also* whiskey excise

exploitation 53
extractive industries 48, 73, 87, 132–133, 170–174, 180

fait divers 182, 184, 186
Faulkner, William 3, 135, 147, 168
Federal Bureau of Investigation (FBI) 148
federal government 7, 11, 13–18, 38, 50, 67, 70, 76, 133, 142, 188, 227
federal regulators 21; *see also* revenue officers; revenuers
Federalists 12, 18
First Street 120, 125
Fisher, Stephan L. 187
Fisher-Wirth Ann 200
Flatt, Lester 171
Ford [Motor Company] 72, 74
Ford, Thomas R. 91, 115
Fordism 59
Foucault, Michel 1, 4–5, 8–9, 17–18, 23–25, 28, 30, 34, 40, 45–46, 51, 53, 59, 76, 79, 93, 101, 106, 108–109, 116, 118, 122–123, 141–144, 146–149, 152–159, 173, 182–184, 188, 200–221
Founding Fathers 10, 12–13, 18, 50
Fowler, Gary L. 44, 59, 112
Fox, John, Jr. 33, 168–169, 171, 181–184, 1963
Fox-Genovese, Elizabeth 93
French Broad River 53
French Broad Trail 197
Friends of Liberty 8, 17
Frog Mountain 63–64, 134, 139–140, 144–145, 150–151, 153, 156, 160, 162–163, 184
Frontiersman 9, 11, 14–15, 17, 22
Frost, William Goodall 168, 180–181, 183, 196

Gabriel's Rebellion 93
Gallatin, Albert 51
Gardiner, Elaine 139
Gaskie, John J. 45, 51, 57–58
Gatlinburg, TN 131
Gaventa, John 35, 57, 93, 133
Gay Street 114, 117
Genovese, Eugene D. 93
Gibson, Mike 184, 196
Gifford, Jefferson 4, 41–42, 72, 76, 81, 83–85, 174, 189–190, 192
ginseng 49, 71, 187, 211
Gordon, Colin 30
Grainger County, TN
Grammar, John M. 69, 139, 195, 201, 216, 227
Graniteville, SC 95, 101, 105
Graniteville Factory 96, 98
Grant, Natalie 33, 67–68, 72, 208, 227
Gray, Richard 114, 119
The Great Depression 42, 132, 202
Great Smoky Mountains National Park 142
Green Fly Inn 35, 41, 64
Greenville, SC 53, 101, 113
Greer, John 63, 65–66, 138, 145, 153–155, 157–159, 161, 166
Gregg, James 29, 101–108, 127

Gregg, Mrs. 104–105, 107–108
Gregg, William 95–98, 100–102, 104–105, 111
Griffith, Andy 138
Grim Triune 197, 201–202, 204, 218, 220; *see also* spectral magi
Guillemin, George 55, 67, 77, 121, 145, 159–160, 199, 227
Guinn, Matthew 172, 183

Hall, Wade 5
Hamilton, Alexander 7–18, 21, 24, 37, 227
Harkins, Anthony 5, 168, 170–172, 175, 193, 196, 198, 209, 228
Harney, Will Wallace 32, 168
Harpe Brothers 201
Harris, George Washington 32–33, 121, 135, 139, 168, 194, 196
Harrogate, Gene 81–85–115, 118, 120–129, 187–188, 193–194, 228
"Harrykin" (Hurricane) wilderness 70, 135
Hartigen, John, Jr. 136
Hattiesburg, MS 163–164
Hee Haw 2–3, 138
hegemony 25, 141–143, 146, 150, 154–155, 166
Heller, Kevin John 141, 154
Henley Street Bridge 78, 213
Herring, Harriet 89–90, 96, 99, 101–102, 105–106, 109–111
high sheriff 137; *see also* Turner, Fate
Hillary, George A. 52, 113
hillbilly 2–4, 24, 30, 33–34, 37–38, 55, 81–82, 92, 107, 121, 131, 133, 135–136, 138, 149, 151, 165, 168, 170–175, 180–181, 185, 193–194, 203, 205, 210, 215, 227–228
hillbilly diaspora 87–88, 112, 211; *see also* Appalachian diaspora
hillbilly music 171
Hiroshima 209
History of Sexuality 25, 46, 79–80, 142, 189
hog drive 193, 228
Hogeland, William 10–12, 16
Holloway, David 5, 48, 162, 172, 216, 220–221
Holme, Culla 4, 35, 54–56, 60, 62, 187–188, 193–194, 197–206, 220, 228
Holme, Rinthy 35, 54–55, 179, 197, 199–201, 204–206
Hooper (the ragpicker) 120, 124–126
Hooper, Johnson 168
Hume, David 12
Hundley, D.R. 168, 175

iconoclasm 173, 183
incest 194, 200
Indian 177; *see also* Cherokee; Native American; noble savage; red man
indigenous people 13
infanticide 200, 202
internal colonialism 23
internal periphery 23
Interstate [highway] system 43
itinerant millhands 199

Jack the Ripper 163
Jackson, Andrew 177
Jameson, Fredrick 172, 220
Jason (*Friday the 13th*) 163
Jefferson, Thomas 18, 50–51, 177–178
Jefferson County, TN 127
Johnson, Gerald, W. 99
Johnson, J. Stoddard 182
Johnson, Junior 74, 188
Johnson, Lynden Baines 60, 171, 183, 198
Jones, Abednego (Ab) 62, 117–118
Joyce (Sutree's prostitute) 171

Kartiganer, Donald 3
Kennedy, John Fitzgerald 56, 171, 198
King's Mountain 139, 178
Kirby, Ruebel 144, 153; *see also* dumpkeeper
Knox County, TN 84, 184
Knoxville, TN 36, 44, 51, 60, 62, 73–75, 78–79, 81–83, 88, 90, 92–93, 113–118, 121, 124–125, 127–130, 139, 158, 160, 171, 184, 213
Kohn, Richard 13, 17

Lang, John 150
late-capitalism 216
League, D.W. 100–101
Leatherstocking Tales 139
Ledford, Katherine 10–11, 175, 177
Lee, Henry "Lighthorse" 16
Legwater [Deputy] 72, 77–79, 81
Lemert, Ben 100, 106
Leonard [the catamite] 120, 126
Lewis, Helen 50
Lewis, Ronald 38, 114, 167, 169
Li'l Abner 171–172, 201
Lilienthal, David 112
Lilley, James D. 5
Lippencott's Magazine 32, 168
Little Rock, AR 196
local color 32, 33–34, 38, 167, 169–170, 180–181, 189
Long, Jim 118–119
Long, Junior 118–119
Longley, John Lewis, Jr. 92, 115
Longstreet, Augustus B. 168
Lovingood, Sut 32, 121, 139–140, 173, 194, 196
Luce, Diane 5, 32, 37, 65–67, 69–70, 73, 80, 106–107, 133, 135, 138, 150–151, 158, 165, 186, 197, 198, 203–205
lynch mob 138, 155, 158
Lyotard, Jean-François 208

Madness and Civilization 158–159
Malazia, Emil 50
Marius, Richard 60, 118
McAnnally Flats 36, 44, 60–63, 75, 82, 91–92, 114–120, 122–125, 128
McCarthy, John Francis 224
McCoy, Clyde B. 91
McDonald, Michael J. 60, 113–114, 117, 121, 124
McEvoy, Martha 101, 105–108, 129–130, 227

McEvoy, Maryellen 104
McEvoy, Patrick 100, 102–108, 111
McEvoy, Robert (Bobby) 35, 102, 104–108
McEvoys 29, 36, 100–101
McKenna, Frank 43–44, 51
McWhiney, Grady 53, 228
Mechanicsville 60, 91, 114, 117
Memphis, TN 159
Menzer, Joe 80
Metress, Christopher 195–196
Michael (Native American) 119
mill operatives 90, 96, 108–109; *see also* mill workers; millhands; operatives
mill owners 101, 106; *see also* operators
mill village 90, 92–93, 97, 99, 101–102, 104, 106–112, 117; *see also* cotton mill village; textile mill village
mill workers 89; *see also* mill operatives; millhands; operatives
Miller, Wilbur 9
millhands 86, 93, 97–98, 104, 106, 110–111; *see also* mill operatives; operatives
Mississippi River Valley 197
Mitchell, Broadus 94, 96, 98, 100–101, 106
modernism 172
modernity 39, 67–68, 70, 84–85, 88, 173, 181, 187, 191, 219
modernization 22, 40, 48–49, 86, 220, 222, 224
Monroe, Bill 171
Moonlight Diner 122
Moonlight melonmounter 115, 121, 193, 228
moonshine 33, 47, 74, 81, 183, 188
Morgan, Arthur 112
Morgan, Wesley 197, 213
Morris, John W. 212
Morris, Robert 11–12, 178
Mother She 117
The Mountain Boys 172, 201
Mountainview 60, 114
Mulefoot hog 53, 197–198; *see also* Ozark hog
Murphree, Mary Noailles 32–33, 169, 181, 184, 196
mussel brailing 127; *see also* musseling
musseling 128; *see also* mussel brailing
Myers, Michael (*Halloween*) 163
mystical primitivism 55
Mythoclasm 195, 197, 207

Nagasaki 209
NASCAR 74, 80, 131, 188
National Parks System 142
Native American 176–178; *see also* Cherokee; Indian; noble savage; red man
necrophilia 134, 137, 161
Neville, John 16
New Deal 49, 142
New Mexico 207
Newitz, Annalee 139–140, 145
Newman, Monroe 51, 56, 58–59
"Nigger" John 147

Index

911 emergency response 45
No Country for Old Men 224
noble savage 176; *see also* Cherokee; Indian; Native American; red man
Noe, Kenneth W. 180–181

Oak Ridge, TN 68, 87, 113, 208
objective dependency 23
O'Connor, Flannery 135
Oklahoma State University 197–198
operatives 96, 98–99, 101, 104–106, 110; *see also* mill operatives; mill workers; millhands
operators 89, 96, 108, 110–111; *see also* mill owners
out-migrants 59, 136
out-migration 57–58
Ownby, Arthur 4, 35, 40, 42, 49, 54–56, 67–73, 75, 81, 83–85, 135, 157–158, 173, 187–189, 191–192, 209, 211, 227; *see also* Uncle Ather
Ozark Mountains 195
Ozark pigs 198; *see also* mulefoot hogs

panoptic gaze 117–118
panopticism 36, 97
panopticon 27, 109, 159
Parham, Billy 224
Parton, Dolly 131
paternalistic despotism 101
Pepper, Barry 139
Petros penitentiary 76, 86, 128; *see also* Brushy Mountain penitentiary
Pickens, SC 100
piedmont 89, 107, 219
Pigeon Forge, TN 131, 184
pocketknife society 64, 132–133, 141, 151, 153, 161, 163, 185–186
police 44, 47, 49, 61–62, 64–66, 73, 76–77, 85, 99, 117–118, 120, 124, 126, 155
postmodernism 172, 207
Power/Knowledge 25, 30, 37, 45, 53, 60, 116, 147, 152–153
Precourt, Walter 47–48, 54, 87, 97, 178, 180
President's Appalachian Regional Commission (PARC) 56
Prohibition 14, 21, 42, 73–74, 76
Pulitzer Prize 207
Pusser, Buford 138

Quinn, Tarzan 116–117

Ragan, David Paul 22, 67, 77, 84, 227
Ragged Man 103, 105
Raitz, Karl B. 131, 143, 176–177
Rattner, John Wesley 1, 67, 69, 76–78, 80, 82, 84–85, 174, 187, 189–190, 192, 202, 212, 224
Rattner, Kenneth 35, 41–42, 56, 69–70, 72, 74–75, 80, 82, 187–189, 191–192, 202, 220
Rattner, Mildred 80, 190, 192
recidivism 29, 123, 144, 146, 149
Reconstruction 9, 86, 91

Red Branch 42, 69, 71, 75–77, 82, 114
red man 176; *see also* Indian; Native American; noble savage
Red Mountain 68
Reed, John 24, 31
Reese 120, 127–128
Reese, Wanda 127
Reese, Willard 127
regional cities 35, 112; *see also* regional urban centers
regional urban centers 112–113; *see also* regional cities
reprobate 148–149; *see also* delinquency
Requiem for a Nun 147
revenue officers 188; *see also* federal regulators; revenuers
revenuers 21, 33, 126; *see also* federal regulators; revenue officers
Revolutionary War 139, 178
Roediger, David R. 94, 176
Rotech, Warren 45, 51, 57–58

Salstrom, Paul 53, 86, 227–228
Sandell, Jillian 134, 162–163
Savannah, GA 214
Saving Private Ryan (film) 139
Scraggs, Romeo (Lem and Luke) 201
Scruggs, Earl 171
Second Creek 115, 117
See Rock City 212
Semple, Ellen Churchill 182, 196
Sergeant York (film) 139
Sevier, John 178
Sevier County, TN 63–66, 78, 131, 133, 135–138, 140–141, 144–147, 150, 153, 162, 165–166, 184, 186
Sevier County Courthouse 131, 148, 185
Sevierville, TN 144, 158, 160, 162, 184
Shackelford, Laurel 71, 107
Shapiro, Henry D. 28, 32–33, 133, 136, 167, 169–170, 179, 181, 185, 188–191
Shelton, Frank W. 120, 125
Simpson, William Hayes 89, 94, 96, 99, 106
Slaughter, Thomas 8–10, 12, 50
Slotkin, Richard 33, 38
Smokey Mountain Market 118
Snuffy Smith 17, 195, 227–228
Snuffy Smith 174, 196
social contract 147
social uplift 21; *see also* benevolent organizations; benevolent societies; denominational benevolence; denominational philanthropists; denominational uplift
Southern Literature 172
Southern Renascence 172, 183
Southwestern humorists 139, 168
spectral magi 203; *see also* Grim Triune
Spenser, William C. 202–204
Spielberg, Steven 139
Squire Salter 199, 202
Stallybrass, Peter 142

Stewart, Kathleen 41–42, 56, 64, 83, 133, 155, 161
The Stonemason 224
subversivo 77
Sullivan, Walter 184
Sunset Limited 224
surveillance 16, 26, 115–116, 120, 128, 143, 152, 167
Suttree, Cornelius 2, 35–36, 44, 61, 81–84, 115, 117, 120, 122–129, 139, 171, 194, 212, 222
Swine in America 197
Sylder, Marion 4, 35, 41–42, 47, 55–56, 58, 62, 73–76, 79–85, 174, 187–190, 192, 211

tableau vivants 27
Tanner, Simpson Bilbo 99
Tennessee River 1, 82, 113, 127, 212
Tennessee Valley Authority (TVA) 68, 87, 112, 171
Tennessee wetbacks 57–58, 84, 211
Texas 207
textile mill village 101; *see also* cotton mill village; mill village
Thom McAn shoes 128
Three Forks, PA 16–17
timekeeper 104, 106, 109
Traber, Daniel S. 82–83, 119–120, 125
Trail of Tears 87, 177
Tullos, Allan 95, 99–101, 103, 109
"Tully" letters 37
Turner, Fate (sheriff) 64, 124–135, 138, 144, 148–149, 151–153, 165, 186
Twain, Mark 168

Ulack, Richard 131, 143, 176–177
Uncle Ather 84, 174
United States 7–8, 11–12, 16, 22, 30, 34, 37, 43–44, 48, 50–52, 137, 178, 208–209, 211–212
University of Tennessee 114

Vietnam War 177
voyeurism 146, 150, 155

Walden's Creek 184
Wallach, Rick 5, 209–210
Waller, Altina L. 189, 214
Walls, David S. 30, 89
Walsh, Christopher 22, 24–25, 29, 31, 40, 46, 61, 68, 70–71, 101, 106, 115, 119, 128, 137, 155, 173, 191, 196, 209
War of Poverty 183
Washington, George 7, 9, 12–13, 16–17, 50–51, 177
Watkins, Virginia McCoy 91
Watson, Daddy 120, 124–125
Watson, Jay 4
Webb, Paul 172, 201
Weinberg, Bill 71, 107
Weller, Jack 21, 43, 52, 55, 59, 68, 97, 110, 115–116, 127, 185
Wheeler, William Bruce 60, 113–114, 117, 121, 124
whiskey excise 9–10, 12, 14, 16–18, 22, 24, 205; *see also* excise tax
Whiskey Rebellion 7–9, 11–13, 15–19, 21, 50, 76, 93
whiskey rebels 126
whiskey runner 75–76; *see also* bootlegger
Whisnant, David E. 140, 177, 180
White, Allon 142
White Caps 65, 135, 138, 149, 152–154, 159, 162, 164–166
white privilege 94–95
Williams, Cratis 92
Williams, Hank 171
Williams, John Alexander 43, 47, 86, 93, 99
Williamson, J.W. 170, 181, 183, 228
Wilson, Darlene 169
Woodmason, Charles 168, 175
workhouse 122–124
World War I 114
World War II 43, 82, 87, 113, 139, 201–202, 209

Yeats, William Butler 207
Young, Thomas D., Jr. 116

www.ingramcontent.com/pod-product-compliance
Ingram Content Group UK Ltd.
Pitfield, Milton Keynes, MK11 3LW, UK
UKHW041939140426
5217IPUK00014B/570